THE RIFLE BOOK

The Rifle Book

By JACK O'CONNOR

Second Edition, Revised

ALFRED A. KNOPF: NEW YORK

1964

L. C. catalog card number: 62–11053

THIS IS A BORZOI BOOK,
PUBLISHED BY ALFRED A. KNOPF, INC.

PUBLISHED OCTOBER 14, 1949
SECOND EDITION, REVISED AND ENLARGED, 1964

For my two boys,
Jerry and Bradford,
who both love the rifle
and who are good shots and hunters

Preface
TO THE REVISED EDITION

Since this volume was first published, there has been more activity among rifle and ammunition manufacturers in the United States than in any similar period during this century. New models for old calibers in all of the actions—slide, lever, and bolt—and a host of fascinating and useful new cartridges have been developed. When *The Rifle Book* was first published, the drift toward high-intensity cartridges was noticeable, and as this new edition goes to press, high velocity is definitely in the saddle. Indeed, high-intensity loads have become so popular that a good many hunters who would be better served by slower loads and heavier bullets have taken to the magnums. The American shooter has probably never been more over-gunned since the days of The Big Fifty.

During the same period there have also been new developments in the smaller calibers, especially, of course, in the field of six millimeter. *The Rifle Book* has now caught up with the most recent new cartridges. It attempts to reflect all of the most recent developments, and in doing so reflects, I hope, the interests and queries of the many riflemen whose questions I have answered over the years as an arms and ammunition editor.

1964

Introduction

To me the rifle has always been the most romantic of all weapons, and of all rifles the one I love most is the rifle for big game. Some may have the same sort of feeling about other weapons, but I do not—to the same extent, anyway. The handgun I associate with the target range, with plinking at tin cans on Sunday afternoon picnics, with an occasional potted cottontail or grouse. When I think of the shotgun, I see warm September days in wheat stubble with swift doves angling in against clouds piled high and white in the blue sky of late summer, hear the roar of a covey of flushing Gambel's quail in some wide arroyo, or see again the V of wild geese and hear their lonely cries. But the rifle— Ah, that's something!

I like a handgun. I hold a shotgun in high regard; but rifles—well, I love the darned things. To me they stand for wilderness, mystery, romance . . . the brown bighorn ram high on a rocky comb, the flash of a whitetail's fan as he bursts out of his cover and dashes for safety, the big hulking moose stalking on long, stilt-like legs through the spruce timber . . . high mountain passes, glaciers, timber-line basins, green, lush, smooth as an English lawn, where a grizzly bear digs for marmots and the soaring eagle whistles.

Because I love rifles and because I love wilderness country I have carried my rifles all over the North American continent, from the hot, dry, barren sheep mountains of northwest Sonora to the glaciers of the Yukon. In the rack is an old beaten-up Springfield sporter. It is scarred and battered and its third barrel is now so worn that it won't keep its bullets in a two-foot circle at two hundred yards. Once down in Mexico the front saddle cinch broke, and the runaway horse battered its poor stock terribly. Another time in the same country when I was hunting sheep a rotten granite ledge gave way with me and I had to

[ix]

drop the rifle to save myself. The stock is badly cracked and held together with a bolt, the checking is smooth, and the rifling has gone. But I'll always keep that rifle. I shot my first elk with it on the Mogollon Rim of northern Arizona, my first grizzly with it in western Alberta. I have carried it in Sonora, Arizona, Wyoming, British Columbia, Alberta, and the Yukon. It has five grizzlies to its credit, and I feel the same way about it that a horseman feels about an old but much loved mount.

Another favorite of mine is an old .270. I can never take it out of the cabinet without thinking of where that rifle and I have been together and of the game I have seen through its telescope sight. With it I shot my first Canadian bighorn, my first moose, my first goat, and my first white Dall ram. . . .

Anyway, this is a book about rifles and the shooting of rifles. The accent is on rifles for hunting, rather than for competitive target shooting. I myself am more interested in hunting, and I think most potential readers of this book are.

This is not a profound book and wasn't planned to be one. It is a book, however, that has grown out of many years' experience on the range and in the hunting field with many different rifles, and it is intended for those who share my interest and enthusiasm in these most interesting of all firearms.

If this book helps the beginner understand and handle his rifle better, it will be successful.

Contents

CONTENTS

Note

ABOUT THE ILLUSTRATIONS

The illustrations for this book—except for the diagrammatic drawings that are printed with the text—are all grouped together for convenience of study. They will be found immediately before the first page of the text.

THE RIFLE BOOK

Of all the game for the rifleman in North America, the mountain sheep is considered the greatest trophy because of the tiresome climbing, the meticulous stalking, and the precise shooting that sheep hunting entails. Here Jack O'Connor comes down from a sheep mountain in the Yukon with the head of a big Dall ram. This was taken on a trip made in 1945. The rifle used was the custom-built .270 stocked by the late Alvin Linden. The scope was a 2½-X Lyman Alaskan, and the Remington Core-Lokt bullet was used.

This is the Model 94 Winchester with the serial number 2,500,000. It is a .30/30. Most of the two and a half million Model 94's that have been manufactured in the past sixty-five years or so have been .30/30's.

Here is a beautiful German single-shot rifle built on a hammerless, single-shot action similar to those used on American single-barrel trap shotguns. It has double-set triggers and is chambered for the German 5.6 x 35-R, which is similar to our .22 Hornet cartridge.

LEFT: HOW CARTRIDGES ARE NAMED: *Left to right: The .25 Remington Auto or .25 Remington rimless cartridge, so named because it was developed by the Remington Arms Co. first for the Model 8 Remington automatic rifle. The .30/30, a rimmed cartridge so named because it is a .30-caliber with a case capacity of 30 grains of black powder. The .30/06, so named because it is the U.S. military cartridge, caliber .30, Model 1906. In Europe it is called the 7.62 x 63 because that is the bore diameter and case length in millimeters.*

RIGHT: TYPES OF CARTRIDGES: *Left to right: The rimless .30/06 cartridge loaded with a full metal-cased bullet; the rimless .257 Roberts cartridge for varmint and deer hunting; the rimmed .22 Savage High-Power varmint cartridge; the rimmed .22 Hornet varmint cartridge. The first two cases head-space on the shoulder, the last two on the rim.*

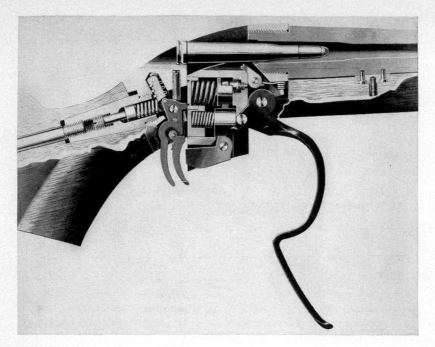

A new American single-shot falling-block action for varmint and target rifles developed by Jerry Gebby, the designer of the .22 Varminter cartridge, and associates. As this is written, the action is not yet on the market.

A beautiful varmint rifle built by Neidner Arms Corporation of Dowagiac, Michigan, on a British Farquarson falling-block single-shot action.

A Model 98 Mauser military rifle.

The Winchester Model 70 varmint rifle with the heavy 26-inch barrel. It is chambered for the .243 Winchester and the .220 Swift.

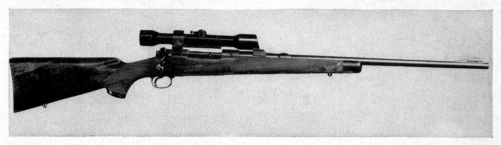

The ultimate in a fine modern bolt-action rifle: a Winchester Model 70 in .270 caliber, restocked in European walnut by the late Alvin Linden, and mounted with a Zeiss four-power scope on Stith Streamline mounts, incorporating windage.

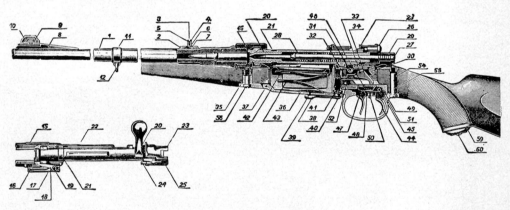

A cutaway view of the Mauser action, reprinted from a prewar Mauser catalogue.

A sporting rifle stocked by Keith Stegall, of Gunnison, Colorado, fitted with a G-88 scope on Redfield Jr. mounts and a muzzle brake.

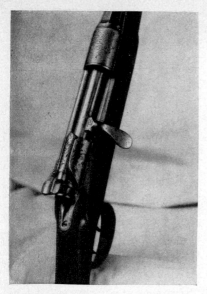

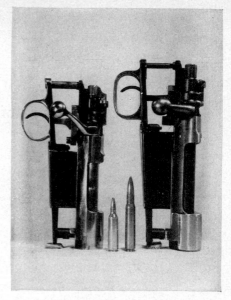

The action of a fine Mannlicher-Schoenauer sporter, showing the characteristic Mannlicher split bridge and the "butterknife" bolt handle.

A standard Model 98 action for the .30/06 cartridge (right) and the shortened and lightened version of the same action (left) for the .22/250 cartridge. The work was done by the Columbia Gun Company of Spokane, Washington.

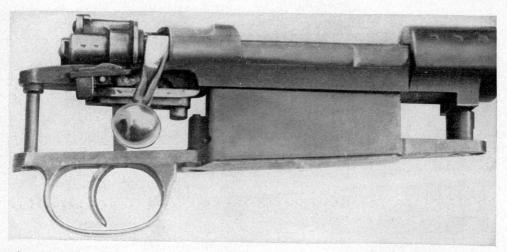

A Model 98 Mauser action with bolt handle altered and side button safety fitted by the Anderson Gun Shop, of Yakima, Washington.

TYPES OF BULLETS *Left to right: (1) .45-caliber revolver bullet with lubricant in grooves, cast from alloyed lead. (2) 150-grain spitzer full metal-cased M-2 .30-caliber government bullet for .30/06. (3) 150-grain Remington Bronze Point bullet for .30/06 and .300 Savage. (4) 180-grain .30/06 Winchester pointed expanding bullet. (5) 180-grain Remington .30-caliber Bronze Point. (6) 300-grain .375 Magnum. (7 and 8) 177-grain 7-mm. bullets made in Germany by D.W.M. (9) 300-grain .333 Jeffery (British) bullets. (10) 220-grain Western boattail bullet for the .30/06. (11) 175-grain 7-mm. bullet. (12) 250-grain Barnes soft-point spitzer bullet for the .375 Magnum. (13) 180-grain .30-caliber soft-point. (14) 150-grain .30-caliber Western open-point. (15) 130-grain Winchester-Western Silvertip .270 bullet. (16) 125-grain cast, lubricated, gas-check bullet for the .270.*

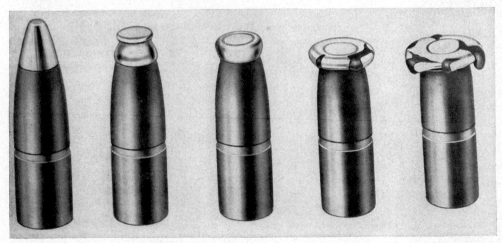

Steps in opening up of a Winchester-Western Silvertip bullet.

Silvertip bullets taken from game.

Right: Component parts of a center fire cartridge. Left to right: case, bullet, powder, primer.

TYPES OF BIG-GAME BULLETS *Left to right: 300-grain .375 Magnum soft-point; 250-grain .375 Magnum bullet in spitzer soft-point, manufactured by Fred N. Barnes, Durango, Colorado; Winchester-Western Silvertip 220-grain .30-caliber bullet; 220-grain Western soft-point boattail .30-caliber bullet; 180-grain Winchester .30-caliber soft-point; 180-grain .30-caliber Remington Bronze Point; 150-grain Remington Bronze Point; 130-grain Winchester pointed expanding .270 bullet.*

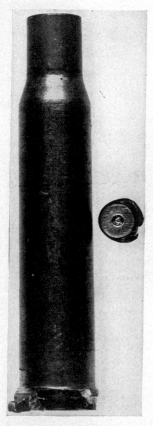

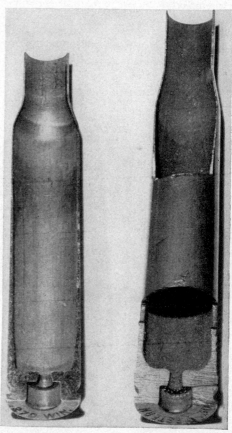

Left: A .30/06 case with the primer separate. At right showing very high pressures, which, as a matter of fact, partially wrecked the rifle. Notice how distorted the primer, which was blown from the case, is.

Right: Sectioned cartridge cases. Left, the .270 Winchester, a rimless case. Right, the .300 H. & H. Magnum case, which is belted. Notice how enormously thick the "web" of the Magnum case is.

SOME BIG-GAME CARTRIDGES *Left to right: (1) .300 Weatherby Magnum. Cases for this cartridge are obtained by firing a standard .300 H. & H. cartridge in a .300 Weatherby chamber. The brass expands to give more powder capacity and a sharper shoulder. Greatly stepped-up velocities with the same bullets can be obtained in this case. (2) .270 Weatherby Magnum. This cartridge is a high performer. It is based on a shortened, necked-down, and blown-out .300 H. & H. case. With it standard .270 W.C.F. ballistics are stepped up 150–200 foot-seconds. (3) The standard .30/06, loaded in this instance with a 220-grain bullet. (4) The standard .270 Winchester loaded with the 130-grain Silvertip. (5) A 7-mm. Mauser loaded with the 175-grain bullet. (6) A .257 Roberts.*

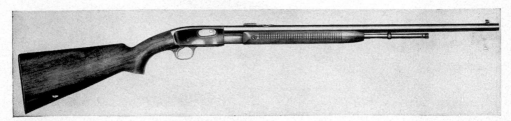

The pump-action .22 is a favorite for plinking and small-game hunting. This is the Remington Model 121-A, manufactured for many years. Previously called the Model 1912, but the stock and other details have been changed.

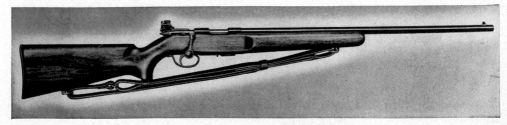

The Remington Model 521-T, a moderately priced, boy-sized target rifle, and a very good one.

The Remington Model 40-X "Range Master" .22 target rifle with heavy barrel.

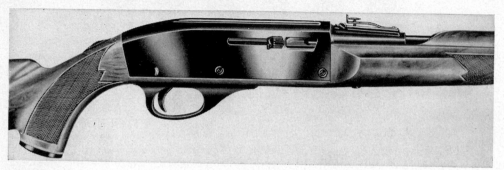

The Remington Nylon 66 .22 auto-loading rifle uses structural nylon in working parts and has a plastic stock.

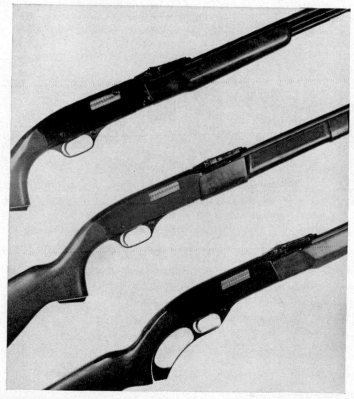

Three .22 rifles of the new Winchester 200 line introduced in 1963. From top to bottom: the Model 200 semiautomatic, the Model 270 slide-action, and the Model 250 lever-action. All three handle short, long, and long rifle cartridges interchangeably. These rifles are designed for mass production with modern manufacturing methods.

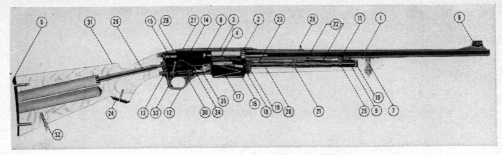

Winchester Model 100 semiautomatic rifle for the .308 Winchester cartridge.

The Mossberg No. S-108 receiver peep sight for the Model 125 rifle. A simple sight, inexpensive to manufacture yet workable.

An inexpensive and light single-shot .22 rim-fire rifle like this Stevens is a good one for a boy to start out with.

A Winchester Model 57 Sporter equipped with a Stith Bear Cub scope and Stith mounts.

An inexpensive little Winchester single-shot for the beginner.

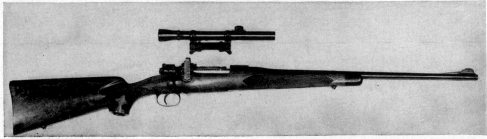

A beautifully designed and executed stock for a light .30/06 sporter on an FN Mauser action made for Jack O'Connor by Alvin Biesen, of Spokane, Washington. Data: length of pull, 13½ inches; drop at comb, just to clear bolt; drop at heel, only ½ inch more than at comb; pitch down from 22-inch barrel, 4 inches; circumference of pistol grip at "small," 4¾ inches. Barrel by W. A. Sukalle, 1120 E. Washington St., Phoenix, Arizona. Lyman Alaskan scope with Griffin & Howe mount. Lyman 48 receiver sight.

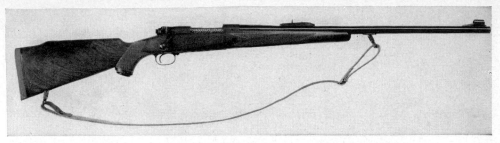

Winchester Model 70 in .458 African caliber.

Jack O'Connor's .415 Rigby is based on a converted Model 1917 Enfield action rebarreled by the Apex Rifle Company of Sun Valley, California, with stock work by Al Biesen. The scope is a Weaver K-1 on a Griffin & Howe slide mount.

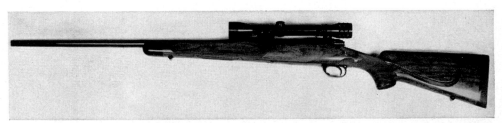

Winchester Model 70 in .338 remodeled and restocked by Al Biesen. Scope is a Redfield 4-X Bear Cub on a Tilden mount.

The BSA bolt-action sporter made in England is imported into the United States in various calibers from .243 to .458 W. C. F.

A detachable magazine is a feature of the Remington Model 742.

A fine custom-grade Model 70 Winchester .270 owned by Dr. Russell Smith, of Barron, Wisconsin.

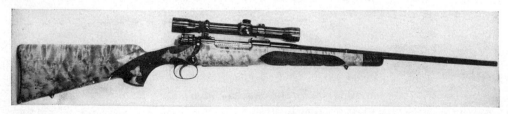

A .257 based on a G.33/40 Mauser action with a Weaver K-4 scope on Tilden mounts. It was stocked for Jack O'Connor in bird's-eye maple by Alvin Biesen.

A .250/3000 on a short Mauser action restocked by the late Bob Owen.

A Model 721 Remington in .300 Holland & Holland caliber, owned by Dr. Russell Smith, of Barron, Wisconsin. It has a Stith Master mount with a Stith Bear Cub scope. It was restocked by A. D. LeFor, of Dickinson, North Dakota. I do not consider that carving has any place on a fine rifle stock, but some like it.

This is probably the handsomest Model 110 left-hand Savage ever built. Stocking and remodeling was done by Al Biesen.

Two great men in the custom gun field: Emil Koshellek, of Stevens Point, Wisconsin, a famous metalworker; and the late Alvin Linden (right), one of the most versatile stockers ever to practice the trade in the United States.

Workman at the shop of Griffin & Howe in New York City engaged in engraving the receiver of a bolt-action rifle.

An example of German carving on a Mauser sporter.

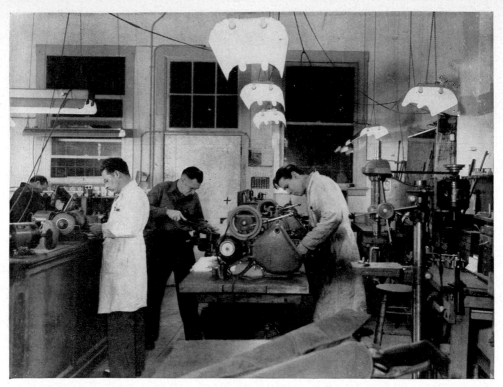

The custom gunshop of Roy E. Weatherby at South Gate, California.

A Remington Model 721 in .270, stocked for E. C. Quinn of the Dodge Motor Company by Alvin Biesen.

The bottom of a fine single-shot varmint rifle based on an Enfield action, stocked by Alvin Linden.

Different views of a fine Mannlicher-style Model 70 Winchester, with a 22-inch barrel, stocked by the late Alvin Linden.

Workman at Griffin & Howe checking the stock of a bolt-action rifle.

Showing the placement of the swivel and barrel band on Jack O'Connor's fine .270, stocked by Alvin Linden. With the left hand tight behind the swivel, this does not cause sling tension to pull the barrel down.

A fine example of custom stocking done by Charles Goueleke, of Green Bay, Wisconsin. The action is a short Mauser.

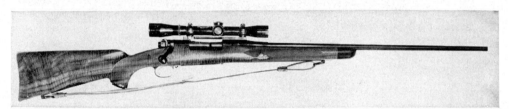

A .280 Remington on a Model 70 Winchester action, owned by Fred Huntington and stocked by Dale Goens.

A superb .270 on a Mauser action with German double-set triggers. The stock work by Al Biesen.

Details of cheek piece, grip, and checking on Jack O'Connor's old .270 on a Mauser action stocked by the late Alvin Linden.

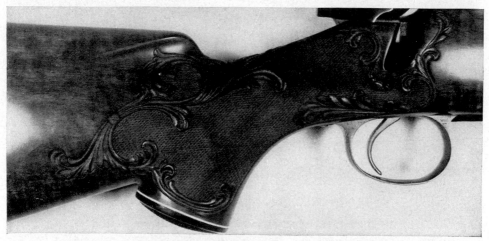

Details of the woodcarving at the pistol grip of a stock made by Reinhart Fagjen of Warsaw, Missouri.

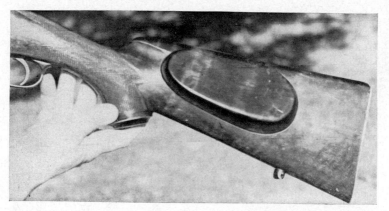

At one time this type of cheek piece was greatly favored, but now the most popular is the Schuetzen cheek piece as shown in Jack O'Connor's .270 by Alvin Linden.

BORESIGHTING—
CENTER TARGET IN MUZZLE,
CENTER MUZZLE IN BREECH

BORESIGHT
TARGET

How bore sighting is done. The rifle is put in a vise so that the center of a bull's-eye at about forty feet can be seen through the bore when the bolt is removed. Then the reticule in the scope is so adjusted that it rests on the same bull. Then the first shot will be on the target, and refinements in sighting can be made.

Probably the worst of all sights—the Rocky Mountain Buckhorn, complicated enough as it is, but complicated more with the White's diamond. However, many love them.

A better rear sight. At least, this one does not have the useless ears of the Buckhorn to blot out the game.

1. BLUNT PICKET POST AND CROSS WIRE
2. BLUNT PICKET POST,
3. SHARP PICKET POST AND CROSS WIRE
4. SHARP PICKET POST
5. TAPERED POST AND CROSS WIRE
6. TAPERED POST
7. CROSS WIRES

Type of reticules available in the Lyman Alaskan scope. I am partial to either the tapered flat top post with cross wire or the plain cross wire.

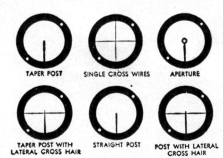

TAPER POST   SINGLE CROSS WIRES   APERTURE

TAPER POST WITH LATERAL CROSS HAIR   STRAIGHT POST   POST WITH LATERAL CROSS HAIR

Type of reticules available in Lyman target scopes.

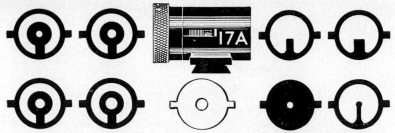

Type of apertures available for the Lyman 17-A front sight.

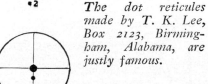
#2

The dot reticules made by T. K. Lee, Box 2123, Birmingham, Alabama, are justly famous.

Below: A typical ramp front sight. This one is on a Remington rifle. For ordinary hunting, a 3/32-inch gold bead is best.

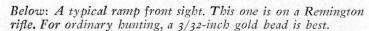

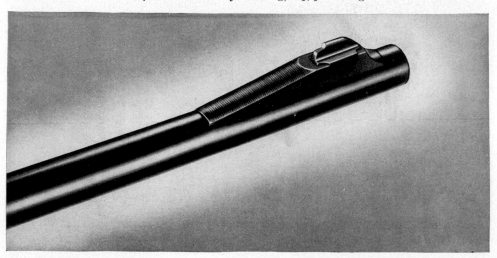

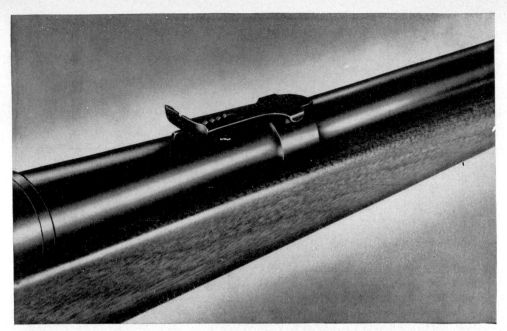

Here is a typical open rear sight with no provision for windage at all except driving the slot back and forth, and no provision for elevation except crude steps. Such a sight should be replaced with a micrometer adjustable receiver sight.

The fine Redfield Series 70 receiver sight on a Remington Model 30 rifle. This is an excellent sight for either hunting or target shooting.

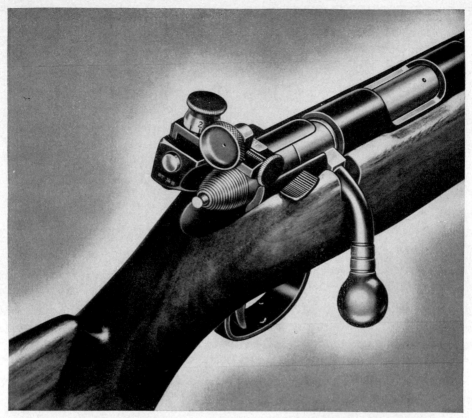

An adjustable Lyman target sight on a Remington .22 rifle.

Jerry O'Connor shooting Jack O'Connor's .300 Magnum rifle, which is based on a Magnum Mauser action. The scope is a Weaver K-4 on Redfield Jr. mounts.

Eleanor O'Connor shooting Jack O'Connor's old .30/06 Springfield with a Hensoldt 2¾-X scope on a high Griffin & Howe double-lever mount. This was considered a red-hot outfit back in the 1920's.

These two Model 70 Winchesters were built for Prince Abdorreza, brother of the Shah of Iran, by Al Biesen. The top rifle shows the Bausch & Lomb Var 8 on a Bausch & Lomb mount.

Princess Peri Sima and Prince Abdorreza Pahlavi of Iran with a Patterson eland shot in Tanganyika with a .375 Magnum by Holland & Holland.

Jerry O'Connor shooting a .270 on a Mauser action with a Stith S-4 scope on Stith Streamline windage mounts.

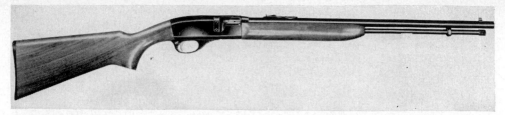

Remington Model 522 .22 auto-loader is a man-size rifle with a man-size stock.

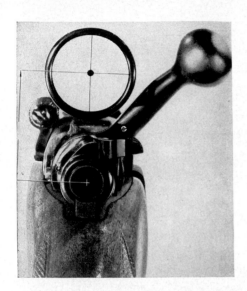

Left: The way the Lee dot reticule looks to the man shooting the rifle.

Below: The Redfield 102-N receiver sight on a Model 81 Remington automatic rifle.

Marlin Model 88-C .22 with Weaver B-4 scopes and Weaver mounts.

Over a million Stevens Model 87 .22 auto-loading rifles have been sold.

The famous Redfield Junior mount with a Texan scope on a Remington Model 30.

A good way to pick out your scope is to line them all up, properly focused on the same target, and then take the one that seems optically the best.

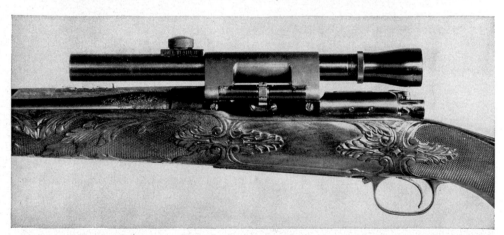

A Lyman Alaskan scope mounted on a restocked Model 70 Winchester with a Pachmayr Lo-Swing mount.

This popular .22 was built for Sears, Roebuck by High Standard.

A fine .30/06 Springfield with Weaver K-2.6 scope and Stith Streamline mount. The stock was made of Tiger Flame maple by the late Alvin Linden.

Remington Model 742 semiautomatic rifle. It is chambered for high-intensity cartridges such as the .308, .30/06, and .280.

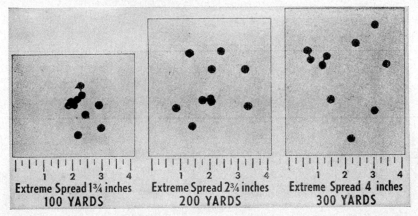

1 2 3 4	1 2 3 4	1 2 3 4
Extreme Spread 1¾ inches	**Extreme Spread 2¾ inches**	**Extreme Spread 4 inches**
100 YARDS	**200 YARDS**	**300 YARDS**

Typical groups shot with the 180-grain Winchester Silvertip bullet in .30/06.

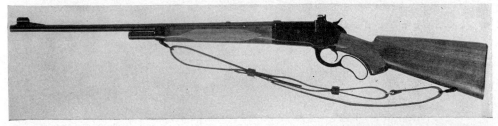

Winchester Model 71 lever-action rifle in .348 caliber, fitted with receiver sight and gun sling. This is a fine, fast-handling woods rifle for any game up to grizzly bear and moose. It is now obsolete.

Al Ronstadt, now of Mexico City, sights in a varmint rifle on a bench rest using a bedroll to simulate the rifle held by the left hand.

Some varmint cartridges, left to right: .22 Hornet, K Hornet, .218 Bee, Improved Bee, .222 Remington, .219 Zipper, Improved Zipper, .220 Swift.

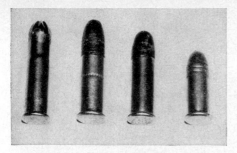

.22 RIM-FIRE CARTRIDGES *Left to right: .22 long rifleshot shell, .22 long rifle, .22 long, .22 short.*

Right: The principal varmint of the Southwest is the jackrabbit. Here Bradford O'Connor holds up one he got with a Remington 513-S.

Taking a shot at a prairie dog with a .22/250. This rifle weighed about eleven pounds and was very accurate.

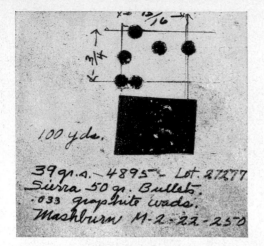

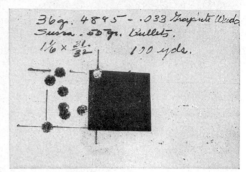

39 gr. a. — 4895 — Lot. 27277
Sierra 50 gr. Bullets.
.033 graphite wads.
Mashburn M-2-22-250

100 yds.

36 gr. 4895 — .033 Graphite Wads
Sierra 50 gr. Bullets.
1⅙ × 31/32   120 yds.

Groups shot with a .22/250 made by the Mashburn Arms Company of Oklahoma City. These small-bore varmint rifles give astounding accuracy.

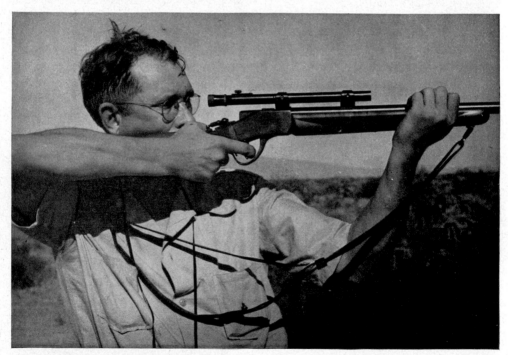

A .22/3000 of the 2-R variety on a Sharps-Borchardt action once owned by Jack O'Connor. It was fitted with a Weaver 440 scope and was a great little rifle for running jacks.

A coyote is a destructive predator and fair game for a varminter with anything from a .22 to a .30/06. This Arizona coyote was killed with a scope-sighted .30/06 rifle.

SOME GOOD VARMINT CARTRIDGES *Left to right:* .22 Hornet, .218-Bee, .25/20, K-Hornet, 2-R Lovell, Maximum Lovell, .22/250, improved .219-Zipper, .220 Swift, .250/3000, Savage, .257 Roberts.

Right: A big Southwestern antelope jack shot at 200 yards by Jerry O'Connor with a .257.

A Czechoslovakian .22 Hornet rifle on a special short Mauser action with set triggers and fitted with a 10-X Unertl target scope.

This prairie-dog hunter has had good luck with his .220 Swift.

Wherever he is found, the whitetail deer is a grand game animal and gives the hunter a run for his money. This Arizona whitetail was taken at about 250 yards across a canyon with a .270.

The lever action is fast to operate for deer hunting. Here a hunter slams down the loop lever of his Model 99 Savage.

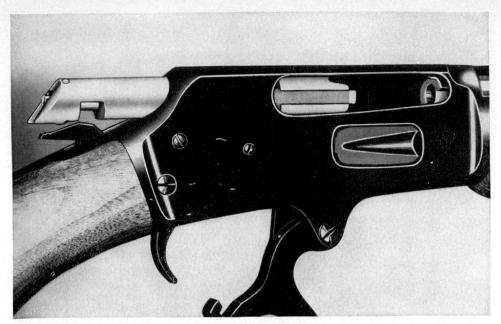

This is the action of the Marlin lever action, which, unlike the Winchester, ejects at the side. With minor changes it has been a deer hunter's favorite for a couple of generations.

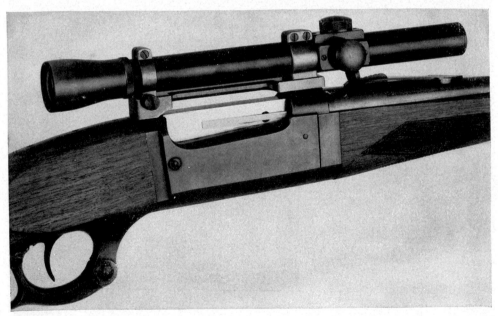

Here's another old favorite for the deer hunter, the Model 99 Savage with a Redfield Jr. mount and a 2½-X Lyman Alaskan scope.

SOME GOOD ALL-AROUND CARTRIDGES *Left to right*: 8-mm. Mauser, .30/06, .300 Weatherby Magnum, .270, 7-mm., and .30/40 Krag.

The .30/06 is a very versatile cartridge, which can be used on anything from deer to Alaska brown bear and moose shown here. Left to right: .30/06 cartridges loaded with the 150-grain Remington Bronze Point, the 180-grain semi-spitzer soft point, and the 220-grain Remington Core-Lokt.

This barren-ground caribou with the extraordinarily heavy and massive head was shot in the Yukon with a scope-sighted .30/06.

GOOD DEER CARTRIDGES *Left to right: .30 Remington, .35 Remington, .30/30, .25 Remington, and .300 Savage.*

A rifle to be used in bad weather should have a quickly detachable scope mount like the Model 70 here fitted with a Jaeger side mount with a G-88 scope, which can be removed so the Lyman 48 can be used.

The floor plate of a highly engraved Model 70 Winchester in a .270 belonging to Dr. Russell C. Smith.

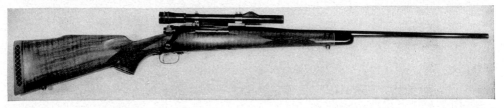

A fine all-around rifle that will take care of any North American big game: a Model 70 Winchester rechambered to .300 Weatherby Magnum and fitted with a Stith Bear Cub scope on Redfield Jr. mounts.

Here Frank Golata, famous Dawson Creek, B.C., guide and outfitter, takes a crack at a bull caribou near the head of the Prophet River in northern British Columbia.

Field Johnson, Yukon Indian guide, with a big Alaska moose shot with a 130-grain bullet in the .270.

This grizzly was killed with the 180-grain Remington Core-Lokt bullet in the .30/06 over on the bar of the Generc River in the Yukon.

Taking a shot with a British .470 double-barrel Nitro-Xpress rifle, used by the British for the largest game.

SOME BRITISH BIG-GAME CARTRIDGES *Left to right: .470 Nitro-Xpress, .416 Rigby spitzer, and .416 round-nose soft-point. Both used on Magnum bolt-action rifles, the .275 H. & H. rimless belted, which is used for light plains game.*

The business end of a .470 double-barrel rifle owned by Jack Holliday, of Indianapolis, Indiana, and Tucson, Arizona. This is Jack doing the pointing.

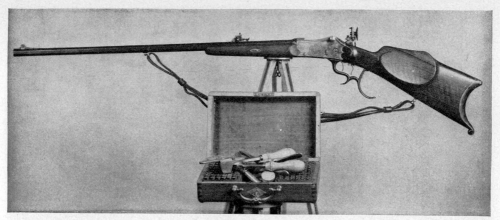

A German Schuetzen rifle for offhand shooting, chambered for the 8.15X46-R cartridge, which was a favorite with German target shooters.

Bullets recovered from big game during the course of a hunt in the Canadian Rockies, showing the mushrooming effect.

O'Connor with a 44¼-inch Tanganyika sable shot with a .300 Weatherby Magnum.

Herb Klein, world-famous hunter, shot this excellent greater kudu in Tanganyika with a .300 Weatherby.

A group like this from a bench rest at 200 yards will really give a man confidence in his rifle.

In offhand shooting the left hand can be well forward if the rifleman is shooting rapidly and swinging the rifle at running game.

Adjusting the loop of the sling high on the upper arm.

Taking a shot at a big bull caribou from a sitting position on the caribou range in northern British Columbia. Notice that the feet are well apart and that the elbows are well over and inside the knee for steady holding.

Doug Wesson, of the Smith & Wesson factory and former manufacturer of the concern, demonstrates his prone position on an Arizona range.

A good offhand position for stationary game or target shooting: left hand far back, left elbow straight under the rifle, right elbow high and parallel with the shoulder.

This group is right at 200 yards with the center of impact about six inches from the middle of the ball.

This group, shot from the sitting position with sling at 200 yards as one would do in the field, shows the center of impact to be just right. The rifle was a .300 Weatherby Magnum. The three shots in or touching the X-ring were the first three fired, by the way.

A coat over an ammunition box makes a poor substitute for a sandbag, but in this case it had to do.

Two Arizona deer hunters congratulate each other on a buck mule deer shot running at about 150 yards in this big open basin.

A big Stone ram with a 41½ curl, shot near the Prophet River in British Columbia with a .270.

An Osborn caribou shot with a 180-grain Remington Core-Lokt bullet in .30/06 at about 175 yards.

A big Dall ram shot in the Solomon Mountains of the Yukon with a 130-grain bullet in the .270.

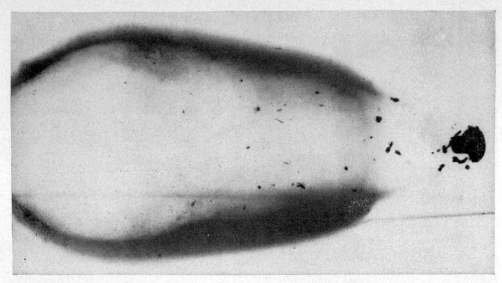

A bullet passing through gelatin, which was a good substitute for flesh. It shows the tremendous disrupting power of the modern high-velocity bullet.

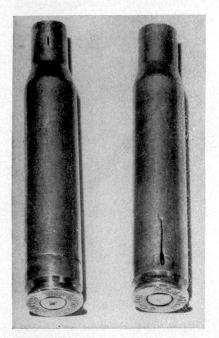

The cartridge at the left shows a partial head separation close to the head. In other words, the cartridge is pulling in two. This can be a sign either of excessive head space or brittle brass caused from repeated full-length sizing. The case also shows a neck crack, which may come from long storage or from repeated working by sizing in reloading. The longitudinal crack of the right-hand cartridge comes from improperly annealed brass, combined perhaps with a somewhat sloppy chamber.

Right: A good rifle scabbard for a scope-sighted rifle, showing how the scabbard protects the rifle well over the comb.

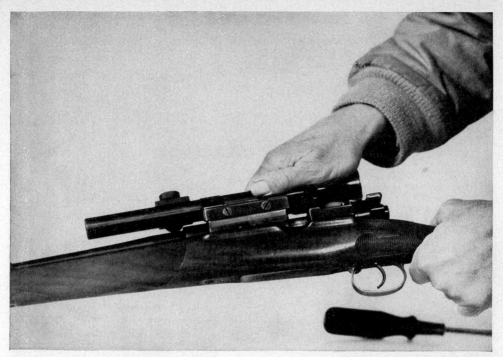

If a rifle suddenly becomes inaccurate, one should always check the scope mount to see if any play in the scope can be detected.

The guard screws of a bolt-action rifle should be kept tight if the rifle is to deliver its best accuracy.

*A big buck desert mule deer shot in southern Arizona by **Carol Lemon**, of **Tucson**, Arizona, with a .30/06.*

A rifle case like this is fine for carrying an extra rifle on a pack horse or transporting a rifle as personal luggage by train or plane.

A pack outfit in British Columbia. Note that the rifles are carried high, but to the rear on the right side to balance the saddle on those round-backed northern nags.

Adjusting elevation on the Lyman Alaskan scope.

The screw in this little Remington .22 and in other similar .22's should be kept tight for the best accuracy.

Breaking bottles is a fine way to show boys the necessity of squeezing them off.

⋅⋦ CHAPTER I ⋧⋅

What Is a Rifle?

Most readers of this book already know what a rifle is, but I suspect that any one of them would have to pause and consider if he was asked to give an airtight definition.

Suppose he said: "It is a weapon with a rifled barrel." How would that be? Not very good. There are many weapons with rifled barrels besides those we commonly know as rifles—cannon used in the field, on airplanes, and on ships of war; heavy and light machine guns; the so-called submachine guns; even pistols and revolvers.

So let us work out a definition here.

A rifle is a firearm with a rifled barrel, designed to fire one projectile at a time and to be operated by one man from the shoulder and with the use of both hands.

That definition is fairly inclusive. It rules out shotguns, even though a few shotguns have been manufactured with rifled muzzles to spread the shot pattern, because shotguns shoot from a few large buckshot to several hundred small birdshot at a time. Actually, however, a British Paradox or other gun with a rifled muzzle is in fact a rifle when it is used with a conical bullet or a round ball. Our definition also rules out pistols and revolvers, since they are designed as one-hand firearms. Machine guns have rifled barrels, but they are operated by a crew of from two to several men. We might also try making our definition a bit tighter by saying that a rifle can be fired but once for each time the trigger is pressed, because no truly automatic *rifle* has ever

[3]

been manufactured. Possibly this would be a wise addition to our definition, since the submachine gun or machine pistol fills all other requirements for the rifle except that it fires automatically.

Firearms with rifled barrels have been made for many hundreds of years, since it soon became known that a bullet has to spin in order to stabilize itself and fly accurately. But getting a bullet down a rifled barrel from the muzzle rapidly enough to make the rifle a practical military and sporting weapon was a problem that was not solved until the eighteenth century in America. Until not much more than a hundred years ago all military shoulder arms were smoothbore *muskets*. When the Americans at the Battle of Bunker Hill were told to hold their fire until they saw the whites of their opponents' eyes, they were receiving very good advice indeed, because if they had fired sooner they would have wasted most of their shots.

Early rifles, with a few experimental exceptions, were all muzzle-loaders. For many years the bullets, which in order to take the rifling had to be larger than the bore diameter, were pounded down onto the powder with a ramrod and mallet. It was a slow and difficult job. American pioneers learned to make the ball about bore diameter and then patch it with greased linen or buckskin and slide it down the barrel. The tight fit of the patch imparted the spin of the rifling to the bullet, and forcing the patch down the bore cleaned out the powder residue every shot.

The *breech-loader* became practical some time before the outbreak of the American Civil War, with the perfection of the famous Sharps rifle. During the Civil War *repeating breech-loaders* came into use with the Spencer and the Henry. In the United States in recent years the only single-shot rifles manufactured by the large companies are inexpensive .22's. All other rifles are repeaters of some kind.

The typical feature of all rifles is, of course, the barrel, into which spiral grooves known as "rifling" have been cut. Barrels are a piece of steel with grooves cut to impart spin to a bullet.

In modern rifles, barrels run from 18 and 20 inches in those weapons designed for brush hunting and short ranges generally to 30 inches in some heavy match rifles. If a rifle has an especially short barrel, it is sometimes called a *carbine*. The little Winchester-designed .30 M-1 carbine, used in World War II, is an example. It uses a light cartridge with a maximum accuracy range of about three hundred yards, and it is used by troops whose primary purpose is not fighting, but who must fight occasionally in performance of other duties. The barrel is short and the weapon itself is short and handy.

The usual sporting rifle has a barrel about 24 inches long. As a rule nothing in particular is to be gained by using a shorter or a longer barrel. A rifle with a 24-inch barrel is handy on horseback and in the brush and it is long enough for mountain shooting. The shorter a barrel is, the greater the muzzle blast and recoil. The shorter it is, the lower the muzzle velocity. Instrumental velocities for various cartridges are taken in barrels of specified length. Standard for the .30/06 or .270, and indeed the majority of American cartridges, is 24 inches.

Like all other human beings, American riflemen are faddists. Some years ago featherweight rifles were very popular. Owners of 1903 Springfields took them to gunsmiths, had the barrels cut off to 20 inches, turned down, the actions lightened by taking off metal here and there. If they could come out with a seven-pound .30/06 they were happy. Those rifles were not very satisfactory in a caliber so powerful. Velocity was lower, accuracy was poorer, because of the shortened sight-radius, recoil was unpleasant, and the muzzle blast would knock the ears off a brass monkey. Now the tendency is in the other direction.

The barrel is the very heart and core of the rifle. It is from the barrel that the rifle gets its name. Important though it is, however, the barrel is but one part of the rifle.

In order to function, the barrel must be screwed into an *action*, which supports the rear of the cartridge and which causes it to fire through the trigger and firing-pin mechanism. The action may be repeating or single-shot, but at the present time few single-shot actions are made. It may be operated by a lever, of which the trigger guard is part, as in the Winchester, Marlin, and Savage lever-action rifles. It may be operated by a bolt, as with all Mauser-type actions, with the Savage sporter actions, and the many seen on .22 rifles and on various military rifles. A slide-handle may be the means of inserting fresh cartridges and ejecting fired cases, as in the Remington line of pump- or "trombone"-action high-power rifles and in .22 repeating rifles manufactured by almost all American makers.

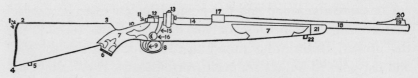

NOMENCLATURE OF THE RIFLE

1 Butt plate *2* heel of stock *3* comb *4* toe of stock *5* rear sling swivel *6* pistol grip cap *7* checkering design on grip and fore end *8* trigger guard *9* trigger *10* grip *11* cocking piece *12* bolt sleeve *13* rear receiver sight *14* bolt *15* bolt handle *16* bolt knob *17* receiver ring *18* barrel *19* ramp sight base *20* front sight *21* fore-end tip *22* front sling swivel.

In addition, semiautomatic, self-loading or autoloading mechanisms are manufactured in calibers from the tiny .22 to the powerful .30/06. In that case the rifleman needs only to pull the trigger. The mechanism ejects the fired case, inserts a new cartridge, and cocks the firing pin. All "automatic" .22 rifles, the Winchester self-loading big-game rifles (.32, .35, .351, and .401), and the Remington autoloading rifle in .30 and .35 Remington rimless are operated in one way or another by recoil. The Johnson semiautomatic rifle is also recoil-operated.

The United States military rifle known as the M-1 or Garand, after its inventor, is operated by powder gases taken off through a port near the muzzle. The little M-1 .30-caliber carbine developed for the army by Winchester is also gas-operated, as is the

Winchester experimental rifle in .30/06 caliber that was submitted to the government in competition with the present M-1.

If the rifle is a repeater, it must have a *magazine* of some sort. One of the most familiar is the tubular magazine fed through a gate in the receiver, as in the Winchester and Marlin lever-action rifles. This type of magazine has two disadvantages, however. One is that it must lie beneath the barrel, and therefore the stock cannot support the barrel as it does in rifles of the bolt-action type. More serious is it that the bullet of one cartridge must press against the primer of the cartridge immediately ahead of it.

Consequently round and flat-pointed bullets must be used in tubular magazines because of the danger of the recoil firing the primer. Ballistically, round-nosed bullets are not so good and flat-pointed bullets are even worse because they lose velocity very rapidly. The magazines of the obsolete Models 14 and 141 Remington trombone-action rifles carried their cartridges in a spiral and hence sharp-point bullets can be used. Like the other type of magazine, however, this lies beneath the barrel and hence the fore end cannot support it.

The Model 99 Savage line of rifles uses a spool type of magazine, as does the Austrian Mannlicher-Schoenauer. Each cartridge is carried in its separate compartment beneath the breech bolt. Another type of magazine is the clip, in which the cartridges are carried in a single line, one above the other. Today it is seen in most .22 bolt-action rifles. The Savage and Winchester rifles for the .22 Hornet cartridge also use it, and it is seen in various obsolete and semi-obsolete military rifles like the Model 88 Mauser, the old .41 Swiss, and the 7.62 Russian military rifle.

For rimless military-type cartridges the world's most popular magazine is the staggered box magazine as seen in all Mauser-type actions—the Springfield, Remington 30, 720, 721, and 722, 1917 Enfield, 98 Mauser, and Winchester 54 and 70. Cartridges are carried in two rows. They are fed up by a strong spring

[7]

pushing a follower. The action is with rimless cartridges simple, reliable, and almost foolproof.

Every rifle must have a barrel, an action, and also a stock. Lever- and pump-action rifles have two-piece stocks; so do single-shot rifles like the Winchester 85, the Stevens 44 and 44½, and the former Stevens Walnut Hill line, the Sharps Borchardt. The Remington pump and autoloading high-power rifles have two-piece stocks, and so do some .22 self-loading rifles. All things being equal, the one-piece stock is the most satisfactory, since it supports barrel and action and welds the whole rifle together. However, the actions that are held to the butt stock by a long strong bolt as in the Savage 99 actions and some of the single-shots compare very favorably with the bolt actions for accuracy.

The Classification of Rifles. Here I might as well explain some of the various terms used in relation to rifles. Among the most common are "small bore" and its opposite, "big bore." In the United States the term "small bore" usually refers to the .22 rim-fire caliber. Indeed, an official small-bore match is always a .22 match. For sporting purposes the term is extended to include rifles of .25 caliber. A rifle that is anywhere from .22 to .25 may legitimately be called "small bore." The "big bore" rifle, in the United States anyway, can refer to anything from a .270 up to .375 Magnum or .45/70 but official big-bore matches are fired with rifles using the .30/06 cartridge, which is the government military rifle cartridge.

Until the middle 1890's most sporting cartridges utilized black powder and gave velocities running from 1,300 to 1,500 foot-seconds. Then the new, much smaller smokeless-powder cartridges at considerably higher velocities were developed— the .30/30, the .303 Savage, .30/40 Krag, 7-mm. "Spanish" Mauser, etc. All had velocities with fairly long bullets that ran around 2,000 foot-seconds. To distinguish them from their black-powder predecessors, they were known as *high-velocity* or "high power" cartridges. The pressures for these cartridges ran somewhere between 35,000 and 42,000 foot-pounds.

Early in the present century cartridges with still higher velocities and higher pressures were developed—cartridges like the .30/06, the .270 W.C.F., the .250/3000, and .300 Savage. To distinguish these cartridges the term "high intensity" was sometimes used. Velocities ran from 2,700 foot-seconds with the 150-grain bullet of the old .30/1906 Springfield load to 3,140 with the 130-grain bullet in the .270. Pressures also ran a good deal higher—from 48,000 to 50,000 pounds per square inch. Hence the term "high intensity."

The term "magnum" is a British importation and is rather generally used in England where we formerly used the not particularly popular term "high intensity." In England a magnum cartridge is simply one that gives higher than ordinary velocities. I believe Americans first became familiar with the term when the first Holland & Holland Magnum rifles were imported. Wildcat cartridges made by various gunmakers and based on the belted Holland & Holland case are usually called "magnums"—the .280 Dubiel Magnum, the .270 Ackley Magnum, the .257 Weatherby Magnum, etc. The term is quite loosely used, however, as we have seen. That great Smith & Wesson revolver cartridge, which is really an overgrown .38 Special, is known as the .357 Magnum and the various hot-shot wildcat .22's are often referred to as magnum .22's.

Rifles can also be classified by their use. A "small game" rifle for use on edible game animals like cottontails and squirrels is always a .22 light enough to be portable as compared with the very heavy target .22's, which often weigh ten or eleven pounds. The term "deer rifle" usually refers to a light rifle of medium power to be used on deer at short and medium ranges. Such a rifle is the Model 141 Remington pump in .30 Remington caliber, the Model 99 Savage in .250/3000, or the Model 94 Winchester for the .30/30 cartridge. The term "big game

[9]

rifle" usually refers to a rifle to be used on animals larger than deer at longer ranges. Such a term can apply to the .30/06, the .270, or the .348 Winchester Model 71.

"Varmint rifle" refers to a specialized rifle to be used at relatively long ranges on inedible pests like jackrabbits, woodchucks, prairie dogs, crows, and harmful hawks. Varmint rifles are usually chambered for cartridges which drive light bullets at high velocity so that the explosive effect of the bullet will make one-shot kills even though the game is badly torn up and also so that these bullets will disintegrate when they hit the ground and not be dangerous in thickly settled farming country, where varmints are so often hunted. Often varmint rifles are made quite heavy and use scopes of 6-X or even higher because precise aim must be taken at small marks rather far away. The term "bull gun" simply means a target rifle with an especially heavy barrel. A bull gun will weigh twelve to fifteen pounds. It is used only on the range and is not carried as is a hunting rifle.

CHAPTER II

Cartridges and Chambering

SOME years ago I wrote an article for the arms and ammunition department of *Outdoor Life* on the good little .257 Roberts cartridge. In discussing its possibilities for the handloader I mentioned the fact that .257 rifles had the standard .25-caliber bore and groove diameter and hence the handloader could use any .25-caliber *bullet*. For more than a year thereafter I received letters from disappointed hunters who had bought .257 *rifles* and were bitterly disillusioned when they discovered their rifles would not handle *cartridges* for the .25/20, .25/35, .25 Remington Self-Loading, .250/3000, and so on.

To many, a *cartridge* is a *bullet*. In fact, one might say that to a man who knows little of firearms a cartridge is always a bullet. One war poster said: "A War Stamp will buy a Bullet to Defeat the Axis." The illustration, however, showed not *bullets* but .50-caliber heavy machine-gun *cartridges*. Many times I have heard people in sporting-goods stores ask for .22 *bullets* or .30/30 *bullets* when, of course, they meant cartridges.

A bullet is but one part of the complete cartridge. Other parts are the case to contain the powder charge and fit the chamber of the rifle, the powder charge itself, and the primer to ignite it. When a blow is struck the primer by the firing pin of the rifle, a hot jet of flame, which ignites the powder, results. The powder begins to burn, and the expanding gases push the bullet into the barrel, where the lands of the rifling impart a

[11]

spin to it that it keeps as it goes through the air toward the target. The fired case is then ejected. With a center-fire cartridge, as we shall see, the spent primer can be removed, a new primer, new powder charge, and new bullet inserted. The *case* can then be used again. That is impossible, however, with a rim-fire cartridge.

First let us look at the cartridge cases themselves and see how they are classified. The first successful metallic cartridge cases were made with the priming mixture distributed around a fold in the head—in other words, in the rim. Only a handful of rim-fire calibers are now manufactured, and the only ones that seem destined to survive are those in the .22 rim-fire line—the .22 Short, .22 Long, and .22 Long Rifle. Besides .22's the only rim-fire cartridges now regularly made are the .25 Stevens and the .32 Short and Long. The old .41 Swiss military cartridge, which hung on for a long time, is now obsolete. The .25 Stevens may be given a brass case and stepped up in velocity to fill a gap between the .22 Long Rifle high-speed and the .22 Hornet center-fire cartridge, but the others seem headed for the graveyard.

Very early in metallic cartridge history the center-fire primer came into being. Separated from the case, it is a little pellet of sensitive explosives enclosed in copper or brass and it is inserted into the primer pocket of the cartridge case after the case has been manufactured. For many years primers contained potassium chlorate, which attracted moisture and caused rust, and even today the famous Frankfort Arsenal No. 70 primer used in the government M-1 cartridge is a primer of this type. Other priming mixtures contained mercury and made the cartridge cases brittle. Now, with but few exceptions, all center-fire cartridges made by private manufacturers are primed with non-corrosive, non-mercuric primers from which both potassium chlorate and mercury have been eliminated. Primers are made in various sizes and of various degrees of hardness for large rifle cartridges, for small rifle cartridges, for handgun cartridges, and for shotguns. Anyone attempting to reload should be certain that he is using a primer of the correct size and of the proper composition, else he will run into trouble. Lists of the correct primers to use in all calibers are available in the *Ideal Handbook*, published by the Lyman Gun Sight Corporation, Middlefield, Connecticut, and in the *Belding and Mull Handbook*, published by Belding & Mull, Philipsburg, Pennsylvania. Each costs fifty cents. No handloader should be without them, and they contain much information useful to any lover of firearms.

Cartridge cases are classified, then, by the character of their primers—rim or center fire. They are also classified by shape—straight, straight taper, or bottleneck. The .22 rim-fire cases are straight, the .32/40 a straight taper, and all modern military-type cases (.250/3000, .30/06, etc.) are bottlenecks.

Cases are also classified by the character of the head. The oldest type of center-fire case is rimmed. A portion of the head projects from the body, as is also true with all rim-fire cases, and keeps the case from entering too far into the chamber of the barrel. Cases for the famous .30/30, the .30/40, .45/70, .22 Hornet, and .218 Bee are examples of the rimmed, center-fire case.

The rimless case was brought about by the two-column magazine of the Mauser action. It has a rim, true, but it does not project beyond the body of the case. With rimmed cartridges the rim serves to keep the cartridge from entering too far into the chamber. With the rimless cartridge this function is performed by the *shoulder* of the case. Consequently all rimless cases are also of bottleneck shape.

There are two other types of modern cases in use today—the semi-rimmed case and the belted case. Both are attempts to preserve the virtues of the rimmed case with its ease of head spacing and still have it function easily through a Mauser-type magazine. The semi-rimmed case, which is used in the obsolete 6-mm. U.S. Navy, the .280 Ross, and the Japanese 6.5-mm. Arisaka, is often taken for a rimless case, but a close look will show that the rim is a bit wider than the body of the case, enough so to halt the progress of the case into the chamber without having to depend on the shoulder as does the true rimless case. Although it is semi-rimmed, the .220 Swift case head spaces on the shoulder.

The belted type of case uses another device—a belt of metal just forward of the extractor groove which stops the progress of the case into the chamber and controls head space. This "belt" is the invention of Holland & Holland, the famous British firm of gun- and rifle-makers in London, and is used by them for their .240, .275, .300, and .375 Holland & Holland Magnum cartridges. The last two, by the way, have been Americanized, and Winchester Model 70 rifles are now chambered for them. The .275 cartridge was also made in limited numbers by the Western Cartridge Company of East Alton, Illinois, for made-to-order rifles, and it is entirely possible that the Model 70 rifle will in time be chambered for it or something similar.

This rimless belted case has all the virtues of the rimmed case, with ease of head spacing, and is proof against the careless hand-loader's shortening head space by unskillful full-length resizing. It also has the rimless case's virtue of working perfectly in a double-column Mauser-type magazine. It is undoubtedly the best case in the world and it will be used for the new ultra-powerful cartridges that will eventually come along in factory production. Today many advanced wildcat cartridges are based upon it.

CHAMBERING

The enlarged portion at the rear of the barrel is known as the chamber. It is shaped, of course, to fit the cartridge that is to be fired in it. The forward portion of the chamber is known as the "throat," and the portion at the end of the throat where the rifling begins is called the "bullet seat" or "leade." It is here that the bullet touches or nearly touches the lands of the rifling. In an experimental type of barrel called the "free-bored barrel" the throat extends several inches up into the barrel, and is, of course, free from rifling. Exponents of free-boring claim that this gives higher velocity and lower pressures with the same powder charge as the conventional throat and that it enables one to use stiffer loads of powder and get much higher velocity. Free-boring with a vengeance is seen in the Mossberg Targo gun, which is smooth-bored like a shotgun to handle .22-shot cartridges. It can be converted into a rifle, however, by screwing a few inches of rifled barrel on the end of this smooth bore. Accuracy with the rifled device installed is surprisingly good. Free-boring may be heard of more in the future.

The most widely accepted belief is that the bullet should touch or almost touch the lands for the best accuracy, and most factory rifles are designed with this in mind. In some factory rifles, however, like the Model 70 Winchester for the .257 cartridge, the magazine is so short that sharp-pointed bullets cannot be seated far enough out in the neck of the case to touch the lands. This makes the bullet jump through the unrifled throat before it engages the lands. Almost all owners of .257's report the best accuracy when the bullet is seated to touch the lands, and they also report less throat erosion with the bullets so seated.

Some cartridges were originally designed with long bullets loaded far out of the case, and it is impossible to seat lighter bullets so they touch the lands. Consequently throat erosion is bad, because the powder gases rush past the bullet before it engages the rifling, and the accuracy life of the barrels used with the shorter bullets is not long. Examples of cartridges so designed are the 7×57-mm. "Spanish" Mauser and the 6.5-mm. or .256 Mannlicher-Schoenauer. With any bullet there is some leakage of gas at the throat and it is particularly bad with bullets of the boattail or "tapertail" variety. To lengthen barrel life but cut down on throat erosion many handloaders use grease and graphite wads at the base of the bullet. The theory is that these wads seal off the gas, and actually they do seem to prolong the accuracy life of the barrel and are especially helpful in such calibers as the .220 Swift and the .22 Varminter.

What Head Space Means

Most rifle-owners have heard of head space, but very few indeed know exactly what it means. Once a friend of mine went to a sporting-goods store to trade in a Springfield sporter on a Model 70 Winchester. The clerk, who wanted to make a good deal for his firm, glanced at my friend's Springfield and said he could not give him much on it because it had "head space." Pale and trembling, my friend brought his rifle to me, convinced that for years he had been taking his life into his hands every time he fired his rifle.

"Has this rifle got head space?" he demanded.

"All rifles have head space," I responded.

I checked the head space of his rifle. It closed on the "go" gauge and did not close on the maximum gauge, so the head space was normal, or somewhere within the 6/1,000 limits of the .30/06.

Now, just what does this mysterious term "head space" mean?

Simply this: When a cartridge is fired in the chamber of a rifle, the brass case expands to fit the chamber, and the head of the case comes back against the bolt face or the face of the breech-block. The space existing between the head of the case and the face of bolt or breech-block is this thing called "head space." Some is necessary because there are certain limits to the precision with which cartridges can be manufactured. There are also limits to the precision with which a rifle can be chambered and with which bolts can be manufactured.

As we have seen, some device on the cartridge case itself is necessary to arrest its progress into the chamber, because if it goes too far, the condition known as excess head space results.

With the rimmed and semi-rimmed case this function is performed by the rim, with the belted case it is performed by the belt, and with the rimless case it is performed by the *shoulder of the case*. In certain straight rimless cases like the .45 automatic pistol cartridge, the mouth of the case coming in contact with a shoulder in the chamber controls head space.

Now let us take a look at rifles for the .30/06 and .270 cartridges, because head-space requirements for each are exactly the same. The .270 is only a .30/06 case necked down with the same shoulder angle. A new barrel in .30/06 or .270 has been made up, threaded, fitted to the receiver, and rough-chambered. The gunsmith now runs a *finish reamer* into the chamber, takes a few turns, then picks up a minimum head-space gauge (1.940) to see if he can close the bolt on it. If he can, he then tries the maximum gauge (1.946) to make sure he has not run the reamer in too far and given the rifle excess head space. If the bolt will close on the 1.940 gauge and not close on the 1.946 gauge, head space is within the permissible limits of 6/1,000 of an inch. These figures represent the length of the .30/06 and .270 cases from the head to a predetermined point on the shoulder.

Now, let us say that the chamber of the rifle is short and the bolt will not close on the 1.940 gauge. Then cartridges will seat with great difficulty and some makes of ammunition will not seat at all. Pressures will be higher than normal. I once had a .30/06 the bolt of which would not close on the 1.940 gauge. It would accept Remington and Frankfort arsenal ammunition, but not Western or Winchester ammunition. I once got a Western case stuck in the chamber and removed it only with the greatest difficulty. I took the rifle back to the maker and stood over him until he ran a reamer into it until it would close on a 1.940 gauge.

Besides the minimum (1.940) gauge and the maximum (1.946) gauge, the army uses another called the "no go" (1.950) gauge. When a bolt will close on that gauge, the rifle is removed from service and the condition corrected.

Results of Excess Head Space

It is very important that the space between the head of the cartridge and the face of the bolt or breech-block be within certain limits; in other words, to have what is known as normal head space. As we have seen, too little leeway between cartridge and bolt face results in higher pressures and difficulty in seating cartridges. Excessive head space may result in a blown-up rifle. When a rifle is fired, the brass case expands to make a tight fit in the chamber. Its entry into the chamber in a rimless case has stopped when the shoulder of the cartridge hits the shoulder of the chamber. Friction causes the brass of the body of the case to cling to the walls of the chamber, and hence the expansion must be backward to the bolt face. This stretching can take place within certain limits, but if it is excessive, the head of the case is apt to blow off. Since the case itself, not the action, seals off the gas of the burning powder, a ruptured case will let it go. Sometimes the rifle will be wrecked, the floor plate bulged, the stock shattered, and a storm of gas and brass fragments thrown into the shooter's face. In the case of the .22 rim-fire, the unsupported head where the priming mixture lies usually ruptures and gas and brass come back into the shooter's face.

Normally a rifle can have a good deal of excess head space and nothing will happen, since the strong, springy brass of the case will expand and seal the action against the gases without rupturing. Sooner or later, however, a brittle or very soft case will come along and then there will be trouble.

As we have seen, this thing called head space is relative, since it is the distance between the head of a particular cartridge and the face of the bolt. In the same rifle, firing cartridges from the same box, head space would vary, because cartridges vary within established limits in their dimensions. To illustrate this business of relativity further, let us say that we have a rifle with a little excess head space and fire a cartridge in it. The case expands without rupturing to fit against the bolt face. We reload that cartridge by neck-sizing only. When we again fire that reloaded cartridge, head space is normal, since the case has already been expanded to fit that particular chamber. The first time head space was excessive, the next time practically zero.

There is small chance of excess head space being developed from use by a bolt-action rifle of the Mauser type in which the bolt is locked at the head. Such rifles with excessive head space are examples of careless chambering when the barrels were installed, or the bolts and receivers have not been properly hardened and have set back. However, lever-action rifles using rimless cartridges with relatively high pressures, like the old Model 95 Winchester for the .30/06, can develop excessive head space because the continual pounding of the head of the case will in time set the face of the breech-block back. The same thing will happen in the Model 40 and 45 Savage bolt-action sporters, which are not of the Mauser type, with locking lugs at the head of the bolt. The condition can develop in any lever-action rifle, although in most of them it takes place very slowly because pressures for most lever-action cartridges are fairly low. I have even seen excessive head space develop in high-grade .22 rifles through the use of thousands of rounds of high-speed ammunition, and many cheap .22's leave the factory with excess head space that can be measured not in thousandths of an inch but apparently in tenths of an inch.

This problem of head space is the reason why barrels and bolts are not strictly interchangeable. If a man has a Model 70 .30/06 Winchester rifle with a worn barrel, let us say, he simply cannot order a barrel from the Winchester factory, screw it in, and then go merrily on his way. That *might* work, but the chances are that it will not. If several barrels are available to try, it is probable that one of them will fit in any particular action so that the bolt will close on the 1.940 gauge and not close on the 1.946 gauge. Bolts vary too, and if several bolts are available the gunsmith can probably find one that, using the same barrel and receiver, will close on the minimum gauge and not close on the maximum gauge.

Let us suppose that our gunsmith has only one barrel and one action to work with and head space is excessive. He must then cut off one thread, rethread, and rechamber, just as if he had made the barrel up from a blank. As this is written, just after World War II, hundreds of barrels of various kinds are being fitted to actions for which they were never intended—1917 Enfield barrels to 99 Savage, Mauser, and Springfield actions, Model 70 Winchester barrels to Mauser actions, and so on. If this is done by competent gunsmiths with good reamers and head-space gauges and the knowledge of how to cut threads, it is in most cases all right.

The owner of an old rifle that has seen much use should have the head space checked. Gauges for the .30/06 and .270 calibers are widely distributed and can be purchased not only in maximum, minimum, and no-go lengths but in intermediate lengths for five dollars or so. Other gauges, unfortunately, are *not* widely distributed, and I have a hunch that even some barrelmakers are without them. Instead of using gauges, they rely on using cartridges, trying the smallest factory cartridge they can find for the minimum gauge and the largest (longest) for the maximum. It will most often be necessary for the owner of a rifle of some other caliber to send it to the factory to be checked.

Once upon a time I went into the rifle department of a sporting-goods store with head-space gauges in my pocket. I checked three old Model 95 Winchesters and an ancient sporting Springfield, and all four would close on the field (1.950) gauge. I afterward heard that the continual pounding of the head of the case coming back violently against the bolt face crystallized one of the locking lugs of the Springfield and it sheered off, fortunately with no bad results for the user.

Before we get off this subject, let me warn against the careless full-length resizing of cases. With some tools it is possible to move the shoulder of the case back until the space between the bolt face and the head of the resized case is very great, even though with normal cases the head space in the particular rifle would be well within standard limits. I have caught friends of mine full-length resizing and moving the shoulder so much that it could be detected with the naked eye.

We have devoted most of our time to the discussion of the head-space problem in rifles for rimless cases, and the effect of this all-important shoulder. In rimmed, semi-rimmed, and belted cases, as we have seen, head space is controlled by the thickness of the rim or the belt and *not* by the shoulder. Consequently it is possible to reshape the case by altering the chamber. For example, the .22 Hornet case, which is tapering and has a very gentle shoulder, is reshaped or "blown out" into entirely different K-Hornet cases with straight sides and a sharp shoulder simply by firing a regular Hornet case in a K-chamber. Likewise the .25/20 repeater is converted into a .25 Dean by the same method, and many wildcat cases on rimmed, semi-rimmed, and belted cases are "fire-formed." The .22 Arrow is a fire-formed .220 Swift case, and plenty of powerful wildcats are made from fire-formed .300 Magnum cases.

How Cartridges Are Named

We have dealt with the inseparable subjects of head space and chambering together, as part of the discussion of cartridges as a whole. Now let us see how cartridges are named. The first method of naming cartridges was to give the bore diameter in hundredths of an inch, followed by the capacity of the case in grains of black powder—information that was worth something at the time because black-powder cartridges were filled to the base of the bullet with powder. Examples of this type of nomenclature are the .45/70, .38/55, .45/90, and .50/110. When the first smokeless-powder cartridges came along, the same system was followed for the earlier ones—.30/30, .30/40, .25/35, and others. Often in black-powder days the weight of the bullet was tacked on after the bore diameter and powder capacity, as in .45/70/405 and .38/72/275. Occasionally the length of the case was given as well, such as .45 Sharps, 3¼ in.

Whereas Americans gave the bore diameter in hundredths of an inch, the British used thousandths, and a .25-caliber became a .250, a .30-caliber a .300, and a .28-caliber a .280. We have to some extent adopted this, as is illustrated in the .270 Winchester and the .300 Savage.

The British service rifle (.303 British) actually has a bore diameter of .303 and a groove diameter of .311 or .312, and consequently so do the five-groove 1917 Enfield barrels originally manufactured in this country for the British but adapted to the .30/06 cartridge. The British left-hand twist and oversize bore were retained. The .303 Savage, however, is a standard .30-caliber with a bore diameter of .30 and a groove diameter of .308.

On the European continent, where the metric system of measurement prevails, it is customary to give the bore diameter in millimeters followed by the length of the case in millimeters. For example, the cartridge that we call simply the 7-mm.—because it is the only 7-mm. cartridge regularly loaded in the United States—is sometimes also known here as the 7-mm. "Spanish" Mauser, because Americans first encountered it in the war with Spain. In Europe it is known as the 7 × 57-mm. because the case is 57 mm. long. A millimeter is equivalent to .0394 inches. A 6.5-mm. is a .256-caliber, a 7-mm. a .276, an 8-mm. a .315, a 9-mm. a .354, a 9.3 a .366, and a 10.75 a .423. The Russian military cartridge, which is used to some extent in this country, is 7.62 mm., or approximately a .30-caliber. The Japanese use two military calibers: a 6.5-mm. (.256) and a 7.7 or what we would call an oversize .30-caliber (or .303).

In Europe many cartridges are made in rimless form for Mauser-type actions and in rimmed form for single-shot and double rifles and combination guns. In that case the rimmed form is followed by a capital *R*, as in 6.5 × 52 R, or 7 × 57 R (the rimmed form of our own 7-mm. "Spanish" Mauser).

Representative European calibers are: 8 × 57 (the German service cartridge), 9.3 × 72 R, 8 × 57 R, 7 × 64, 6.5 × 53. In Germany the .30/06 cartridge, for which the German gunsmiths made rifles, is called the 7.6 U.S.A., or the 7.62 × 63.

This story may seem complicated even now, but the plot thickens. Some calibers are named, *not* for their *bore* diameter, but for their *groove* diameters. The .257 Roberts cartridge is an example. It is a standard .25 with a bore diameter of .25 and a groove diameter of .257. Another such cartridge is the .348 Winchester, which is a .34. Still another is the common run-of-the-mill .22 rim-fire, which has a bore diameter of .218–.219, and a groove diameter of .222–.223. Exceptions to this method of naming the .22's are the .218 Bee and the .219 Zipper, both of which are named for *bore* diameter, because the world was so very full of various kinds of .22's, including the .22 Hornet, the .22/3000 Lovell, and other special cartridges.

Furthermore, data of various kinds, fanciful names, and heaven knows what are often added to either groove diameter or bore diameter. Very common designations are "R.F." and "C.F.," which mean rim-fire and center-fire respectively. For example, .25 Stevens R.F. means that the cartridge is a rim-fire, and .270 W.C.F. means Winchester Center Fire. The .22 W.R.F. cartridge is an oversize .22 with a groove diameter running between .2255 and .226. The .22 Savage Hi-Power is another odd-size .22, with a groove diameter of .226.

In the case of the .250/3000 Savage, the 3000 means that the muzzle velocity of the original 87-grain bullet was 3,000 foot-seconds. The .30/06 got its name because it was the .30-caliber U.S. military rifle cartridge modified to its present form in 1906. However, the .30/06 has been called the .30 U.S. Government, to distinguish it from the .30/40 or Krag cartridge, which was sometimes called the .30 Army or .30 U.S.A.

The .257 Roberts gets the second part of its name from the

man who evolved it, just as the wildcats are usually named for their inventors—.270 Ackley, .400 Neidner, .22/3000 Lovell. The names Bee, Zipper, Thunderbolt, and Swift are, of course, descriptive names with sales appeal. The term Magnum is loosely used and simply means a powerful cartridge of high velocity, as in .300 Holland & Holland Magnum (rifle), .357 Magnum (revolver).

Now add the fact that many calibers are actually misnamed, and the first figure in the name stands for neither bore nor groove diameter. Most .38-caliber revolver cartridges are really .35's with groove diameters of around .357. Actually the .357 Magnum is the only ".38" that sails under its true colors. The old .35 Smith & Wesson auto cartridge was not a .35 at all, but a more or less standard .32 pistol cartridge, and .32 pistol cartridges are really oversize .30's, with groove diameters of .311–.312. The .38/40 is neither a .38 nor yet a .35. Instead it is really a .39 caliber with a groove diameter of .401, the same as that of the old .41 Colt cartridge.

The famed fo'ty-fo' is not a .44 but a .42, and the groove diameter of the .44/40, the .44 Russian, and the .44 S. & W. Special is .427.

Well, that's how cartridges are named. It's all very simple when you understand it!

NECESSITY FOR USING CORRECT CARTRIDGES

In my job as an arms and ammunition editor I am constantly getting queries about the correct size of cartridges to use in various rifles. There is a notion, a hold-over from muzzle-loading days, that if a bullet fits the bore, all is well. Nothing could be farther from the truth. For example, people want to know if .300 Magnum cartridges could be used in a .300 Savage rifle, or vice versa—if .303 British cartridges can be used in a .303 Savage.

A person could not even begin to get a .300 H. & H. Magnum

case into a .300 Savage chamber. The .300 Magnum case is a very long belted case, one third again as long as the .300 Savage. The .303 British case is a much longer one than the .303 Savage, and it of course would not go in the .303 Savage chamber.

I constantly hear of people firing .300 Savage cases in the chambers of 7.7-mm. Arisaka Japanese army rifles. It has been done. How it happens, in spite of the fact that the .300 Savage case does not fit the Arisaka, is that the extractor holds the case for the blow of the firing pin, and the .300 Savage case wedges to some extent into the 7.7 chamber. There is absolutely no control of head space, however, and when the case is fired it blows completely out to fit the Arisaka chamber. Eventually the man who persists in doing that is going to have a serious accident. People can do many foolish things and get away with them for a time. I have seen .257 Roberts cartridges fired in a 7-mm. Mauser chamber. The head space is about the same, and the neck under the pressure will expand to fit the 7-mm. throat; of course the accuracy, however, would be exceedingly poor.

A .270 cartridge can be fired in a .30/06 chamber because head-space specifications for the two cartridges are exactly the same, but the .277 bullet in the .30-caliber barrel would simply wobble from side to side, and nothing can be hit.

After the first World War a good many .30/06 rifles were blown up by using in them 8-mm. Mauser cartridges, which looked something like .30/06 cartridges. An 8-mm. cartridge cannot be inserted into the chamber of a good .30/06 rifle, but in an old .30/06 where the bullet seat is worn out and excessive head space has developed, that is possible. That oversized bullet of about .323 fired in a .30-caliber bore will result in a blown-up rifle. Another bad piece of medicine that causes blown-up rifles is firing a .35 Remington cartridge in a .30/06 chamber.

With a rimmed case one cartridge can be fired in another chamber if the rim thickness, which in this case controls head space, is the same and the bullet is not too large. For example, a .219 Zipper cartridge could be fired in a .25/35 chamber. The reverse is not true, because the .30/30 W.C.F. bullet is oversize for the Zipper barrel. Rims on American rimmed cases are thicker than the rims on most rimmed German cases, and consequently it is impossible to close up most foreign rifles on an American rimmed case inserted in the chamber.

Often people are confused by the fact that cases fired in one rifle cannot be inserted in the chamber of another rifle of the same caliber. As we have seen, cases expand to fit the chamber under pressures from 30,000 to 50,000 pounds. When a larger case is fired in a chamber, it assumes the exact dimensions of that chamber. No two chambers, even though they are made with the same reamers, are exactly alike, and a case fired in a rifle with a slightly larger chamber will not fit in a rifle with a slightly smaller chamber. On my rack I have three .270 rifles. All of the chambers are within permissible limits. Bolts of all three rifles will close down on the minimum 1.940 gauge, but will not close on the maximum 1.946 gauge. However, one rifle has smaller chamber dimensions than the other two, and one larger dimensions than the other two. Cases fired in rifle number 1 will work nicely in rifles number 2 and number 3. Cases fired in rifle number 2 will not work in rifle number 1, but will work in rifle number 3. Cases fired in rifle number 3 will not chamber in rifle number 1 or number 2. If the reloader wants to use in his rifle cartridges that have been picked up indiscriminately after having been fired in various other rifles, he will have to full-length resize all of those cases in order to bring them back to minimum dimensions.

The Types of Actions

SINGLE-SHOTS AND DOUBLES

IN SPITE of the fact that single-shot rifles are pretty much a thing of the past, the type still has its admirers. The American single-shot actions developed at a time when the existing repeaters had not been perfected and could neither handle long and powerful cartridges for really big game nor hold their own in accuracy. The result was that the more serious rifle nut of the seventies, eighties, and to some extent nineties was a single-shot fan. He did his grizzly, elk, and buffalo hunting with the strong, accurate single shots, and also his target shooting.

Single-shot actions perfected in those days were the Sharps, the hammerless Sharps-Borchardt, the Remington-Hepburn, the Remington-Rider rolling-block, the Stevens 44½, and the famous Winchester Model 1885. At a time when black-powder cartridges were reaching the peak of development, so were these single-shot actions. In England the Farquarson action was used as a basis for many high-power big-game rifles, and in Switzerland the Martini was a favorite for target work. Germans also made many fine single-shots for target shooting. The better actions like the Winchester high side-wall version of the Model 1885 and the Farquarson are very strong actions, even by today's standards. One by one those actions became obsolete, however, and today not a single single-shot falling-block action is being made anywhere in the world, except in Switzerland. The

Winchester Model 1885 was discontinued about 1917, and as this is written not even the British are making the Farquarson.

Today rifle nuts who are also varmint hunters often get old single-shot actions and have them rebarreled and adapted to handle high-velocity varmint cartridges like the .22 Hornet, the .218 Bee, the .219 Zipper, and various wildcats. Many of these jobs are very fine and very accurate, but the sad fact is that the single-shot will not do anything that a good repeater will not— *and* it will not repeat. Particularly when equipped with a telescope sight, the single-shot is difficult to reload. I had a fine 2-R Lovell on a Sharps-Borchardt action at one time. I sold it because getting that second shot off took too darned long. On the target and on animals like prairie dogs and woodchucks where a fast second shot is not necessary, the single-shots are all right. The conservative British use them for big-game hunting, too; but for that work most hunters prefer repeaters.

The double-barrel rifles are typically British. They are made for everything from the .22 Savage Hi-Power on up to the terrific .600 Nitro Express cartridge and used for everything from crow shooting to elephants. They are built on exactly the same actions used for double-barrel shotguns and they cannot stand very high pressures. That is the reason the British use cordite powder, which gives relatively high velocity for the pressure developed.

The big double has its advantages. The second shot can be taken very quickly, and in hunting dangerous game in heavy cover this is probably a great advantage. The British say that even if one barrel goes bad, there is still another. The doubles are also alleged to have the great advantage of a quiet second shot without any rattle of the rifle action, and they are supposed to point quickly and naturally like a shotgun, as they probably do— if the hunter is used to twelve-pound shotguns.

But the doubles also have very real *disadvantages*. It is difficult to get the two barrels to shoot together. Then if the powder charge or bullet weight is changed, the barrels seldom shoot together. Replacing barrels is exceedingly expensive. Furthermore, the hunter who fires his two shots at a dangerous animal then has to reload.

The big double is probably a dying form of rifle and few will be made henceforth, as the European sportsmen who used them probably aren't going to do much big-game hunting.

In the United States a few muzzle-loading doubles were made. Colt turned out a few in .45/70 caliber, and as an experiment Winchester made a couple in .405 Winchester caliber on Model 21 Winchester shotgun actions.

THE PUMPS

No type of action is more common or more typically American than the pump, which is also called the *slide* or *trombone* action. It is the favorite action for repeating shotguns. Remington, Winchester, Savage, Stevens, Marlin, and Ithaca have all made repeating shotguns using this method of operating the repeating mechanism. Many models of .22 rifles have also used it.

Next to the semiautomatic, the slide action is the fastest of all actions, particularly for the man who has not taken time out to practice with the slower lever action and the still slower bolt action. Tens of thousands of little pump-action .22 rifles have been manufactured and sold. Most of them have ordinary tubular magazines that will handle .22 short, long, or Long-Rifle cartridges interchangeably, but one old model of the Savage pump used a clip magazine. Some of these .22's had hammers, some were hammerless. They were all takedowns. Those ejecting at the side and having solid tops are suitable for scope mounting.

From the expert rifleman's standpoint, none of these little pump .22's are any too accurate, and a man entering a match with one would be hopelessly handicapped. They are excellent boys' rifles, however. Tens of thousands of youngsters have learned to shoot with them.

In former years Marlin made a pump-action hammer-type rifle for the .25/20 and .32/20 cartridges. It was discontinued sometime about 1930 as sales fell off. Remington also made a pump for those cartridges, a hammerless, side-ejecting, solid-top job; but it too was discontinued. Those little pumps for the pest cartridges are excellent for casual shooting at coyotes, foxes, wild turkeys, and other game and varmints of medium size. Because of the takedown construction, however, none of them had the accuracy demanded by the growing army of hardened and sophisticated varmint hunters. This, coupled with the fact that neither the .25/20 or the .32/20 has the flatness of trajectory of the later varmint cartridges like the .22 Hornet and the .218 Bee, put the little pump rifles on the road to obsolescence.

The Remington high-power pump-action rifles are unique. They are hammerless, side-ejecting, and solid-breech. As a consequence they mount hunting scopes well, and many hundreds if not thousands have been so equipped. The man who uses a pump-action shotgun and who likes to shoot fast and throw plenty of lead is well fixed with one of them.

These Model 141 Remington rifles have a unique spiral magazine under the barrel so designed that the bullet of one cartridge does not rest on the primer of another. Consequently cartridges with pointed bullets can be used—something that is not true of the straight tubular magazine.

When the second World War was over, the Remington management was not particularly happy about the line of rifles they had been manufacturing. They were expensive to make and the pump and automatic rifles were not adapted to the more modern cartridges.

So the famous old Model 141 was scrapped and the Model 760 pump or slide action rifle replaced it. The new action had multiple locking lugs at the head of the breech bolt turning into a receiver slotted to receive them. Instead of the spiral magazine, the Model 760 uses a detachable box-type magazine which carries the cartridges in staggered rows like the Mauser. The action is very strong and is well adapted to the high-intensity cartridges for which it was designed—the .280, .30/06, .308, and .270.

The Model 760 is a rifle not for the dyed-in-the-wood gun nut, the accuracy enthusiast, the handloader, or the varmint hunter. Instead it is for the once-a-year hunter who buys his ammunition ready made, who is not a crack shot, who believes in plenty of fire power, and who does not like the bolt action. With their two-piece stocks these rifles are generally not as accurate as good bolt-action rifles in the same caliber. However, they are accurate enough for big-game hunting. They lack the camming power of the bolt action and they do not seat or extract oversize or dirty cases as well as the bolt. A bolt-action man myself, I have never owned one but I have shot several for groups in .280 and .30.06 calibers. Groups run 2½–4 inches at 100 yards.

THE LEVER-ACTIONS

The Winchesters: The Spencer and Henry lever-action repeating rifles came into being during the American Civil War, but the history of the Winchester lever-action rifles really begins with the famous old Model 1873, which at one time or another was made in a long line of calibers from .22 short and long to .44 W.C.F. The '73 in .38/40 and particularly .44/40 caliber probably killed more game in the period from the middle seventies to the middle nineties than all other models of American rifles combined. It was considered a great advantage by frontiersmen to have a rifle and a revolver taking the same ammunition, so the .44/40 rifle along with the .44/40 Colt Frontier revolver was practically standard equipment in the early days in the West. The rifles had a large magazine capacity and the ammunition was relatively light, so a large supply could be taken.

The Model 73 was followed by the Model 76, which was simply the 73 on an enlarged scale designed to handle more powerful cartridges needed by the elk and buffalo hunters of the West—cartridges such as the long-obsolete .45/75.

The next in the long line of Winchester lever-actions was the famous old Model 1886, which was made up until 1936, when a modernized version of this same action, the Model 71, for the fine .348 cartridge, came out. But more of that later. The 86 first came out for the .45/70 cartridge, which was the .30/06 of its day, a powerful, widely distributed cartridge, which on the frontier could usually be caged from the military. In later years it was brought out for such cartridges as the .38/56, the .38/70, the .40/65, .40/82, and .45/90. After smokeless powder came along, the 86 action was equipped with a nickel steel barrel chambered for the .33 Winchester cartridge, which is still loaded and uses a 200-grain bullet at a velocity of 2,200 foot-seconds.

The 1886 was a great favorite of the big-game hunters of the Rocky Mountains from New Mexico to the Yukon all during the eighties and nineties. It was a great elk and grizzly rifle— one used by Theodore Roosevelt in his days on the plains. The action is one of the smoothest ever produced by Winchester.

The Model 92 Winchester action is a small version of the 1886 designed to handle short cartridges like the .32/20, .25/20, .38/40, and .44/40. Before World War II it was adapted to the .218 Bee as well as to the older cartridges and was brought out with a new stock as the Model 65. It is now obsolete for all calibers and probably will never again be made.

The best seller of all time in the Winchester line is the famous Model 94. It came out in 1894 for the .32/40 and .38/55 black-powder cartridges, and then the following year for the .30/30 W.C.F., the cartridge that was the first smokeless-powder sporting cartridge made in America. With its relatively light bullet, high velocity, and flat trajectory it took the sporting world by storm and made all the grand old black-powder cartridges obsolete almost overnight. Later the .25/35 and .32 Winchester Special cartridges were brought out and found their admirers, but the .30/30 continued to reign as favorite. The Model 94 in the carbine form with the twenty-inch barrel is still being manufactured and is still popular.

The last version of the Model 94 was the Model 64. It was made in .30/30, .25/35, .32 Special, and a high-velocity caliber known as the .219 Zipper. The Model 64 has been discontinued and the only surviving Model 94 is the carbine.

All of these rifles are hammer top-ejectors, with tubular magazines. Because the point of the bullet of one cartridge rests on the primer of the cartridge immediately in front of it, sharp-pointed bullets cannot be used. Since these rifles all eject at the top, a hunting scope must be offset to the left so the fired case can be ejected.

These actions will stand pressures of around 40,000 pounds. Because the breech-block does not lock at the head, there is always some spring. Fired cases must be full-length resized before they can be reloaded.

The Model 95 Winchester was brought out right at the tail-end of the black-powder era for powerful black-powder cartridges too long to be handled by the tubular-magazine actions like the 86 and 94. The old 95 has now been obsolete since 1936. It uses a box magazine and an entirely different locking system. Originally brought out for black-powder cartridges like the .38/72 and .40/72, it was adapted to the .30/40 Krag cartridge, then later to the .30/03 and .30/06 military cartridges. It was also made for the .303 British cartridge and the famous .35 and .405 Winchester cartridges.

In those two calibers it was a favorite for elk and moose hunters and for the hunters of the grizzly and the brown bear. Theodore Roosevelt called the .405 his lion medicine, and a long list of sportsmen took Model 95 Winchesters in .30/06 and .405 to Africa with them. For many years the .405 with its 300-grain bullet at 2,220 was the most powerful cartridge made in the United States.

Many factors contributed to the old 95 becoming obsolete. For one thing, the sportsmen of the country were becoming bolt-action minded. For another, Winchester brought out the powerful .300 and .375 Magnum cartridges in the Model 70 bolt-action rifle. Fewer and fewer of the 95 rifles were sold, so finally they were discontinued. Now even the .405 cartridge is no longer loaded.

The Marlin Lever-Action Rifles: Unlike the Winchester lever-action rifles, those made by Marlin have solid tops and eject at the right side. As a consequence, scopes can be mounted low and central over the bore. The action was made in three sizes—the Model 94 for cartridges like the .32/20 and .44/40, the Model 93 for the now obsolete .25/36 and for the .30/30, .32 Special, and .38/55. The Model 1895 was brought out for the .33 W.C.F. and for big black-powder cartridges. It is obsolete.

Now the Marlin Model 39-A is still made for the .22 rim-fire cartridges. It is still a very popular little rifle and the one to be recommended for general plinking and small-game hunting to the man who uses a lever-action big-game rifle and wants some practice. The Marlin Model 36 big-game rifle is a nicely stocked and balanced woods rifle for the .30/30 and the .32 Winchester Special cartridges.

The Model 99 Savage: In spite of the fact that it was designed almost fifty years ago, the Model 99 Savage rifle is still one of the best sellers among rifles for big game. This is due to the excellent original design of the Model 99 action, coupled with a progressive policy in bringing out good new cartridges and redesigning stocks at the Savage factory.

The .22 Hi-Power cartridge was first brought out by Savage —it was the .220 Swift of its day. The .250/3000 cartridge, one of the very finest high-velocity .25's, is another Savage development, and so is the good .300 Savage.

The Model 99 has a spool magazine like that used in the Mannlicher-Schoenauer. Each cartridge fits into a little compartment in the magazine. Spitzer bullets may be used and points are protected from battering. The action is very strong and solid. As the finger lever is closed, the rear of the breech-block rises to wedge itself solidly against the massive receiver. The 99 will handle higher pressures than almost any other lever-action, and because of the solid locking the cases do not stretch to the same extent as they do in the Winchester rifles. I am able to reload my .250/3000 cases without full-length resizing.

The only real fault of the Model 99 Savage action is that it was originally made for short, rimmed cartridges like the famous .303 Savage and the .30/30 W.C.F. Consequently the later rimless high-pressure cartridges adapted to it have had to be short, in order to work through the magazine. Because of the short cases, the powder capacity is limited—and, as a result, performance is limited. Many sportsmen have expressed the desire for a Model 99 Savage rifle to handle long cartridges in the .270–.30/06 class. This, of course, is impossible without a new and longer action.

As the years have gone by, the kinds of steel and the heat treatment of material in the 99 actions have changed considerably, and the corners of the breech-bolt have been rounded. The latest actions are much stronger and tougher than those made around the turn of the century. Consequently the Savage people have a rule that they will not rebarrel their actions to anything but the original caliber.

THE MODEL 88 WINCHESTER

The latest lever-action big-game rifle is the Winchester Model 88, which is chambered for .308, .243, and .284 W.C.F. cartridges, all, like the rifle, developed since the war, and all based on the 7.62 NATO cartridge case—and the 7.62 mm. NATO and the .308 Winchester are identical.

The Model 88 is a hammerless, side-ejecting rifle with a solid top. It is actually a bolt-action rifle operated with a lever, and the bolt locks at the head with three lugs turning into slots in the receiver. The action has considerable camming power and can be used with handloaded ammunition. Also, like the bolt-action, it has a one-piece stock and a detachable box magazine carrying the cartridges in staggered rows.

[35]

THE AUTOMATICS

To the man in the street, the weapon that does everything except pull the trigger is almost universally known as an "automatic." Technicians, however, quarrel with the use of the term. One should, they say, use "semiautomatic" or "self-loading" instead, since there is no truly automatic sporting weapon that fires as long as the trigger is held down. Be that as it may, I shall use the term *automatic* here, since it is the one most sportsmen know.

The advantages of an automatic rifle are many. The principal one, perhaps, is that the automatic enables the hunter to concentrate on the game instead of having to divide his attention by working the repeating mechanism of his weapon. This, of course, is more important to the relatively unskilled man than it is to the expert. The automatic is also helpful in country where shots must be taken in very rapid succession or not at all. Actually, though, the automatic is more of a necessity as a military weapon than as a sporter. For the most part the bag limit of big-game animals is one, and a single well-placed shot will fill the deer hunter's license for the season. In war, however, an unlimited succession of targets may present itself in a very short space of time, as in a charge. The more the rifleman can concentrate on hitting those targets and the less he must think of operating a bolt, the better off he is. A cool, fast expert shot will do very well with a bolt-action rifle in spite of its relative slowness, but the hastily trained conscripts with whom wars are mostly fought are seldom cool, expert shots. Another advantage of the automatic in war is that a man concealed by camouflage or lying in a fox hole can get off several shots in rapid succession without moving or exposing himself. The adoption of our own M-1 semiautomatic rifle, often known as the Garand for its inventor, John Garand of the Springfield arsenal, was a step forward in military armament, and during the war it gave American infantrymen an edge over their foes, whether Japs, Germans, or Italians.

Conservatives opposed the adoption of the M-1 on the grounds that it was less reliable than the Springfield, more complicated, and less accurate, and that it encouraged troops in the front lines to waste ammunition. All of these criticisms are to some extent true. A good Springfield will outgroup an M-1, but the accuracy of the semiautomatic is good enough for battle, even if it may not be good enough for woodchucks. The M-1 is more complicated and easier to get out of order. However, the rifles were kept functioning with proper care even in the jungles of New Guinea and the Philippines. Untrained and undisciplined troops will waste ammunition with anything, but disciplined troops will not —even with an automatic. It is probable that the American M-1 has made every other military rifle in the world obsolete and that the next great war will be fought entirely with semi-automatic infantry rifles. But it is equally probable that for many kinds of sporting use, particularly when precision shooting and telescope sights are in order, the semiautomatic will never be popular.

I am not going to get involved in a detailed analysis of the different self-loading systems. For that the reader should refer to Johnson and Haven's *Automatic Arms*.[1] However, in a book of this sort it would be well to see something of how they work.

In order that a weapon eject the fired case and insert a fresh cartridge into the chamber, it is necessary that the mechanism utilize one of the forces generated when the cartridge is fired. As we all know, these things happen: the burning powder causes a violent expansion of gases, which drive the bullet forward through the barrel and force the head of the case back against the breech-block. We also know that this expanding gas sets up high pressure, which continues down the barrel and then drops

---

[1] Melvin M. Johnson and Charles T. Haven: *Automatic Arms*: Their History, *Development and Use* (New York: William Morrow & Company; 1941).

off rapidly to zero after the bullet leaves the muzzle. All of us have felt recoil, which is caused as a counterreaction by the overcoming of the bullet's inertia and by the impact of the expanded powder gases against the air.

Now let us look at the systems.

A great many rifles and handguns use the blow of the case as it is driven backward by chamber pressure against the breech-block. This utilization of chamber pressure is called the simple "blowback." A breech-block much heavier than the bullet is used, and since there is less inertia to overcome, the bullet moves first. Finally the breech-block begins to move against strong spring tension. It comes backward, taking the case with it. It ejects the case; then the spring brings it forward once more, picking up a new cartridge from the magazine, inserting it into the chamber, and cocking the mechanism. Pulling the trigger to fire another cartridge repeats the performance.

The blowback system with its unlocked breech is a good one in rifles of relatively low power. The Colt Woodsman pistol, the High Standard pistol, and the Winchester, Remington, and Stevens .22's are simple blowbacks. So, too, are the Winchester Self-Loading rifles in .351 or .401, which use straight, short cases with relatively low pressures. As one can see, the use of the simple blowback principle is limited. It has been estimated that if this system were used in the .30/06 the breech-block would have to weigh twenty-seven pounds!

If the blowback principle is used in connection with a mechanical device to slow it up, it is called a "retarded blowback." The Thompson submachine gun has a sliding wedge to do this. The Luger pistol employs a toggle-joint.

Recoil is also utilized. In the short-recoil system the barrel recoils a little way, starts the breech-block moving to eject the fired case and feed in another. The barrel returns to its original place, followed by the breech-block.

In the long-recoil system the barrel comes back much farther. The Remington Model 81 rifle in .25, .30, .32, and .35 calibers is operated on the long-recoil system, and the barrel recoils within a tube, which is often mistaken for a "shotgun barrel" by the uninitiated. The Browning-patent shotguns (Remington, Browning, Savage) also operate on the long-recoil system.

The gas generated by the burning powder is also a source of power. It is taken off through a hole in the barrel. In one system it strikes a piston, which moves a rod, which in turn unlocks and operates the breech-block. Because the gas hits the piston, it is called the "impinging gas" system. Where gas is admitted into a cylinder and allowed to expand against a piston, it is known as the "expanding gas" system.

For many years it was deemed next to impossible to design an automatic rifle light enough to be used as an infantry weapon, because cartridges of the military class are much more powerful and have much greater recoil and higher chamber pressures than do those successfully adapted to light automatics. It is one thing to harness the picayune power of the .22 rim-fire, or even to handle cartridges of medium power like those of the Remington rimless line or the Winchester .351 and .401 self-loading, and yet another to use the much more powerful .30/06, 8 x 57-mm. and other military cartridges. Heavy and light machine guns are something else again, since their parts can be made stronger and heavier to withstand the violence of gas action and recoil. When the United States government was working on the problem, a tentative decision was made to reduce the caliber of the government military cartridge from .30 to .276 and to reduce bullet weight and powder charge greatly to facilitate the design of a semiautomatic. It is lucky that this was not done, because the Japanese .256 Arisaka with its 140-grain bullet at a velocity of around 2,500 feet per second lacked penetration and knockdown power and proved in every way inferior to our own powerful .30 M-2 in jungle fighting; so much so that the Japs brought out a more powerful 7.7 (approximately .303) cartridge for machine gun and infantry rifle and thus complicated their

problems of supply by the use of two different calibers in infantry weapons.

Difficult as the problem of building a light shoulder rifle for
the hot .30/06 cartridge was, it was licked not once but several
times. The most famous rifle of all, of course, is the M-1 or
Garand. It is a gas-operated semiautomatic, which takes the gas
from a port near the muzzle to operate a rod that unlocks a two-
lug bolt. It is fed by a special eight-shot clip. There isn't much
doubt that the M-1 is a better battle rifle than the great old
Springfield or any other rifle of its type, for reasons mentioned
above. Japs and Germans both valued them highly and tried to
infiltrate behind the American lines to steal them. Even the conservative Marines, who clung to the Springfield for some time
after the army had declared the M-1 standard equipment, finally
came around to using them. At first, like any new mechanism,
the M-1 had a good many bugs in it, but gradually these have
been eliminated. It is necessary that the mechanism be kept clean
and oiled and that the gas port be kept free, but earnest G.I.'s
spend long and loving hours on their rifles because they know
that their lives depend upon them.

The chief rival of the M-1 was the Johnson, the invention of
a Boston lawyer who is a rifle enthusiast of long standing and a
Marine Corps reserve officer. Unlike the M-1, the Johnson
operates on the short-recoil system. The bolt turns twenty degrees to unlock while the barrel recoils ⅜ inch. The same system
is also used in the Johnson light machine gun, which is now
standard Marine Corps equipment. During 1939 and 1940 a great
controversy raged as to which was the better rifle, the M-1 or
the Johnson, and even big general magazines entered into it. A
thorough test under field conditions by the Marine Corps showed
that the M-1 was somewhat more reliable, so gradually the shout-
ing died down. The Johnson, however, is a most excellent rifle.
It was made for various foreign governments during the war.

More pleasing to the eye of the rifleman than either the M-1 or the Johnson, both of which look as though they might be carried by Buck Rogers, was the Winchester semiautomatic, designed by Ed Pugsley, Winchester engineer, and David Williams, inventor of the "Floating Chamber" used in the Colt Ace .22 pistol and in the Remington Model 550 .22 automatic, enabling it to take .22 shorts, longs, or long rifles indiscriminately. Like the M-1, the Winchester is gas-operated, but the gas is taken off only six or seven inches from the breech through a small port at the bottom of the barrel. The consequence is a good-looking, conventional-appearing rifle, without the surplus hardware that is characteristic of the Johnson and Garand. The expanding gases strike a piston head and drive it to the rear about $\frac{1}{10}$ inch, sealing the gas cylinder and preventing gas from escaping. Sufficient energy is imparted to the slide during this movement to force it to the rear, carrying with it the bolt-link and bolt. The empty case is ejected and the spring housed in the butt-stock is compressed. The spring-operated bolt then picks up a cartridge from the magazine and returns to position. Since the Winchester is a new and relatively undeveloped rifle, it has plenty of bugs in it, and in the Marine Corps tests in 1941, mentioned above, it did less well than either the M-1 or the Johnson. The bugs will be eliminated in time, no doubt. Its future probably lies in development as a sporting rifle for those who want speed of fire, and it could be made into a handsome sporter not so unlike the Model 70 in appearance. As a military rifle, the Winchester never got off the ground.

The highly successful little Winchester-developed M-1 .30-caliber carbine, which has been used on the battle fronts all over the world, also takes off the gas close to the chamber. The little rifle may possibly be developed and sold as a medium-power weapon for use on such game as coyotes and jackrabbits and indeed would be most excellent for this work at relatively short range. The M-1 carbine cartridge uses a bullet weighing 110 grains at a velocity of only 2,000 feet per second and is consequently of not much greater power than the .32/20. As a matter of fact, the carbine could be adapted to the .25/20, .32/20, or .218 Bee without great difficulty, and there is a possibility that it may be.

Some years before the war the German firm of Kreighoff developed a gas-operated sporting rifle in such calibers as the 7-mm. and .30/06. Gas is taken off into a cylinder near the muzzle and the rifle is said to operate reliably. Few if any of those rifles were imported into the United States and hence little is known about them. The German Army has used limited numbers of rifles called the Gewehr 39, 41, and 43, gas-operated weapons for the military 7.9-mm. cartridge and somewhat similar to the U.S. M-1.

An interesting side light on the reliability of semiautomatic and bolt-action rifles is shown in the Marine Corps tests, during which thousands of rounds were fired through the various rifles under all conditions. The 1903 Springfield, manually operated, bolt-action rifle had 53 malfunctions all together and an average of 3 broken, repaired, or replaced parts per rifle. The M-1 had 370 malfunctions and an average of 12.25 broken or replaced parts per rifle. The Johnsons gave 773.50 malfunctions, with 36 broken parts; the Winchester 892 malfunctions with 36 broken or replaced parts. Only one Winchester, however, finished the tests, since the supply of parts was limited.

Since the war, two gas-operated semiautomatic big-game rifles for high-intensity cartridges have been placed on the market— the Remington Model 740, later revised and call the 742, and the Winchester Model 100. The Remington is chambered for a variety of cartridges—the .30/06, .308, .280 Remington, and the .244 Remington.

Both rifles are light, weighing in the neighborhood of seven pounds. Both are gas-operated, and both lock at the head of the bolt. Both have a handsome streamlined appearance. However, the violence of the automatic action is rough on cases, and neither functions with 100 per cent reliability at high-intensity pressures of over 50,000 pounds. They are deadly hunting weapons but not quite as reliable as the bolt action.

BOLT ACTIONS

The bolt action of the Mauser-type rifle is much simpler than any lever action. An action of this type can be dismantled without tools, to be dried and cleaned. This simplicity is of enormous importance in war and also for the wilderness hunter. Because of the two massive locking lugs at the head of the bolt, the bolt action is much stronger than the average lever action. It will handle cartridges that generate greater pressures and are consequently ballistically more efficient. The bolt action is also more reliable. Because of the great camming power, it will seat over-size cartridges and cartridges that are dirty or corroded. The bolt will extract cartridges that have soft brass cases or cartridges that have been fired with high pressures and are stuck tight in the chamber. Because the bolt locks at the head, the cases do not stretch when fired, and they can be reloaded without full length resizing. As a rule a good bolt-action rifle will give better accuracy than an equivalent lever-action rifle because the cartridge is locked up more firmly and also because the one-piece bolt-action stock supports the barrel better.

The bolt-action rifle, then, because it will handle cartridges of higher pressures and higher performance, is the choice of the long-range mountain hunter who wants the utmost in ballistic performance in cartridges like the .30/06, .270, .300 Magnum, etc. The bolt action is also the choice of the gun nut who reloads his fired cases. Because of its greater simplicity and reliability it ought to be the choice of the wilderness hunter who is a long way from supplies and repairs. Even with factory ammunition, cases sometimes stick in a lever-action rifle, but almost never with a bolt-action.

The bolts will be discussed in detail in the next chapter.

[43]

CHAPTER IV

Bolt Actions Analyzed

THE choice of a rifle action depends on a good many factors —the use to which a rifle is to be put, the type of cartridge to be used, the type of sights wanted, the pressure developed by the cartridge, and so on. No one who deemed speed of fire of first importance would choose a single-shot action, for example; nor would anyone wanting a telescope sight mounted low choose a Winchester lever-action. Likewise the man wanting hairsplitting long-range accuracy would not ordinarily choose a pump or an automatic.

Before the first World War practically all rifles were purchased from a handful of large factories; but in the early 1920's a good many riflemen started having custom rifles built. An action of some sort would be obtained and turned over to a gunsmith, who would fit it with a barrel to the customer's specifications, stock it according to the customer's notion of what fitted him and what he thought beautiful, and equip it with special sights. The firm of A. O. Neidner, of Dowagiac, Michigan, was a pioneer custom gunsmithing concern. So were Griffin & Howe of New York, and the Hoffman Arms Company, first of Cleveland, then of Ardmore, Oklahoma, then finally (through a series of receiverships and changes of management) of Amarillo, Texas. Some gunsmiths bought barrel blanks from the large manufacturers, threaded them to the customer's actions, and chambered them. Others made them up from bar stock.

[44]

Many small custom barrelmakers went into business. Among them were W. A. (Bill) Sukalle, formerly of Tucson but now of Phoenix, Arizona; J. R. Buhmiller of Eureka, Montana; J. E. Gebby, of Dayton, Ohio; and P. O. Ackley, formerly of Trinidad, Colorado, but now of Salt Lake City. Specialists in stockmaking sprang up—the late Alvin Linden, of Bryant, Wisconsin; the late R. G. "Bob" Owen, once of Saquoit, New York, then with the custom department of Winchester, and next in rifle-making again at Port Clinton, Ohio; the late Adolph G. Minar, of Fountain, Colorado; and the late R. D. Tait, of Dunsmuir, California.

These custom stockers and gunsmiths have had a very important place in the recent development of the American rifle, since they have pioneered improvements now incorporated in standard factory arms. The well-dimensioned stocks on the Winchester Model 70 and Remington Model 700 rifles are direct descendants from the stocks turned out to special order by the custom stockers. The methods now employed by the factories in bedding were also worked out by these same custom stockers. Many of the newer and more efficient cartridges now in regular production were evolved by small gunsmiths—among them the .220 Swift, the .22 Hornet, and the .257 Roberts. It was these same custom gunsmiths who were responsible for the development of most telescope sight mounts—the Griffin & Howe, the Neidner, the Pike, the Turner, and others.

These firms all resulted from the great revival of interest in rifles and rifle shooting that grew out of the first World War, and they also helped to stimulate and to carry on this revival.

In ordinary times the man who simply wants a good, efficient rifle for a certain factory cartridge is wise to stay with the products of the large factories. For instance, it is cheaper by far to buy a mass-produced Winchester or Remington bolt-action rifle in a .30/06 caliber than it is to get hold of a 1903 Springfield and have it remodeled and restocked into a sporter. In the former case the rifle will cost from $125 to $150 with a receiver sight, and in the other case one is lucky to get off at three hundred dollars. The same thing holds true with the .22 Hornet, the .220 Swift, or the .257.

I am talking now about the good sensible citizen who counts his dollars. The man of the experimental turn of mind, the gun nut, is in another category. He has his own notions of stock specifications, barrel weight. Maybe no factory cartridge is exactly what he wants. Maybe he simply has a yen to experiment. He is driven by a desire for perfection, and because he wants to feel that his rifles embody his own ideas he gets a creative satisfaction out of them, even though someone else carries out his notions. Such a man is the natural customer of the private gunsmith. He is also the most avid reader of the arms and ammunition departments of the sporting magazines and is the backbone of the rifle-shooting public. May his tribe increase!

In order to have a custom rifle made up, an action of some sort has to be secured somewhere. There are actions and actions, as we saw in the previous chapter, so let us discuss the various types and makes of bolt actions with an eye to their virtues and their shortcomings for serving as the basis for a fine sporter.

The 98 Mauser. The most widely used, the most widely copied, and in many ways the best bolt-action in the world—is the Model 98 Mauser. It is either the action or the ancestor of the actions used in almost all of the recent military rifles. Exceptions are the British short Enfield, the Russian Moussin, the Italian Mannlicher-Carcano, and of course the American M-1 Garand. The American Springfield, the 1917 Enfield, the Model 30 and 721 Remington, the Model 54 and 70 Winchester, and the Japanese Arisaka are simply modified Mausers. The smaller countries, like Mexico, Argentina, and Peru, use straight Mausers, sometimes manufactured locally, but sometimes imported from Germany, Austria, or Belgium. The 1898 Mauser was, of course, the German infantry rifle of World War II.

The home of the Mauser is the Mauser Werke A.-G., Oberndorf a. Neckar, Germany, formerly called Waffenfabrik Mauser, and the so-called "original" Mausers are so marked. However, Mauser actions are made by Kreighoff and Simson in Germany and by various government arsenals. Many were also turned out in Belgium, Poland, and Czechoslovakia as well as in various other countries. The Mausers turned out by the Mexican arsenals are short, but otherwise almost unmodified Model 98's— and are very good actions for short cartridges, by the way. Many high-grade British magazine rifles are turned out in peacetime on Mauser actions; but I do not think any of these actions are manufactured in Great Britain. Instead they are imported from Germany and Belgium.

The commonest example of the 98 action seen in the United States comes from German military rifles. Those made before or during World War I are marked "Gewehr 98" (Rifle, 98), with the German proof marks, serial numbers, the date and the place of manufacture: Berlin, Danzig, Oberndorf, etc. Often these old 98's are rusted and in the haste of wartime production they were not carefully adjusted. They are good, sound actions, however, strong and reliable, a bit soft, but usually well worth working over and adjusting.

The same thing holds true of Mausers used in World War II. Instead of being marked "Gewehr 98" in Gothic characters, they are marked "Mod. 98" in ordinary Roman letters. They are not stamped with the arsenal name (Spandau, etc.) or with the private maker (J. P. Sauer und Sohn). Instead they are keyed with code names for arsenals and makers—*dou, byf, dot*, etc. The code "byf" is for the original Mauser Werke, by the way. Until 1942 these actions were nicely finished, but most of those after that date are pretty rough and many have stamped instead of milled trigger guards. Some, particularly those made in 1944 and 1945, are often so soft as to be useless.

Tens of thousands of these Model 98 rifles were brought back by returning service men and many of them will be remodeled into sporters. Thousands of Czech Mausers marked "BRNO" and Polish Mausers marked "RADOM" and "WARSAWA" (also Model

98's and for the 7.9 Mauser cartridge) have been brought home.

The Polish Mausers have good, sound actions identical with the regular Model 98's except for a slightly larger receiver ring. The Czech VZ 24 action is identical with the Model 98 and usually very well finished. Mauser-action military rifles marked "Modell 24" and with stampings in the Russian alphabet are Yugoslav Mausers made in Czechoslovakia and Belgium and chambered for the regular 7.9 Mauser cartridge. Occasionally Model 1908 Mausers for the 7 × 57-mm. and marked with the Serb coat of arms turn up. These Model 1908 actions are similar to the 98's but slightly shorter, and the Mauser Werke turned out some Model 1908 sporting rifles on that same action. A great many Czech Model 24 rifles for the 7.9 were brought back from Japan. They had been captured by the Japs from the Chinese and in turn were captured by Americans. Mexican Mauser actions are of the short Model 1908 type. Some were produced in Mexico, some in Austria, by the Steyer Werke, and some in Germany.

A very interesting variation of the Model 98 is the Czech VZ 33—a light, small-ring action with the side of the receiver milled away to lighten it and with a hollow bolt knob. It was taken over by the Germans and used by tank men and paratroopers under the name G. (for *Gewehr* or rifle) 33/40. It is a very strong action and especially suitable for building up light .257's, 7-mm's., etc.

All Mauser actions are of ordinary carbon steel similar to S.A.E. No. 1035. They are locally hardened, and except for the rough ones turned out at the end of the war they are suitable for rebarreling. They should give a Rockwell C reading of 20 on top of the receiver, at the side of the receiver, at the bottom of the receiver, and under the bottom lug recess, and the bolt should read C—30 just behind the lugs.

The Mauser-type actions now being imported into the United States from Belgium, where they are made by the great Fabrique Nationale concern, are good sound actions suitable for barreling to any cartridge no longer than the .30/06 or .270, and they come with magazines of various lengths. At the present they are being turned out with bolt handles designed for low scope mounting, the bolt knob knurled, the floor plate hinged, and with the thumb-cut on the side of the receiver omitted. They are excellent actions.

During the German inflation following the first World War thousands of military 8-mm. rifles were converted to sporters, sold cheap to American importers, and peddled in this country for as little as forty dollars, complete with a German sniping scope and mount. Revamped military rifles with barrels lapped out to make them shine and poor sights hastily fitted sold for as little as twenty dollars "new." Some were even converted to two-shot bolt-action shotguns by opening up the inside of the receiver ring so the locking lugs at the front of the bolt were inoperative.

Consequently the Mauser picture is and long has been a muddled one. However, a 98 action properly adjusted is a good one and well worth rebarreling.

The original Mauser factory in Germany turned out 98-type actions in three different lengths with various modifications. It built up complete rifles on all of them, and in normal times it sold the actions in the white to gunmakers all over the world.

The actions come in three lengths—short, standard, and long, or Magnum. The short action is a dainty little thing, the standard action in miniature. Those I have seen have a release lever at the rear of the floor plate. It is suitable for the .250/3000, the .22 Varminter, and other short cartridges with standard heads, and rifles weighing as little as 6½ pounds can be built around it. The standard action is the same length as the regular Model 98. It is a bit short for the .30/06 or .270 cartridges as it stands, and those furnished particularly for the .30/06 have the magazine wells lengthened at the factory. Any competent gunsmith, however, can open up those magazines. The later standard actions turned out by the Mauser Company for sporting rifles have hinged floor plates with a release button in the trigger guard. The third action is the big Magnum action, also with the release button for the floor plate in the trigger guard, but a good deal longer and with a longer bolt-throw than the standard action. The Magnum is suitable for the longest cartridges, like the .300 and .375 Magnum. All of these "original" actions are excellent, but because of the freezing of the mark, high tariff, and probably high mark-ups by the importer, they were very expensive in the last years before the war. A 1939 Stoeger catalogue lists the short and standard actions at seventy and eighty dollars and the Magnum actions at one hundred dollars—all of which explains why the common or garden variety of gun nut is not likely to own a rifle on a Waffenfabrik action.

The "Gewehr" 98 and "Kar" (short rifle) 98 actions of both great wars, however, are well worth good barrels and the time and expense of tuning up and adjusting them. My own favorite .270 Mauser is made up on an old 98 action that was imported into this country right after the first World War as the basis of a cheap 8-mm. sporter with oversize bore and poor stock. Some German gunsmith had pounded out the bolt handle and turned it down to the flat-bolt type. I threw away barrel and stock and had W. A. Sukalle fit a sporting-weight .270 barrel with ramp front sight, checker the trigger, mat the receiver, and adjust the trigger pull to a crisp three pounds. Then I had Alvin Linden fit a beautifully shaped and inletted stock of Bosnian walnut with a Koshollek grip cap and an imported trap butt-plate, and Frank Pachmayr of Los Angeles fit a Noske 2½x scope on Noske mounts with his form-fitting base. The result was a beautiful sporting rifle, as fine as any in the world, one that I have used with perfect satisfaction on many hunting trips.

In many respects the 98 Mauser action is superior to any of the modified Mauser-type actions that followed it. For one thing, it handles escaping gas from a pierced primer or a burst cartridge case better than does any other action. There are two large oval cuts through the bolt into the firing-pin space just back of the locking lugs, which conduct the escaping gas down the left lug race so it can escape through the deep cut in that lug race which is present to enable the shooter to press home a clip of cartridges with his left thumb—a feature not present on the earlier Model 93 and 95 actions, by the way. Furthermore the flanged bolt-sleeve tends to dissipate any remaining gas upward away from the shooter's eyes.

Because of the excellence of the 98 in handling gas and the great strength and ruggedness of the action, it is an excellent one to use with cartridges of high pressure. Once I bought at a bargain a case of old 7-mm. ammunition that had been brought to the border to smuggle to Pancho Villa, the Mexican bandit general, about 1916. It never crossed the boundary and found its way to the market. In 1934, when the stuff was at least eighteen years old and the brass was pretty brittle, I got hold of some and used it for practice in a fine lightweight 7-mm. rifle on a Waffenfabrik action. I thought I had exercised due precaution when I discarded those cartridges with split necks. I hadn't. I was shooting prone when there was a tremendous flash and an explosion right in my face. I opened the bolt and only the rim of the case came out. The head had completely blown off and a tremendous volume of gas had escaped to the rear. With a Springfield that would have resulted in a bulged magazine that would have shattered the stock, and the rifle would have been in a very sad state of repair. That Mauser, however, took it in its stride and was not harmed in the slightest. I had only to get out the remaining part of the case and go on shooting. I buried the rest of that ancient ammunition, however, and never shot another round of it.

The safety lug on the Model 98 is the best found on any bolt-action rifle. It is small, neat, and strong. It is located just forward of the root of the bolt handle and turns down into a recess in the receiver. The Mauser firing pin is one piece, less liable to breakage than those on the Winchester Model 54 and the Springfield and its blow is not cushioned by two-piece construction. Extraction is probably the most positive of any bolt-action and I cannot remember ever having failed to extract a case that remained in one piece—something I cannot say about any other bolt action I have ever used.

The 1903 Springfield. No action has been the basis for more fine sporting rifles in America than the good old 1903 Springfield, and indeed the Springfield arsenal turned out an excellent Springfield sporting rifle, beautifully bedded and tuned up, but in a rather plain, oversize stock during most of the 1920's and early 1930's. At one time this good sporter, with action adjusted to velvet smoothness, with star-gauged barrel, and equipped with a Lyman 48 receiver sight sold to members of the National Rifle Association for only forty dollars. It is not difficult to imagine how happy this made the commercial manufacturers of .30/06 rifles, who have to let the jobber and the dealer in on a small cut, who also have to pay the stockholders an occasional dividend, and who do not have the tax payer as an angel. Probably the manufacture of a *good* sporter by the government was at that time justified, because in many ways the early Model 30 Remingtons and Model 54 Winchesters were terrible turkeys. When the revamped Model 54 known as the N.R.A. model came out, about the same time as the good Remington 30-S, there was no real justification for a government-subsidized sporting rifle, and this famous special Springfield was discontinued.

The Springfield action is a modified Mauser, which was designed at the Springfield arsenal at about the turn of the century by crossing the Mauser with the Krag. Various departures were made from Mauser design, and in every instance the designers laid an egg, as we shall see presently. If these departures were made as an improvement, they failed. If they were made with the worthy notion of avoiding royalty payments to Paul von Mauser, the inventor of the Mauser action, they also failed, since Mauser put the bite on Uncle Sam for a royalty of one dollar for every rifle manufactured for many years.

The Springfield uses a two-piece rather than a one-piece Mauser firing pin. That's mistake number one. The two-piece job cushions the blow of the firing pin against the primer and also makes it a more delicate mechanism, more liable to breakage. No one knows that better than I. In 1939 the firing pin of my old Springfield sporter crystallized and broke. The pin itself wedged in the hole in the bolt face and fired a cartridge when I was pushing the bolt home and before I could turn down the handle. Result: a bulged chamber and ruined barrel, shattered stock, twisted floor plate. *And* a broken thumb almost torn off my right hand, along with a face full of bits of brass and grains of unburned powder. Until that time I had never heard of such an accident, but when I mentioned it in a magazine article, several Springfield users wrote in, saying they had had a similar experience.

The locking lugs of the Springfield are nearer the head of the bolt than on the Mauser—right at the end, in fact. Springfield lugs seem somewhat more liable to breakage.

The safety lug is a big, clumsy hunk of metal on the bolt that does nothing useful except to trip the bolt out to the right in case the lugs let go, as it does not bear against the thin shoulder of the receiver in a properly adjusted action. Actually it is supposed to be $4/1,000$ of an inch away from it. This big safety lug results in a high receiver bridge and the consequently high line of sight of the Springfield.

The Springfield handles escaping gas far more poorly than does the Mauser. It has no cuts in the bolt to carry the gas down the lug race, no flange on the bolt to turn it away from the shooter's eyes, although the head of the cocking piece performs this function to some extent. The Springfield does have a small gas-escape vent at the right of the receiver ring. Recent ones also have a much larger escape vent on the left side, which is a pious idea because it is gas scooting up the left lug race that is more apt to play hob with the shooter.

The Springfield feeds cartridges with various type bullets more dependably than does the Mauser because of the good design of the rear end of the barrel and the magazine throat. Both Mauser and Model 1917 sometimes give trouble with soft-nose bullets.

The Springfield has no thumb-groove for clip loading. Gas is not dissipated there and clip loading is slower, but actually this is of little importance. The safety on the Springfield is of the Mauser type, but is more complicated and has more parts. Not important. Ejector and bolt stop are different but all right.

Actually the Springfield action is a very good one and those seen on military rifles are usually better adjusted than in the case of Mausers. The action is well worth the trouble and expense that rifle-lovers have gone to to make it the basis of fine sporters.

Many different types of Springfield rifles have been turned out—service, sporter, national match, snipers' rifles, and so on; but they do not need to concern us in this chapter except in a very general way. The national-match Springfields have a headless cocking piece and a reversed safety. The headless cocking piece does not divert escaping gas as does the standard one with the knurled knob, and the reversed safety is a general pain in the neck, slow, clumsy to operate for the right-handed man, and confusing to one used to standard Springfield and Mauser safeties. Earlier Springfields had bolt handles that turned straight down, but about 1920 the handles were given a slight slant to the rear to put the bolt knob nearer the hand.

When the manufacture of the semiautomatic M-1 Garand rifle got under way at the Springfield arsenal, all manufacture of Springfields ceased there. The tools, however, were turned over to the Remington Arms Company at Ilion, New York, and Remington brought out war-baby Springfields, used to some extent by the army, particularly in a sniper's rifle, to be sent to China and perhaps other Allied countries. In addition it brought out a special modification of the Springfield to be used as a sniper's rifle, with a bolt turned down *à la* Model 70 for low-mounting of the Weaver 330 and Lyman Alaskan scopes. Differences between the war babies and standard Springfields are the big gas-escape vents on the left side of the receiver and the fact that the Remington-made rifles have a stamped rather than a milled trigger guard, with trigger guard and floor plate in one piece and not detachable, as they were in the old Model 54 Winchesters, which may be justified for speedy war production but will be a pain in the neck to any rifle nut. Incidentally, the Remington-made Springfields have broached rather than bored and rifled barrels, with only two grooves.

Until 1918 all Springfield receivers were made of case-hardened carbon steel. These are the famous "brittle" receivers one hears so much about. Actually thousands of them are in use with the hottest of modern loads and have never given a whimper. They are not so strong and tough, however, as later actions, and with the continual pounding in rifles with excessive head space they have been known to shatter. The firm of R. F. Sedgley of Philadelphia built thousands of Springfield sporters on these old bolts and actions, but they worked out a method of heat-treating them that reduced the brittleness. Before the war the owner of a low-number Springfield could have the receiver heat-treated by Sedgley. From 1918 until 1927 and from No. 800,000 to No. 1,275,766 Springfield used very tough double-heat-treated receivers, and these are perfectly satisfactory. In 1927, with receiver No. 1,275,767, Springfield adopted nickel-steel bolts and receivers, which are still stronger and tougher. Actually, any receiver over 800,000 has a tremendous margin of safety.*

My old Springfield began life as a 1926 N.R.A. sporter. Its receiver is of the double-heat-treated type and its number is 1,273,-272. The two other actions I have are of the nickel-steel type— one numbered over 1,300,000 and the other, evidently one of the last actions turned out by Springfield, over 1,400,000. The first formed the basis for a .257, the second for a .30/06, since my old Springfield has seen better days and I need a spare.

In the years that gunsmiths have been turning Springfield

---

* Receivers made at Rock Island numbered between 285,507 and 219,920 are of the double heat-treated type. Those from 219,921 up are of nickel steel.

rifles into sporters and using the actions as the basis for fine sporting rifles in other calibers, many strange and interesting things have been done to them. In the days before the low mounting of telescope sights it was common to thin down the bolt handle to a smaller diameter and to turn it down closer to the stock. Bolt handles were also sometimes given a further bend to the rear. Today, with the low mounting of telescope sights universal, the bolt handle is commonly cut off and welded on at another angle so it will clear a low-mounted scope, and the safety is modified to operate without a complete ninety-degree turn.

The upper tang, with its rather clumsy shape, is often reshaped to look like that of the Mauser in fine rifles. The trigger guard is often narrowed from front to rear, and occasionally the floor plate is hinged, the forward portion of the trigger guard built up with soft steel, and a release button installed so the magazine can be emptied with one press of the button as in the latest Mausers. The only two gunsmiths I have ever known to do the job are Bob Owen and Bill Sukalle. It has been done to two of my Springfield actions, and these are always confounding gun nuts who examine them. Bolt knobs and safeties are often checkered in fine rifles. Back in the days when the use of the Lyman 48 receiver sight was almost universal, a special straight-arm model was made for custom Springfields with the receiver bridge milled out to take it.

Probably the remodeling of Springfields into custom sporters will never be as popular as it was in the 1920's and early 1930's. A more sensible way for the man with a yen for something special to begin is to buy a standard Model 70 Winchester or Model 700 Remington and have it restocked as his heart desires.

The Model 54 Winchester. Any Model 54 is now an obsolete rifle, and few Model 54's are rebarreled and restocked, since the gun nut will usually choose a Mauser, Springfield, or Model 70 Winchester action for his base of operations.

The Model 54 came out in 1925 because of the demand by returned soldiers for a bolt-action sporting rifle in a .30/06 caliber. The fine .270 cartridge was also introduced with the first 54's.

The 54 is a modified Mauser with Springfield idea incorporated. Gun nuts, however, did not like its awkward reversed safety, its stamped, cheap-looking trigger guard and non-detachable floor-plate. Nor did they like its use of the trigger as a bolt stop, since a trigger properly hardened to keep its pull was apt to snap when the bolt was withdrawn hard. Most astonishing of all was the lack of any provision for escaping gas, but Winchester remedied this free of charge with the older 54's by milling holes at the factory. Otherwise the 54 was and is a strong, smooth-working action of good nickel steel like the later Springfields.

The Model 70 Winchester. Conscious of the shortcomings of the 54, the Winchester designers decided to redesign the whole action, and the Model 70, considered by many the finest bolt-action in the entire world, was the result.

Unlike the 54, the 70 has a handsome milled trigger guard. It also has a detachable floor plate hinged at the forward end, with a release just forward of the trigger guard, not in the trigger as it is in the Mauser. The release is clumsy, slow, and difficult to work and it is to be regretted that Winchester did not spend a few more cents per action to install a release button in the trigger guard as in the latest Mausers. The bolt is handsomely shaped and curved to the rear closer to the trigger. It turns up much lower than does the 54 bolt, but until recently it was still too high for the lowest scope mounting and gunsmiths had to grind it off. The old safety was the worst feature of the action. It was slow, clumsy, stiff, and did not permit the lowest scope mounting. Usually when a low scope is installed, a Tilden, Griffin & Howe, or Pachmayr safety is substituted. The post-war Model 70's have a more civilized safety and a lower bolt lift.

Two holes in the bolt carry escaping gas into the left lug race, and like the Springfield the Model 70 also has a gas-escape vent in the right side of the receiver. Cams shorter than those on the

Springfield permit a very easy bolt lift, and a guide flange on the left side of the bolt makes it quick and easy to operate, with no tendency to cramp or bind. It has a separate bolt stop and does not use the trigger for that purpose. Locking lugs are at the head of the bolt as in the Springfield, but the left lug is not slotted. As a safety lug, the root of the bolt handle turns into a recess in the receiver wall.

The trigger is of new and novel design for a bolt-action rifle. It is not of the double-draw type, but instead gives a crisp let-off like a shotgun trigger. The pull is adjustable within limits by adjusting nuts.

Besides the two guard screws the Model 70 has a third screw midway between them to hold the trigger, which is separate. Experience seems to show that this screw should not be tightened so much as the guard screws for the best accuracy. Instead one should get it just "good and snug" and then let well enough alone.

The Model 70 bolt action is certainly one of the two best actions in the world. It cannot be purchased separately, but the man wanting a de-luxe rifle stocked to his own specifications can get a standard Model 70 sporter or target rifle and go on from there.

The U.S. 1917, the Remington Model 30 and Model 720. The first World War caught the British Army in the midst of a change in their army rifle. They had long seen the faults of the old Lee-Enfield, with its two-piece stock and its one-lug bolt action, unable to withstand high pressures. Consequently an entire new rifle for a brand-new cartridge was designed. The rifle was called the Model of 1914 and the cartridge was a powerful one of 7 mm. or .276 caliber, longer than the .303 British cartridge, rimless, giving a velocity of around 3,000 foot-seconds.

The action is of the Mauser type, but greatly modified. There are two locking lugs at the head of the bolt, and the bolt-handle turning into a cut in the receiver serves as a safety lug. The firing pin is of one-piece construction, but the extractor collar is thin and the extractor itself not stiff. Hence high pressures, rough chambers, and soft brass cases are likely to result in extraction difficulties that may put a rifle out of commission temporarily. Unlike the Mauser, the action cocks on the closing motion of the bolt, a characteristic that is irritating rather than serious. The bolt is of peculiar shape, and unlike the Mauser or Springfield it does not turn up into the line of sight. This, coupled with a "rocker" safety which moves fore and aft, makes low scope mounting possible on the action without alterations. Big clumsy ears project up at the rear of the receiver to protect the rear peep sight. The whole action is big, strong, and massive in the main and is a great favorite to rebarrel to magnum calibers like the .300, .375 H. & H., and .35 Newton.

Since hundreds of thousands of short Enfields were on hand in British arsenals and there was a good supply of ammunition for them, the British never adopted the Model 1914 as the official British army rifle. Remington and Winchester, however, tooled up to make them in this country for the British and adapted them to the rimmed .303 British cartridge. Contracts were about finished when the United States entered the war in 1917. The American government was looking for a source of supply for infantry rifles, since the facilities of the Springfield and Rock Island arsenals were not sufficient to turn out Model 1903 Springfields fast enough. As a result the British 1914 rifle was adapted to the .30/06 cartridge and called the U.S. Model 1917. The bolt face, extractor, and magazine were adapted to the rimless cartridge. The same barrel tools were used, and as a consequence the 1917 rifles have the British left-hand twist and are slightly oversize. The bore diameter is .303 against the .30 of the Springfield, and the groove diameter is .311 instead of .308. During the 1920's and 1930's tens of thousands of those rifles were sold to civilians for $7.50 for a second-hand rifle and $10 for an unused one, and early in 1946 the sale began again. They were restocked by the hundreds and rebarreled to everything from the .22 Varminter to the .375 Magnum. Many gunsmiths made a living by altering them to cock on the opening motion of the bolt, milling the ears off, and installing sporting stocks and sights.

After the war Remington was faced with the necessity of bringing out a bolt-action sporting rifle for the .30/06 cartridge, and since the firm was tooled up to manufacture the 1917, that rifle was used as the basis for the new one. It was called the Model 30 Remington. The first ones had the oversize barrel and left-hand twist of the 1917 and were indeed probably made largely from 1917 parts. The stock was a weird contraption with grasping grooves in the forestock, and like the parent rifle it cocked on the closing motion of the bolt. The next model had a somewhat improved stock, which was still unsatisfactory; it had been altered to cock on the opening motion and a shotgun-type trigger pull had been substituted.

The rifle had plenty of faults, but it did have the virtue of mounting a telescope sight low. Belding & Mull, Philipsburg, Pennsylvania, scope-makers, brought out a Model 30 with a special high-combed stock for scopes, and shortly after Remington made that stock official with the model called the 30-S. By this time it was a fine and satisfactory rifle, in many respects better than the Model 54 Winchester. It was brought out in the .30/06, the .257, and the 7-mm. Mauser. At one time it was also made in the Remington rimless line of cartridges—.25, .30, .32, and .35, but eventually those and the 7 mm. were discontinued.

The last modification by Remington of the old 1917 was the Model 720, which was simply the 1917 modified, with a better-shaped bolt handle, a fine trigger pull, minor changes here and there. Actually it looks very much like the fine remodeled 1917's turned out by ace gunsmiths like Alvin Linden.

The Model 20 Savage. Right after the first World War, the Savage Arms Corporation led the parade in producing bolt-action sporting rifles by turning out the Model 20, the only short, Mauser-type action ever manufactured in this country. It was chambered for the .250/3000 and .300 Savage cartridges. The first rifles were very, very light, weighing only a bit over six and a half pounds.

In many ways the action is an interesting one. The lugs are large and strong and the receiver ring is heavy. The magazine is typically Mauser. The bolt-handle, however, passes through a split in the receiver bridge and consequently the action is not suitable for low scope mounting. The faults of the action make it unsuitable for rebarreling to a high-class expensive cartridge, but anyone looking for a very lightweight rifle in .250/3000 or .300 might consider it, with his eyes open to its shortcomings.

The Remington Model 721. The action of the 721 and, in short form, the 722 was, when introduced, of entirely new design. Instead of having a drop-forged receiver, it has one machined from steel bar stock. Floor plate and trigger guard are a single stamping. Trigger and trigger mechanisms are made of stampings, and the safety looks like the one on the Remington "500" series .22's.

Because the action is cheap-looking, it is not one that the gun nut is going to buy to have a custom rifle built on. It is, however, a very strong action. For one thing, the extractor is a heavy circular spring in the recessed bolt that completely encloses the head of the case. The action should handle very high pressures because of this, as pressure limits have heretofore been set not by the strength of the action so much as by the strength of the brass case.

Model 721 rifles weigh only about seven and a quarter pounds because of the light receivers, yet they are chambered for .270, .30/06, and .300 Magnum cartridges. The Model 722 action (identical except that it is shorter) handles the .257 and .300 Savage cartridges. It could be rebarreled nicely to .250/3000 or .22/250.

The action is locked with two massive lugs on the front of the bolt, as in the Mauser, and the bolt turning down into a cut in the receiver acts as a third, or safety, lug. The magazine is the conventional staggered, double-column Mauser box magazine.

In the spring of 1962, Remington brought out a new bolt action rifle, the Model 700, and it has made obsolete the Model 721, the 722, and the 725—which was a modification of the Model 721. The Model 700 is a handsome rifle with the best-shaped stock Remington has ever put on a bolt-action sporter. It has a Monte Carlo comb, a cheek-piece, and good-looking reversed checkering stamped in with heat and pressure. The fancier model, the BDL has fancier "checkering" and a hinged floorplate. The standard model has no floorplate. The new rifle is made in .222, .222 Magnum, .243, .270, .280, .308, .30/06, .264, the new 7 mm. Remington Magnum, .375, and .458 Magnum. The extractor has been beefed up and checkering stamped on the bolt knob.

The Savage Model 110. The new Savage Model 110 action is the first Mauser-type action turned out by Savage since the Model 1920. The receiver is machined from bar stock and not forged. It is a modified Mauser and it is made in both right- and left-handed models. It has a recessed bolt face, a band-type extractor, and a non-Mauser ejector. The bolt carries an extra pair of lugs behind the locking lugs. They do not lock. Instead they guide the bolt in the raceway of the receiver and serve as a gas shield. The head of the bolt and the receiver are vented for escaping gas.

The Model 110 action is a strong one. As this is written, the rifle around which it is built is chambered for the .30/06 and .270 cartridge and for the .243 and the .308, but the rifle will probably be brought out in .264, .338, and 7 mm. Remington Magnum.

The Weatherby Mark V. After some years of building his Magnum rifles on F. N. Mauser actions, Roy Weatherby redesigned the Mauser action according to his own ideas and called the result the Mark V. He has eliminated the Mauser faults of the partially exposed cartridge case, the wobbly bolt travel, and the wing-type safety. Instead of two lugs, the Mark V has nine.

The bolt face is counter-bored to receive and enclose the head of the cartridge case, and the breech of the barrel is also counter-bored to enclose the portion of the bolt that houses the head of the cartridge case. The bolt lift is 45 degrees instead of 90 degrees of the standard Mauser-type action. Extractor doesn't have the bite area of the Mauser but seems sufficient. Ejector is of plunger type.

The Weatherby action is a very strong one, and with its crisp single-stage trigger, smooth bolt, and good safety, it is entirely satisfactory. The first Mark V actions were made in this country from castings, but the actions are now made in Germany from forgings.

OTHER BOLT ACTIONS

After World War II, shrewd Americans began to import obsolete military rifles and have sold them by the tens of thousands by means of extravagant and colorful advertising.

Some of the rifles are sound enough, in fairly good shape, and American factory ammunition can be obtained for them. The man who buys a Model 1917 Enfield, a good Model 98-type Mauser, or a high-number Model 1903 Springfield in good shape has a basically sound rifle and is justified in spending some money on it. The best of the others have unsatisfactory actions and stocks and sights not suited for sporting use, even if ammunition such as the 7 x 57 Mauser, the .303 British, and the 8 x 57 Mauser are obtainable in this country.

The Swedish bolt-action Mausers in 7 x 55 caliber can be used as they are if the military sights are replaced. Like all Mausers of the Model 93–95 type, however, they are not suitable for pressures of over about 45,000 pounds per square inch. Most of the other imports are junk and poor buys no matter what the cost.

Rifle Barrels

RIFLE barrels are simply pieces of steel with holes in them in which spiral grooves known as rifling have been cut. The conventional process of making a rifle barrel consumes a good deal of time and takes several operations. First a hole is drilled through a steel bar. Then the hole is reamed smooth to what is known as bore diameter. Then the rifling is cut into the barrel, one groove at a time, on a rifling machine. When the rifling is completed, the measurement from the bottom of one groove to the bottom of the opposite groove is known as *groove diameter*. The original diameter of the bore before the rifling was cut is known as the *bore diameter*. As we have seen, the most common practice is to name a caliber from the bore diameter, but a good many calibers get their name from the groove diameter.

There are various systems of rifling. Sometimes the lands are narrow and the grooves are twice as wide or even wider. Sometimes the lands and the grooves are of the same width. In the usual system the lands have sharp corners, but in some systems the corners of lands and grooves are rounded and give the appearance of a worn barrel.

Narrow lands usually give somewhat better accuracy than wide lands and they seem to give lower pressures. But the accuracy life of a barrel cut with wide lands is longer because the lands are less delicate and are not so quickly washed away by erosion. The depth of the grooves varies with caliber. It is the usual practice in this country to cut the grooves for the .22 rim-fire .0025 inches deep. Grooves for the .25 caliber are .0035. The standard .30-caliber groove is .004. It is the American practice to make the groove diameter of the finished barrel the same size as the bullet diameter. The English and Continental practice is to use grooves deeper than the American grooves and a groove diameter greater than the diameter of the bullet. This system does not ordinarily give as good accuracy as the American system, particularly with the hard, tough, jacketed bullet, which cannot upset to fill the grooves. This Continental system, however, produces satisfactory accuracy for most purposes and it gives the barrel longer life than the American system. Old 7.9 German army rifles will give reasonably good accuracy when, according to American standards, they should be pretty well worn out.

The number of grooves varies from two to eight. During the second World War a great many barrels turned out in the United States for the 1903-A-3 Springfield and replacement barrels for the 1917 Enfield were broached instead of rifled and and had two very wide lands. These barrels are not as accurate as four- and six-groove barrels, but for war conditions and for most hunting their accuracy is good enough. The 1917 Enfield rifles made during World War I had five-groove barrels because those were the original British specifications. The lands and the grooves are of equal width. P. O. Ackley, the Trinidad, Colorado, gunmaker, has experimented with three-groove barrels. His theory was that these barrels would give less pressure and higher velocity. He found no particular advantage in them, however. Most high-power barrels of .30 caliber and under are cut with four grooves, and barrels of over that caliber are cut with six. Usually .22 barrels also have six grooves. Some high-power barrels and some .22 barrels have been cut with as many as eight grooves.

It is customary in the United States to give the rifling a right-hand twist. At very long ranges the spin imparted to the bullet by this twist will cause the bullet to drift to the right and it must be allowed for. The exception to this rule is the Colt revolver, which is rifled with a left-hand twist because the Colt revolvers were standardized with that twist when they were made in England. The 1917 Enfields made during World War I have this British left-hand twist.

The grooves are cut with different rates of twist, depending on the length of the bullet in proportion to the caliber and the speed at which the bullets are to be driven. A very long bullet at a moderate velocity requires a very sharp twist or pitch of rifling. For example, the Mannlicher-Schoenauer made in Austria for the very long 160-grain 6.5 Mannlicher-Schoenauer bullet at a velocity of only about 2,100 foot-seconds, needs a twist of about one turn in 7½ inches in order to stabilize that bullet or to keep its point on at game ranges. If that bullet were fired, let us say, in a 1–10 twist, it would keyhole or fly sidewise, and of course the accuracy would be very poor. On the other hand, the standard twist for the little .22 short bullet is one turn in 24 inches. The .22 short bullet weighs only 29 grains. The .22 long rifle bullet weighs 40 grains, and if one is shot in a 1–24 pitch of rifling, poor accuracy and keyholing will result because the bullet is not stablized. The standard pitch for the .22 long rifle is 1–16. Rifles on the American market that are made to handle either short, long, or long rifle cartridges have the pitch of the .22 long rifle, and as a consequence they do not give particularly good accuracy with the .22 short bullet because that short bullet is overstabilized.

The .25/35 uses a relatively long 117-grain bullet at a moderate velocity. The pitch is 1–8. On the other hand, the .257, which was designed for bullets weighing from 87 to 117 grains at much higher velocities, has a pitch of 1–10. It will handle bullets weighing up to 125 grains with good accuracy up to 300 yards, but the 87-grain bullet is less accurate than the heavier ones because it is overstabilized. The .250/3000, which was originally designed for a relatively short 87-grain bullet at a high velocity of 3,000 feet per second has a twist of 1–14. It will handle a 100-grain bullet with good accuracy, but that slow twist will not stabilize a 117-grain bullet.

The .30/06 uses a standard twist of 1–10 because the cartridge was originally designed for military use and the rate of twist established to spin the bullets clear out to a thousand yards or over. When commercial factories took up the cartridge they followed arsenal specifications. As a matter of fact, the pitch of the rifling in the .30/06 is a little too abrupt for sporting use, as the big-game hunter will never shoot at a thousand yards. A twist of 1–12 will stabilize even the 220-grain .30/06 bullet to three hundred yards and more when it is fired at a velocity of 2,400 foot-seconds.

It is generally conceded that with a twist of 1–10 the .270 W.C.F. is not ideal. One can obtain excellent accuracy with bullets weighing 130 grains or over at that twist, but a 1–12 twist gives equally good accuracy with any bullet weighing up to 150 grains and it gives much better accuracy with the 100-grain bullet at very high velocity.

As made by the factories, the .300 Magnum has a twist of 1–10. Most custom barrelmakers cut the .300 with a twist of 1–14 and report better accuracy and somewhat lower pressures. The ideal pitch of rifling should be just fast enough to stabilize the bullet at the range at which it is to be shot. The sharper the twist, the higher the pressure and the greater the strain on the bullet jacket.

Most high-velocity .22's like the Hornet, the Bee, and the Swift have barrels cut with a twist running from 1–14 to 1–16.

When a bullet is fired from a barrel, it loses velocity rapidly, but the spin remains almost constant over game ranges. Let us take a .270 bullet fired at over 3,100 foot-seconds. In every second of its flight it spins well over three thousand times. That's almost incredible. I do not think there is any doubt that the rate of spin of a bullet adds to the killing power to some extent. As the jacket folds back, it is often sharp, and the spinning bullet cuts like a buzz-saw. This was graphically illustrated to me one time when I was hunting whitetail deer in southern Arizona. A good four-point buck got up about two hundred and fifty yards away just under the brow of a hill and started off at a dead run. I managed to get the dot reticule in my scope right on his hind end just as he was about to clear the ridge and I squeezed the shot off. That buck traveled about twenty feet through the momentum of his running. When I got to him I found that the bullet had struck right between the hams, and penetrated right up through the abdomen, and then the whirling bullet with the sharp-edged jacket had simply sawed all his ribs in two on the right side. I found the bullet under the hide of the brisket.

After the round rough billet of steel from which the barrel is made has been drilled, reamed, and rifled, it is known as a barrel blank. Only a relatively few gunsmiths are equipped to turn out complete barrels. Most of them buy rough blanks from men who specialize in their manufacture. In ordinary times these blanks can be bought from the factories like Winchester, Remington, or Savage. They can also be bought from barrelmakers like W. A. Sukalle, 1120 East Washington Street, Pheonix, Arizona; Bliss Titus, Heber City, Utah; John Buhmiller, Eureka, Montana, and others. It is necessary for the gunsmith to turn the barrel to size and weight, and to straighten it so that the finished barrel will be relatively straight. Then he has to thread it to the action to which it is to be fitted, chamber it for the individual cartridge, fit sights, polish it, and blue it. As a usual thing the gunsmith also has to lap the barrel. He will cast a lead lap around a steel rod in the barrel. Then he will coat it with an abrasive and polish the tool marks out of the barrel.

All barrels are not lapped. As a matter of fact, the Springfield arsenal never lapped its barrels, considering lapping an inexact operation. Instead they tried to get the barrels so smooth in reaming and rifling that lapping was not necessary. Nevertheless most custom and factory barrels are lapped, and in most instances careful lapping will improve the accuracy.

Straightening barrels is a very important operation, and

straightening is necessary every time metal is removed from within or without. It is impossible to turn down a barrel on a lathe without getting some kinks in it. Many an amateur has put a barrel on a lathe and merrily turned it down, taking deep cuts, only to find after he was finished that he could practically shoot around a corner with it. When the barrel is turned down, shallow cuts should be taken and the barrel removed from the lathe and straightened after every cut, as every cut taken releases tension within the metal. In fact, some barrelmakers turn a blank to size before they begin drilling. These "pre-turned blanks," as J. R. Buhmiller calls them, presumably never unkink as they heat up. When a barrel has been extensively straightened it will "warp." What is meant is that as the barrel heats up, the shots will string up and down the target. When they get good and hot, many barrels will put their bullets literally inches away from where they put them when they are cold.

The commonest way to straighten a barrel these days is with an overhead clamp. The skilled operator can look through the barrel and by the shadows tell where the kink is. Then he can bear down with the clamp and get the kink out of it. The old method of straightening a barrel was to see where the kink was, then place the barrel between two lead blocks and give it a smart rap with a lead hammer.

Practically all American barrels are round these days, but formerly many of them were made in octagon shape. The octagon-shaped barrel was supposed to be fancy, but the bluing wore off on the sharp edges faster than it wore off elsewhere. The barrel heated up unevenly, and it was heavier than necessary for its strength.

In Europe barrels of various fancy shapes are made. Often the breech portion is an octagon. Often full-length ribs are milled on the barrel. The full-length matted rib is in the opinion of some very handsome. Theoretically anyway, the full-length rib should stiffen the barrel somewhat. Theoretically, also, the barrel would show a tendency to heat up unevenly and change point of impact. Actually, however, the only real disadvantages of a ribbed barrel are that it is expensive to manufacture and that it is heavier than it need be.

Barrels are made with various weights and various contours as well as various lengths. The short barrel is handy to carry on horseback in a saddle scabbard. It is also handy to use in the woods. But the short barrel has its disadvantages. For one thing, if iron sights are used, the sighting radius is shortened and the rifle will deliver less field accuracy. For another thing, the short barrel gives increased muzzle blast. The powder is still burning as it strikes the air. Not only is the muzzle blast actually more severe, but it seems even worse because it is closer to the ears. Furthermore, the barrel shorter than standard has a velocity loss which averages about 25 foot-seconds for every inch cut off the barrel. In a .30/06, for example, where the standard barrel length is 24 inches, a 20-inch barrel would deliver approximately 100 foot-seconds less than the published velocity. Likewise there is a velocity gain with a longer barrel. The .30/06, 180-grain load that delivers 2,700 foot-seconds in a 24-inch barrel will deliver about 2,750 in a 26-inch barrel.

For practical purposes, however, not a great deal is gained through using a barrel longer or shorter than 24 inches. Because it burns a lot of powder and has a loud report and great muzzle blast, the .300 Magnum is usually made with a 26-inch barrel. Heavy bull guns for long-range target shooting are often made with 28- and 30-inch barrels. Since those guns are used from the prone position and are not carried great distances in the field, weight does not make much difference. It is easier to hold a heavy rifle steady than a light one. These long barrels give a greater sighting radius and hence better accuracy for target work.

The standard 24-inch barrel is just about right for hunting. The man who wants an extra-light handy rifle can have a barrel as short as 22 inches in the .30/06 or .270. With the .257, if he wants a featherweight, he can have a barrel as short as 21 or even 20 inches. For cartridges like the .250/3000 and the .25/35, the 20-inch barrel is not bad at all. The man getting a custom-made barrel could well have a rifle for hunting only made with a 22-inch barrel, but if he gets a factory rifle with a 24-inch barrel, I doubt if it is worth the time or money to have the barrel cut off and a new front sight fitted.

As we have seen, the heavier the barrel, all things being equal, the more uniformly it will shoot. It heats up more slowly. It is less sensitive to sloppy bedding. Because it heats up more slowly it will shoot a small ten-shot group, and for that reason experimenters who do a lot of rest shooting favor the heavy barrel. As far as *practical* accuracy goes, however, it is the first two or three shots from a cold barrel that deliver the bacon. The best hunting rifle should deliver those first two or three shots into the same group day after day. If the light barrel is bedded correctly, it will deliver these small groups and as far as accuracy is concerned it is just about as good as a heavy one. The barrel should be of such weight that without a scope sight and sling the hunting rifle would ordinarily not weigh more than about eight pounds if it is to be carried long distances. The target shooter, of course, does not carry his rifle and he can use a very heavy barrel. Many Eastern woodchuck hunters who do not do much walking get rifles that weigh eleven and twelve pounds. The Eastern deer hunter or the Western mountain hunter would kill himself with such a heavy barrel. These big heavy barrels for sporting use sound a lot better in theory than they work out in practice.

Barrels are made to many different contours. Sometimes they slope gradually down from the chamber and then have a straight taper from there on to the muzzle. Sometimes they come down abruptly. The German army had three steps in the Model 98 Mauser barrel. The theory behind this was that the steps controlled the vibrations and made for uniform shooting. Whether that is true or not I am not prepared to say.

In muzzle-loading days barrels were made of soft iron, and

even with the relatively cool-burning black powder, low pressures, and lead bullets the barrels wore out. It was a common thing for a man to start with a muzzle-loader of about .30 caliber. When it got pretty well worn, he would take it to a gunsmith to have the rifling recut. This time the bore would be larger. In the life of a rifle this recutting or "freshing out" would be repeated until the barrel that started as a .30 might end up as a .40. In early black-powder days of factory rifle-production a soft carbon steel was used for rifle barrels. No great hardness was needed because pressures did not run over 25,000 pounds per square inch and lead bullets were not hard on barrels. Steel of more or less the same type is still used for many .22 barrels, because the .22 also uses lead bullets and low pressures. That is one reason why an old soft carbon-steel barrel cannot be rechambered to some modern high-intensity cartridge even though the bore and groove diameter and twist are all right. With the hotter-burning powders, jacketed bullets, and high pressures those soft barrels will wash out in a very short time. For many years the standard steel for high-powered rifle barrels was a carbon steel known as "ordinance" steel. The Springfield arsenal used it. So did Remington and Savage.

For many years the Winchester Repeating Arms Company used nickel steel on the theory that it was less sensitive to erosion and gave longer life to the barrel. As velocities and pressures have gone up, harder steels have been sought. For the last ten years Winchester has been using a heat-treated chrome molybdenum steel which is very hard and highly resistant to erosion. It is generally believed that this step was forced upon Winchester when they developed the .220 Winchester Swift. The first nickel-steel barrels washed out very quickly under the terrific heat and velocity.

The tendency today among certain barrelmakers, particularly those who experiment with ultra-high-velocity cartridges burning great amounts of powder, is to use very hard heat-treated steel into which graphite has been incorporated. The trade name of one of those steels is "Graph-Mo." Just how they are going to work out and whether they are markedly superior to chrome molybdenum is something I do not know.

A famous steel in Europe that was used for barrels on the most expensive rifles was "Poldi Anticorro." This special steel had a high chrome content. Presumably it is very resistant to both rust and erosion. The only Poldi Anticorro barrel that I have had any experience with, however, developed a nice case of throat erosion just about as rapidly as an ordinance-steel barrel would have done. This barrel was in .257 and plenty of hot loads were run through it. At one time the Winchester Repeating Arms Company made a rust-resistant steel for barrels, known as Winchester Rustless steel. The barrels have been discontinued. They were very hard to machine, I understand, and they were actually so rustless that they could not be blued. Instead they had to be copperplated, and the copper turned black. After a little use they would look pretty speckled.

Barrel Life

Many correspondents want to know how long a barrel will last. That depends on many factors. If a barrel is kept clean and cared for, it of course never rusts out—and rust, by the way, is the greatest enemy of rifle barrels. Instead the barrel first begins to show its wear at the end of the throat, or the "leade" where the rifling begins. Instead of being bright and sharp-cornered, the lands begin to wear at the corners. They look abraded or "frosted." A little later they begin to look noticeably dark and rough. This condition is caused by erosion. The powder gases push past the bullet at great pressure before the bullet upsets to seal the bore. These gases have a pressure of from 40,000 to 50,000 pounds in a high-powered rifle. They literally melt away the steel. Often this is complicated by the abrasion of unburned powder gas being pushed and dragged over the lands at terrific speed. As the erosion progresses further, it can be seen for a greater distance up the barrel. Pretty soon the careful marksman may begin to detect a falling off in accuracy. After a certain time the accuracy falls off so much that a new barrel should be obtained.

I am convinced that this erosion can be slowed up to some extent by the use of graphite wads in hand loads. Theoretically, anyway, these wads seal off the gases and keep them from working past the bullet until it is upset and seals the bore. The wax and graphite of these wads probably deposits a thin coating on the steel and protects it to some extent. I do not use these wads in large-caliber rifles as a rule, but I have found that their use pays off in the hot .22 and .25 calibers, like the .220 Swift and the .257 Roberts. These wads also seem to protect the barrel of the lead alloy bullets when they are used and to give better accuracy. A rifle used in rapid fire so that it gets very hot will have a shorter barrel life than ordinary. The rifle used for testing purposes and to fire many ten-shot groups will also show a shorter barrel life. The ultra-high-velocity rifle that burns a lot of powder and forces it through a small bore with terrific velocity will show a shorter barrel life. Some of the super-Magnum calibers will shoot out a barrel in as few as three hundred or four hundred rounds. The ordinary .30/06 should show a good accuracy life to five thousand rounds. The accuracy of the .270 is probably somewhat less because that powder gets a little hotter and moves through the bore a little faster. Actually, however, it takes a lot of shooting to wear out a barrel. Suppose each shot costs a dime, and the accuracy life of the barrel is five thousand rounds. That means that five hundred dollars' worth of ammunition must be put through the barrel, which costs from twenty to fifty dollars—and will cost that much to replace. With low pressures and lubricated lead bullets such as are found in the .22 a modern hard-steel barrel has an almost unlimited accuracy life.

Cartridges, Powder, and Bullets

ANY *cartridge* is composed of these elements: case, powder charge, primer, and bullet. As we have seen, the priming mixture of a rim-fire cartridge is contained within the folded head. In a center-fire cartridge the primer is separate. It is a pellet of priming compound of one sort or another confined within its own little brass container, which contains a built-in anvil. The firing pin of the rifle acts as the hammer. It compresses violently the priming mixture by forcing down the outside portion of the primer against the anvil. This blow sets off the priming compound; the hot gases rush through the flash hole and cause the powder to begin to burn. The expanding gases from the burning powder force the bullet through the barrel and keep pushing it up the bore.

American cartridge cases are made for the primer with the built-in anvil and the single flash hole. European cases use what is known as the Berdan primer. The Berdan primer has no anvil. Instead the anvil is at the bottom of the primer pocket, and European cases have two flash holes instead of one. Consequently American primers cannot be used with European cases, and European cases cannot be used with American-type reloading tools. It is very easy to punch out the primer of an American case, but very difficult to remove a Berdan-type primer from a European case.

American center-fire rifle primers come in two sizes—the

so-called large rifle primer and the small rifle primer. The large rifle primer measures .211 inch in diameter. The small rifle primer measures .175 inch. As a matter of fact, the large pistol and small pistol primers are the same size, but because handgun pressures run much lower than rifle pressures, pistol primers are made of much thinner and softer brass. They cannot be used for full-power rifle loads because they would puncture and not stand the pressure. Furthermore, they are not "hot" enough to ignite a large powder charge.

Formerly Remington and Winchester made large rifle primers which were less "hot" than the standard primers. They were used in such cartridges as the .250/300, .257, and .25/35. Remington called theirs the No. 8½, and Winchester theirs the No. 115. All have been discontinued. Federal Cartridge Company, long a loader of .22 rimfires and shot shells, went into the Primer business, as did Cascade of Lewiston, Idaho. Both produce rifle and pistol primers and also special hot Magnum primers.

Small rifle primers are the Winchester No. 116 and the Remington No. 6½. In the past Winchester made a larger odd-size .30/06 primer, which is no longer manufactured, but that was in the days when it was difficult to develop a non-corrosive primer strong enough for large-capacity cases. The .45 Colt Auto pistol cartridge loaded at government arsenals also used an odd-size primer. The famous Frankfort arsenal No. 70 primer was a large standard-size primer.

Up until the late 1920's all rifle primers contained potassium chlorate, which upon firing became potassium chloride, a substance akin to common table salt. The potassium chloride deposited in the bore of the rifle attracted moisture just as table salt does and caused rust. The tendency to rust was particularly marked in rifles of small-bore capacity like the .22 and .25/20. It was almost impossible to prevent this rust and usually a barrel would be ruined in a few hundred rounds. For a long time the "acid fouling left by smokeless powder" received the blame.

* In 1950 the Remington No. 8½ and Winchester No. 115 primers were discontinued.

When it was discovered that the potassium chlorate was the villain, primers were evolved which did away with that ingredient and which were "rustless." The first successful non-corrosive mixture was Remington Kleanbore. However, most of these early non-corrosive mixtures contained mercury, and mercury causes brass to grow brittle. In the case of the .22 rim-fire cartridge, which is not reloaded, this is unimportant, but handloaders could not use brittle cases that had been fired with mercuric primers. Before long, however, the various companies, led by the Winchester Repeating Arms Company, brought out primers that were both non-corrosive and non-mercuric. With a few exceptions, all center-fire cartridges are loaded with primers of this type today. They are more violent than the old chlorate primers of the Frankfort arsenal No. 70 type and less powder can be used than could be used with the old-type primers.

POWDERS

For many hundreds of years "gunpowder" simply meant a mechanical mixture of sulphur, charcoal, and saltpeter. This was the famous black powder. The rate of burning could be controlled only by the size of the grains, which were known as F.G., F.F.G., and F.F.F.G. Black powder was not ideal. It was very bulky for the amount of energy produced. It was dirty-burning and quickly fouled up a barrel, so that for best accuracy the barrel had to be cleaned every few shots, unless, as with the old muzzle-loaders, a greased patch for the bullet cleaned the barrel while the bullet was forced down the bore. Black powder also gives off a tremendous quantity of smoke, and often the game would be blotted out after the trigger was pulled.

"Smokeless" powder began to displace black powder for sporting use in the late 1890's, and about the same time rifle cartridges began to be designed for smokeless powder. The .30/40 Krag, the 7-mm. Mauser, the .30/30 and the .303 Savage are all examples of these early cartridges designed for the first smokeless powder. The military men of the world took the lead in the use of smokeless powder because of the tremendous advantage armies with rifles that did not smoke would have.

There are two principal types of smokeless powder. One contains nitroglycerin and the other pure nitrocellulose. The powder containing nitroglycerin as well as guncotton is known as double-base powder. The powders of the Hercules Powder Company are of this type. Hi-Vel No. 2, the famous rifle powder, is a good example of a double-base powder. Such powders give higher velocities with lower pressures than do the single-base powders. They are somewhat more erosive on barrels, however, because they burn at higher temperatures. Single-base powders give longer barrel life.

Powders are designed to be used at various pressures—from 10,000 or 15,000 pounds in those to be used in a handgun cartridge to 55,000 pounds in powders designed for the .270 or .300 Magnum. Of necessity the powder used in a revolver must burn very quickly because of the short barrel and the low pressure, since a revolver cannot stand the high pressures. On the other hand it is a great advantage in the case of a strong rifle to have the powder still delivering gas and accelerating the bullet when the bullet is far up the barrel. A rifle cartridge like the .270 or .30/06 demands a slow burning powder.

Some powders are very flexible and, like the famous Hi-Vel No. 2, will burn well at pressures from 30,000 to 50,000 pounds. Some powders are quite inflexible and burn efficiently only within a narrow pressure range. Hercules No. 2400 and Du Pont No. 4227 are small-grained powders for small-capacity rifle cartridges. A full charge of such powders in a case of the capacity of the .30/06 would blow up the strongest rifle ever made. On the other hand some powders are very slow-burning, and of the powders now in use Du Pont No. 4350 is the slowest burning of all.

The rate of combustion of a powder is determined by its

composition, the size of the grain, the perforation of the grain, and the coating. Some powders are made in the form of perforated rods so that the grains burn inside as well as out and continue to give off a steady flow of gas instead of the gas lessening as the diameter of the burning grain decreases. In a book of this sort one cannot get too technical about powders but every rifleman should know that powders differ vastly and because a powder gives increased velocity in one cartridge it is no sign that it will in another. Often just the opposite is true. A slow-burning powder like Du Pont No. 4350 may give increased velocity with heavy bullets in a large-capacity case but much lower velocities in a smaller-capacity case. Some large-grained slow-burning powders can be put in a small case and not even burn. The changing around of powders is extremely dangerous. Many a rifle has been blown up because amateur reloaders have removed powder from shotgun shells or revolver cartridges and attempted to reload rifle cartridges with it.

The selection of the proper kind of powder has a great deal to do with accuracy, as anyone who has experimented by reloading his own cartridges will testify. American powders are the best in the world, the only powder-makers who can compare with them being the Germans. Most of the increased efficiency in the older cartridges can be credited to the skillful technicians in American powder plants.

A book or, for that matter, several books could be written on powders alone. There are powders for every class of cartridge—powders to be used only in shotguns, powders to be used only in handguns, powders to be used only in small rifle cartridges, powders to be used in rifle cartridges of large capacity, powders that do their best work in a straight case, powders that are seen at their best in a bottleneck case. There are powders in the form of long rods of large diameter, in long rods of small diameter, in short rods of large diameter and of small diameter. There are flake powders and ball powders. The famous British cordite is a nitroglycerin double-base powder in the form of long cords. The powder is loaded into the case before the case is necked down. There are reasons for all of these differences in the appearance of powders, and no one should attempt to use a powder until he knows its characteristics.

BULLETS

The original bullet was simply a round ball of pure lead. Used in a smoothbore musket, such a bullet was smaller than the bore so it could be dropped down on top of the powder charge. Of course such a bullet was very inaccurate, and in the days when the musket was the military weapon, opposing armies literally shot in each other's faces so they would be sure of hits. Rifles were invented many years ago, but they were never popular for military use because pounding the bullet down into the tight rifling took too long a time. The American frontiersman solved this dilemma along in the eighteenth century by putting a greased buckskin or a linen patch around a ball that was about bore diameter and then pushing the ball down on top of the powder charge with one sweep of the ramrod. The greased patch cleaned out the fouling of the black powder each time; then when the rifle was fired, the patch, which fitted tightly, caused the bullet to take the rifling and spin. As soon as the bullet and patch left the muzzle, the patch dropped off and the bullet went on its way, spinning so it would fly straight.

In spite of the terrific execution the backwoods American marksmen made during the Revolutionary War, the armies of the world did not adopt the rifle until about the time of the American Civil War. Then conical bullets with hollow bases were adopted. They were smaller than the bore, but the blow of expanding gases "upset" or expanded them to fill the bore to the depth of the grooves.

The bullets for the early breech-loading rifles were of alloyed lead with grooves in them for some sort of lubrication so that the rifle barrel would not lead. Bullets were also wrapped with paper to serve the same purpose—to keep the lead from rubbing off against the barrel. Sometimes these lead bullets were cast with hollow points—or cavities in the noses. These bullets would expand when they struck flesh, and tear a much larger hole and give greater killing power than a bullet without this cavity point.

These lead lubricated bullets are still seen in revolver cartridges. They are still cast at the factories in big gang molds that will cast from twenty to forty bullets at a time. Most revolver bullets are "inside lubricated"; that is, the lubrication grooves are under the case so that the grease will not rub off if the cartridge is carried in the pocket. The ordinary .22 bullet is a lead bullet lubricated with grease. The hollow-point bullet is of the same sort that was used in the large-caliber express rifles of the 1870's. Of late years, however, the cartridge companies have loaded .22's with dry wax as lubricant or they have copperplated the bullets. In either case the bullets do not have the annoying habit of picking up dust or grit. As far as the actual shooting goes, however, these bullets are as a rule not quite so accurate as the old-fashioned greased bullets and they are slightly harder on the barrel.

With the development of smokeless powder, velocities took a decided jump and pressures rose. It was found that the greater heat of smokeless powder fused the bases of lead bullets and also that they would not stand high velocities, as they tended to strip in the rifling. Gas checks, which are simply little brass cups fitting over the base of the bullet, were developed to protect the bases from the hot gases. Even at that, though, there is a limit to the speed with which even a lubricated, gas-checked bullet that has been cast of hard alloy can be driven.

As a consequence, the early smokeless-powder cartridges like the 7-mm. Mauser, the .303 British, the .30/40 Krag, and the .30/30 Winchester were given jackets or *envelopes* of metal. If the bullets were intended for military use only, the forward portion was completely enclosed in metal and the base was usually left unprotected. The point of the bullet was left round because that was the form of bullet point used with the black-powder rifles. When the early smokeless-powder bullets were made for sporting rifles the base was enclosed with metal and the lead core was exposed at the front end. This is the familiar form of the soft-point bullet. Various metals have been used for bullet jackets. Popular for many years was a mixture of copper and nickel known as cupronickel or German silver. Jackets in some European countries were even made of mild steel. Velocities of early smokeless-powder cartridges ran from 1,800 to 2,200 foot-seconds and cupronickel jackets were entirely satisfactory.

Shortly after the turn of the century, however, bullets were lightened and velocities speeded up. In 1905 the Germans adopted an 8-mm. bullet weighing 154 grains, with a sharp point, which they called "spitzer." Instead of driving a 236-grain bullet at around 2,100, they drove that 154-grain bullet at about 2,850. The result was a much flatter trajectory and because of this a longer potentially deadly range. The Americans followed suit with a 150-grain bullet in the .30 caliber army cartridge, which had been adopted with a 220-grain bullet in 1903 for the 1903 Springfield. The lighter bullet was given a velocity of about 2,700 foot-seconds, and this combination became the famous .30/06. Then at that much higher velocity it was found that cupronickel jackets left much metal fouling. It would first be detected by lumps on the lands near the muzzle where the velocity was high. If not removed, it built up until accuracy fell off badly. For this reason all owners of high-velocity rifles in those days had to clean them periodically with ammonia dope— a messy and annoying procedure. After the first World War the Western Cartridge Company of East Alton, Illinois, brought out a non-fouling jacket material of copper, lead, and zinc, known by the trade name of "Lubaloy." Various other non-fouling jackets have been worked out and now cupronickel is no longer used except by the ultra-conservative English. The government uses a mixture of copper and zinc known as gilding metal, and even pure copper jackets are used.

A certain amount of the jacket material rubs off in the bore now, but instead of building up in lumps, it leaves in the bore a very thin copper plating, which can be removed with a brass brush or with some ammonia dope like Winchester Crystal Cleaner.

MODERN SPORTING BULLETS

The sharp-pointed or "spitzer" type of bullet is the best for longer-range shooting with the modern high-velocity rifle because such a bullet retains its velocity, its shocking power, and its energy farther than round-nosed bullets of similar weight. For short and medium ranges, however, this sharp point is not necessary, and most bullets for rifles of medium velocity like the .30/30, .32/20, etc., are still made with round noses. A round- or flat-nosed bullet is necessary for rifles with tubular magazines because the bullet of one cartridge rests on the primer of the cartridge in front of it. A bullet with a hard, sharp nose might fire the primer when the rifle recoiled. An example of how a cartridge is handicapped by being used in a rifle with a tubular magazine is the Winchester .348 cartridge with a 150-grain bullet at a velocity of 2,880. The nose of this bullet must be flat because of the magazine of the Model 71 rifle, and as a consequence the bullet loses its velocity with great rapidity. Most sporting bullets are made with flat bases, since over sporting ranges the front end of the bullet is far more important than the rear end. Once a bullet falls below the speed of sound, however, it is the rear end of the bullet that is important, and various military bullets have been made with boattail or tapertail bases. Such a bullet is useful for machine-gun barrages at very long range, but the boattail does not form a good gas seal and with it barrel life is shorter. The 172-grain M-1 bullet used by the United States Army between the two World Wars had a nine-degree boattail base. It was decided, however, that the bullet was too hard on barrels and too difficult to manufacture in great quantities. It was abandoned before the second World War broke out. The famous 180-grain Western boattail bullet has been abandoned because the boattail is of no advantage in sporting use, even though it was a good point for advertising and selling.

All things being equal, the longer a bullet is in proportion to its diameter, the deeper it will penetrate into flesh and the better it will hold its velocity. This length in proportion to diameter is generally known as "sectional density," but sectional density is really figured on the weight of the bullet as compared to its diameter. Obviously a bullet made of bronze in proportion to one made of lead and jacketed with gilding metal would not have the same sectional density because it would be lighter even though the proportions were the same.

The long, rather round-nosed bullet is best for use in heavy timber because the round-nosed bullet does not deflect nearly so much on twigs and branches as the sharp-pointed bullet. One can make a rule about like this: the lighter the bullet, the higher velocity, the sharper the point, the thinner the jacket, the more the bullet is deflected by brush. A round-nose or flat-point bullet with rugged construction and fired at moderate velocity will get through the brush on a straight line quite well, but the lighter, high-velocity, sharp-pointed bullet will be badly deflected.

The bullet should not only strike the game but expand to rupture and destroy tissue and should yet penetrate into the vitals. Some animals are lightly constructed, with thin skins and small bones. Other game animals are large, with heavy hides and massive bones. Obviously the sort of bullet that is ideal for one type of shooting cannot possibly be ideal for another. A bullet that will penetrate through the rib cage of a small whitetail deer or an antelope and then blow up in the lungs is likely simply to blow a saucer-sized hole on the shoulder of a moose or elk and wound painfully without killing. On the other hand, a bullet that gives good performance on an animal like a moose or an Alaskan brown bear would be apt to drive clear through a light, fragile animal like an antelope or a whitetail without doing much immediate damage. It is a strange paradox that a bullet that will perform ideally on a moose will only wound the much smaller whitetail.

The tendency of a bullet to expand is controlled by several factors—the speed at which it is traveling when it strikes, the thickness of the bullet jacket, the hardness of the lead core, the amount of lead exposed at the nose, or the character of the expanding-device. A bullet traveling at 3,000 foot-seconds when it strikes will expand much more violently than the same bullet traveling at 2,000 foot-seconds. A bullet encountering great resistance will expand quicker than one encountering a little resistance. Bullet design has been a serious problem. Early soft-point spitzer bullets for the .30/06 proved unsatisfactory for heavy game because they tended to go to pieces too rapidly. Often bullets have been designed with jackets that were too heavy, with hollow points that were too small. They would drive right on through light game without expanding enough. Hunters of the enormous African game like rhinos, hippos, and elephants have found that in most instances they cannot use any type of expanding bullet because if they do they cannot get sufficient penetration. Most hunters of these largest of all game animals in Asia and Africa use what we call full metal case bullets and what the British call "solids" to give maximum pentration through enormously heavy hide and in heavy bone. America, however, has no game of that class, no game on which a properly designed expanding bullet will not function well.

Various schemes have been evolved to make bullets expand. As we have seen, the oldest is the soft point, but a soft-point spitzer bullet batters badly in the magazine from recoil. An obvious thing to do is to cover the soft point with a very thin jacket of some metal. That has been done in the Winchester pointed expanding bullets of .25, .270, and .30/06 caliber. Another scheme is to have a hollow in the point. The famous 180-grain Western open-point bullet is an example of this. Various other bullets of round-nosed, semi-spitzer, and spitzer shapes have been made with this hollow point. Another scheme is to retain the hollow point and also retain the sharp point of the bullet by having a metal cap over the hollow point. This scheme has been utilized by various loading companies. The Remington Arms Company has long used a sharp-pointed bronze wedge thrust into the nose of the bullet. This famous "bronze point" expanding bullet is of a very effective design. When the wedge strikes flesh, it drives back into the bullet, splits the jacket, and opens it up.

In recent years the loading companies have experimented with bullet construction in an attempt to get bullets that would expand quickly and easily up to a certain point and then expand no farther. The famous Peters belted bullet and the Remington Core-Lokt bullets have belts toward the forward end which stop the expansion at a certain point so that much of the base remains to drive on through the game. The rather complicated Winchester-Western Silvertip bullet is also a controlled-expansion bullet. The Core-Lokt bullets have soft points or hollow noses. The Silvertip is a soft-point with the point covered and protected by a thin jacket of nickeled gilding metal. Those two bullets are among the most satisfactory for all-round use. They expand up to a certain point and then drive on through. I have shot Remington Core-Lokt bullets clear through a moose from side to side and have found the bullets perfectly expanded under the hide on the opposite side. I have driven the 180-grain Core-Lokt bullet clear through both shoulders of a big grizzly and have seen the bullet kick up dust on the opposite side. I have shot caribou with the Western Silvertip and have found the bullets under the hide on the far side. It is my impression that the Core-Lokt will penetrate somewhat more deeply than the Silvertip, but with either bullet the penetration is entirely satisfactory even with the lightweight 130-grain .270 bullet.

For long-range open-country shooting at animals of light and medium weight the best bullet is the one that expands easily. The bullets with heavy jackets and small hollow points often do not expand satisfactorily on light game even when driven at high velocities. Many years ago I put three bullets into the chest of an antelope and the exit holes on the far side were no bigger than the bullets. No expansion of any sort took place. At various times bullets, now discontinued, have been put out that expanded very poorly on light game, just as bullets have been put out that penetrated very poorly on heavy game.

One of the quickest-killing bullets I ever used was the Barnes 120-grain soft-point spitzer bullet driven in a .270 at a velocity of about 3,250. With it I shot about twenty whitetail deer and antelope and I believe every one I hit was dead before it struck the ground. Those bullets would blow up in the chest cavity and simply wreck it. I have never seen more deadly bullets for light game.

One of the best-designed of all bullets to be used on light and medium game was the 130-grain Winchester pointed expanding bullet for the .270. As we have seen, that bullet has a soft point protected by a thin copper jacket. When that strikes at .270 velocities it expands violently, yet the last third of the bullet has a very thick and heavy jacket, which ensures good penetration.

The choice of bullets, then, is something which should not be taken lightly. Not long before I wrote this I had a letter from a man who denounced the .348 Winchester cartridge. He said he had shot and wounded several deer and always had a long chase before he could dispatch the animals. He had been using the 250-grain Silvertip bullet on whitetail deer which would not dress out at much more than 125 pounds. He was shooting those bullets through the deer with a minimum of expansion. If he had used the 150-grain soft-point at much higher velocity, those deer would have been killed like dynamite. He was using a bullet designed for moose and grizzly on light animals. Often hunters use 220-grain .30/06 bullets, designed for the deepest penetration, on small game with poor results. They then blame the caliber instead of themselves. Likewise they use light, high-velocity bullets that expand readily on the heaviest game and then protest at the results. Actually the construction of the bullet has more to do with penetration than weight and sectional density. A 220-grain .30/06 bullet with a thin jacket and a great amount of lead exposed at the nose will give poorer penetration than a strongly constructed 180-grain .30/06 bullet like the Core-Lokt or Silvertip. The 130-grain Silvertip and Core-Lokt .270 bullets will give much deeper penetration than slower 150-grain soft-point .270 bullets. The bullet, then, is an exceedingly important factor in the effectiveness of any cartridge.

CHAPTER VII

Cartridge Design

THE first cartridges—the word comes from the French *cartouche*—were simply packets of cloth or paper containing a ball and powder. The shooter tore the packet open with his teeth, poured the powder down the muzzle, used the covering for wadding, then dropped or pounded the bullet down on top of it.

The first metallic cartridges that contained primer, powder, case, and bullet all in one unit were rim-fires. The case was made of copper. The priming mixture was within the folded head that formed the rim. Gradually these larger rim-fire cartridges became obsolete and were replaced by rimmed center-fire cartridges with a separate primer, which was pushed into a primer pocket in the head of the case. As the necessity for stronger cases was seen, the heads were made thicker and were simply not folded.

The conventional .22 cartridge still has a folded head. For many years the case was made of copper, but when velocities were speeded up from 1,000 foot-seconds to over 1,300, it was found necessary to make the case of brass rather than the old-fashioned and much softer copper.

Rimmed cases have many advantages. The progress of the cartridge in the chamber is stopped by the rim. More of the case is supported by the chamber itself than with the later rimless cartridge. The rimmed case, however, does not work satisfactorily through the staggered Mauser-type box magazine, and the

[89]

rimless case is really an evil forced upon the rifleman by the excellent Mauser action. To overcome this difficulty with the rimless case in which the rim does not project beyond the body of the case, two other types of cases have been designed—the semi-rimmed case, in which the rim projects enough beyond the body of the case to stop its progress into the chamber, and the belted case, in which head space is controlled by a belt just forward of the extraction groove. Either of these cases will work through a Mauser-type magazine. Examples of the semi-rimmed case are the .38 Auto Colt, the 6.5 Arisaka, the old 6-mm. Lee-Navy, and the old .280 Ross. The belted cases are the .275, .300, and .375 Holland & Holland cases and the various wildcats designed from them.

Besides the character of the rim, cartridges are classified by the shape of the case. Some cases, like the .22 for example, are straight. Some have a straight taper from the rim to the mouth. Others are bottleneck cases with the body of the case much larger than the neck. In addition the slope of the shoulder varies greatly. Some shoulders have a very gentle slope, some a very abrupt one. Experimenters have tried various curves and slopes of shoulder in an attempt to cause powder to burn more efficiently.

Some cartridge cases have very thick "webs" and are made to withstand very high pressures. Some have much thinner webs. This should be taken into consideration by the handloader. Although the .257 case is simply a necked down 7-mm. Mauser case, the web of the .257 case is a good deal thicker than that of the 7-mm. The .220 Swift case, which was designed for pressures running up to 55,000 pounds, has a very thick web. It is fatal to use a case designed for moderate pressures with high pressures. For example, much trouble with ruptured webs has been encountered in using old .25/20 single-shot cases in such high-pressure cartridges as the 2-R Lovell. Most of the big old black-powder cartridges had straight cases, and as a consequence the case capacity in grains of black powder was usually given—as in .45/70 and .45/90. Sometimes the case length was given in inches. Just so long as the caliber was correct, shorter cases, if they were perfectly straight, could be used in a longer chamber, just as a straight .38-caliber revolver case can be used in a longer chamber. For instance, the .38 Short Colt case can be used in the longer .38 Long Colt chamber. The .38 Long Colt case can be used in the still longer .38 Smith & Wesson Special chamber and the .38 Smith & Wesson Special case can be used in the .357 Magnum chamber. The introduction of the bottleneck case complicates matters, however, for, of course, a bottleneck case or a straight taper case cannot be used in a straight chamber even though the bullets may be of the same size.

Another example is the use of the .22 Short and the .22 Long in the .22 Long Rifle chamber. Those cases vary only as to length. The .22 Short case is the shortest. The .22 Long takes the same case length as the Long Rifle, but the over-all length of the cartridge is shorter because the .22 Long uses a .22 Short bullet in a .22 Long Rifle case.

The shape of the case has a great deal to do with the type and the amount of powder that can be used. The smaller the capacity of the case and the more nearly straight it is, the faster-burning the powder must be. For instance, a straight revolver case of relatively small capacity requires a small-grained fast-burning powder, which will give reasonably high velocity with very low pressure. The large-capacity bottleneck case requires a slow-burning powder, which is most efficient at a much higher pressure. The pressure for the ordinary revolver runs around 15,000 pounds per square inch. Medium-capacity slightly bottlenecked cartridges of the .30/30 class give pressures of around 38,000 pounds per square inch. Medium-capacity slightly bottlenecked cartridges of the .30/30 class give pressures of around 38,000 pounds per square inch. The large-capacity greatly bottlenecked cases like the .270, .30/06, etc., require much slower-burning powders because their pressures run around 50,000 pounds per square inch. It would be useless to try to burn powder designed for the .270 in a .22 Hornet case, and such powder would even give rather poor results in a .30/30 case. On the other hand, if one should fill a .270 case with powder designed for the .22 Hornet, the powder would detonate or explode instead of burning and blow the rifle up.

Case Design. Let's look at some of the factors in case design. In the first place the size of the head is important. If we were to design a cartridge for the Model 94 Winchester action as Winchester did when it brought out the .219 Zipper, the head size would have to be that for which the action was made—in other words, like the .30/30, .32 Special, or .25/35. The over-all length of the cartridge would have to be such that it could function through the particular magazine. That is why those enthusiasts who want the Savage Arms Corporation to bring out a Model 99 Savage in .270 W.C.F. will be disappointed. The over-all length of the .270 cartridge is simply too great. Because of the Model 99 magazine the .300 Savage cartridge had to be designed for an over-all length not greater than that of the .250/3000. First, then, the designer of a case must fit it to some existing rifle action. Besides the breech pressure, which is equal in every direction, there is also a factor known as *back thrust.* All things being equal, the larger the area of the head of the case, the greater the back thrust on the face of the bolt or the breech-block. Even though the chamber pressure of the 2-R Lovell wild-cat cartridge is high, the back thrust on the breech-block does not amount to much because of the small head of the case. On the other hand, the back thrust on the face of the breech-block is quite high with the .348 Winchester cartridge because the head of the case is very large. Chamber pressures in the .348 actually run lower than they do in the little 2-R Lovell, but back thrust is enormously greater because of the very large head of the .348 case.

There are many other factors in cartridge design. Let us go back to the .348 again. If we examine the cartridge case we notice that it is quite sloping. The sloping body of the case in combination with a rather gentle shoulder angle makes for lower pressures. It also makes for easier extraction. For this reason cartridges designed for a lever-action rifle usually have to be given some slope to the body or extraction difficulties are encountered. This slope, however, which makes extraction easier, also increases the back thrust on the bolt of the breech-block. For this reason one should never fire a rifle of this type with an oily chamber because oil in the chamber keeps the expanding brass from clinging momentarily to the chamber walls at the point of highest pressure and greatly increases this back thrust.

Because of the camming action, bolt-action rifles of the Mauser type have much greater power to extract a fired case or to seat a fresh cartridge. As a consequence, cartridges for actions of that type can be designed with practically no taper of the body. This has its advantages. A case of this sort greatly decreases the back thrust of the bolt, and hence much higher pressures can be handled.

As we have seen, a gentle shoulder slope decreases pressures, but it tends to cause the powder to burn in the rifling instead of in the cartridge case itself. This tends to increase throat erosion and shorten barrel life. As an example of this the .220 Swift as developed by Winchester gives shorter barrel life with its relatively gentle shoulder slope than do the "blown-out" or "improved" versions of the Swift with the sharper shoulder or such high-velocity .22 center-fire cartridges as the .22 Varminter or .22/.250, which has a 28-degree shoulder. The sharper shoulder also seems to give somewhat better accuracy and to burn powder somewhat more uniformly. This is generally believed to be the reason why the Swift gives the best accuracy only with maximum loads, whereas the .22 Varminter is very accurate with almost any load.

In recent years there has been a tendency on the part of experimenters to use exceedingly sharp shoulders—40 degrees or so. There is no doubt that these sharp shoulders create a turbulence within the case which consumes the powder there and gives higher velocity for less powder. It is also highly probable, however, that many of these experimental wildcat cartridges are developing very high pressures. There can be no other way to account for the fact that some of those cartridges will produce as high velocities as others with only two thirds of the amount of powder. This turbulence is producing high velocities, but probably very high pressures as well.

The very sharp shoulder has the disadvantage that often cases are hard to seat because it is difficult for the camming action of the bolt to shorten a stretched case a little bit, something that is possible with the less abrupt shoulder. From what I have seen, I seriously doubt if a shoulder sharper than 28 degrees pays off.

In the past, when the first smokeless-powder cartridges were designed, many of the necks were very long. Perhaps the best design is simply to have the necks long enough so that the longest bullets will not fit down into the powder space.

Up to a certain point it can be said that the more powder used in relation to the bullet, the higher the velocity will be. Simply taking a case and necking it down to smaller caliber for a lighter bullet has resulted in many high-speed cartridges. One of the earliest high-velocity cartridges was the .22 Hi-Power as developed by the Savage Arms Company. It was a .25/35 case necked to .22. The .256 Newton case was a .30/06 case necked to .256, and the .270 Winchester case is simply the .30/06 necked down to .270 with the same slope of shoulder retained. The .220 Swift is the old 6-mm. Lee-Navy case shortened and necked to .22, and the .257 is the 7-mm. case necked to .25. The .218 Bee case is the .25/20 repeater case necked to .22, just as the wildcat 2-R Lovell case is the old .25/20 single-shot case necked to .22.

One would think, then, that the more powder capacity in relation to the bullet weight, the greater the velocity. Very early, however, it was discovered that there is such a thing as *bore capacity*. It is possible to use only about so much powder for a certain bore. Gases can get through an aperture of a certain size only so fast. Putting more gas behind that aperture simply raises pressures without raising velocity. Many years ago A. O. Neidner of the Neidner Arms Company developed a cartridge known as the .25 special or the .25/06. It was simply the .30/06 case necked to .25. Results were disappointing. In spite of the much greater powder capacity, the velocities produced were very little better than were obtainable with the .250/3000 Savage and its much smaller case. In recent years the same lesson has been learned over and over again. The .300 H. & H. Magnum case necked to .22 did not produce velocities any higher than those of the .220 Swift with much smaller powder capacity. There also seems to be a relation between bore capacity and powder capacity as far as accuracy goes. For example, a powder capacity about like that of the .250/3000 case seems to be just about right for the high-speed .22, and the case capacity of the .30/06 is right for a bullet of .270 or 7 mm. All things being equal, this relationship between case capacity and bore capacity seems to produce the best results.

Pressure Dope

When a cartridge is fired, it generates pressures that act equally in every direction. As we have seen, they not only force the bullet down the bore, but force the head of the case back against the bolt face, and the sides of the case against the chamber. There is no very good way to measure these pressures, in spite of the fact that pressure figures for various cartridges are quoted. When pressures are taken, the cartridges must be fired in a special pressure gun, which has a hole drilled through the barrel into the chamber. A steel piston is fitted into this hole. When the cartridge is fired, the pressure exerted operates this piston, which in turn crushes the little cylinders of lead (which is used for low pressure) and copper (which is used for high pressure). The shortening of these crushed cylinders is measured in thousandths of a inch, and then a formula is used to translate this shortening into pounds per square-inch pressure. This method of determining pressures is by no means ideal. Some time a different method may be worked out.

Pressures in shotguns run from 8,000 to 12,000 pounds per square inch. Ordinary revolver loads run around 15,000 pounds per square inch. The hottest handgun loads and loads for old black-powder rifles run up around 25,000 to 30,000 pounds per square inch. Permissible pressures for lever-action rifles run around 38,000 pounds per square inch, with the exception of cartridges for the .250/3000 and the .300 Savage, which will take over 45,000 pounds per square inch. Pressures for modern bolt-action rifles using good thick barrel cases run up well over 50,000 pounds per square inch.

The size of a cartridge case does not necessarily have much to do with the pressures. For instance, the tiny .22 Hornet cartridge is loaded to the same pressure limits as the .30/40 Krag—about 42,000 pounds per square inch. Some of the little .22 wildcats develop very high pressures.

The limiting factor for pressures in the modern bolt-action rifle is not the rifle itself but the brass cartridge case. Even with the most modern cases, with plenty of brass, the safe pressure limit is still about 55,000 pounds.

Many factories control the pressures developed in a cartridge case. All things being equal, the more densely the case is loaded, the higher the pressures will be. The finer-grained the powder, the higher the pressures will be. A case can be filled full of a large-grained slow-burning powder like Du Pont No. 4350 and then the bullet seated on it so that the powder is compressed and there is no air space whatsoever. If the bullet is not excessively heavy, the pressures will be within normal limits. On the other hand, if a fine-grained quick-burning powder like Du Pont No. 4227 or Hercules No. 2400 was used in that manner, the pressures would be terrific and would blow the rifle up. The sharper the shoulder slope, the higher the pressures will be, all things being equal. The greater the bearing surface of a bullet—and by that is meant the portion of the bullet that comes in contact with the bore—the higher the pressure will be. A hard, tough jacket on a bullet will cause higher pressures than a soft jacket. Modern non-corrosive primers develop high pressures themselves, and one cannot use nearly so much powder safely with them as one could with the old potassium-chlorate corrosive primers. Different makes of cartridge cases of the same caliber vary in thickness and powder capacity. A load that would be perfectly safe in a case of one make might not be in a case of another.

Primers can tell the intelligent shooter a good deal about pressures. If the primer is completely flattened out, pressures are on the high side. If, in addition to this sign, the primer extrudes up around the firing pin, the pressures are too high.

One of the first signs of too high pressures is extraction difficulty. The high pressure has literally glued the pliable brass case into the reamer marks of the chamber. This will also happen even with normal pressures if the brass case is too soft. Sometimes the gas will escape around the edges of a primer—a condition known as "primer leak." This is a sign of high pressure, or soft brass, or both. With many custom-made rifles, chambers are too tight, and in these a load that would be perfectly all right in a normal chamber will give pressures that are too high. A bullet seated too deeply will increase pressures, and a tight throat will do the same thing. On the other hand, when the "leade" or the point where the bullet contacts the rifle becomes worn, pressures fall off and more powder can be used. A loose bore lowers pressures. Likewise a tight bore raises them. For example, the original Model 1917 Enfields were rifled oversize for the standard .30-caliber bullet. The groove diameter is about .311. When .308 bullets were fired with ordinary .30/06 standard loads, they gave lower pressures in those old 1917 barrels than they did in the tighter standard .30/06 barrels in the 1903 Springfield, or in a Model 54 and Model 70 Winchester.

The Rifle Stock

THE rifle stock as it is seen on the American hunting rifle today is the result of a long evolution. At first the rifle stock was
simply a handle to hold the gun barrel and mechanism, but very
soon craftsmen began using fine wood and checkering and carving the stocks. Guns made many hundreds of years ago in Europe
show painstaking care in stock work.

Stocks on the distinctly American muzzle-loading "Kentucky" rifles for many years set the style in rifle stocks. They
were designed to be used only in the offhand position with rifles
of relatively light recoil but considerable weight. The butt plates
were small and curved. The butt stocks themselves were quite
thin and small considering the weight of the rifle. Drop at both
heel and comb was excessive, making a Kentucky almost impossible to shoot in anything except the offhand position.

Stock design of factory sporting rifles was derived from this
Kentucky style, and for many years the stocks of most factory
rifles had too much drop and they retained those little curved
rifle-butt plates. In rifles of light recoil shot only from the offhand position they did reasonably well, but they were uncom-
fortable from sitting and from prone, and a rifle with heavy
recoil became very painful to shoot because excessive drop ac-
centuates recoil and the points of the rifle-butt plate dig into the
shoulder. The stock for the Model 1903 Springfield is a very
poor one—too short and with excessive drop at both comb and

heel. The British-designed stock for the 1917 Enfield is just about as bad. Stocks on many rifles of heavy recoil gave the shooter a bad beating. Because of its stock the old Model 95 Winchester in a .405 caliber was a terror and even the little Model 94 Winchester carbines in .30/30 kick out of all proportion to the foot-pounds of free recoil.

A properly designed stock should have a comb high enough to keep the eye comfortably and firmly along the line of sight because the cheek pressed against the comb is a great aid in keeping a rifle steady. In fact, this comb height is one of the very important elements of stock fit. The well-designed stock should be reasonably straight with drop at heel of no more than one inch greater than drop at comb so that the recoil comes back in a straight line with a steady push instead of throwing the comb up to hit the jaw. The well-designed stock should have a correctly shaped pistol grip to support the right hand and leave the trigger finger free and uncramped to control the trigger. It should have a relatively full fore-end to aid in rapid swinging of the rifle and also to enable the shooter to take up some of the recoil with his left hand. Furthermore, the fore-end of the well-designed stock should support the barrel and dampen the vibration. Lever-action rifles, pump-action rifles, and most semiautomatics have two-piece stocks. This tends to give the rifle more or less of a hinge in the middle and it is one of the reasons why the average lever-action rifle is not as accurate as the average bolt-action. Winchester lever-action rifles have the butt stock held to the action with tang screws. The most rigid two-piece stock is that seen on the Model 99 Savage. The butt stock is held to the action with a long, strong screw passing through the butt stock.

Modern American stock design began along about 1910 and the best type of stock as seen today is a process of evolution since that time. A handful of skilled marksmen were very discontented with the stocks on factory rifles. Among them were Colonel Townsend Whelen, the shooting writer and army ordnance officer, Stewart Edward White, the novelist, and the late

[99]

Captain E. C. Crossman, gun editor. They bought Model 1903 Springfields from the army and had them restocked by various gunsmiths. Those first stocks for the Springfield differed from the ordinary factory stocks in that they had flat, wide butt plates to distribute the recoil evenly over the shoulder, high combs, relatively straight butt stocks, and good hand-filling fore ends. Many of them also had cheek pieces which helped to support the rifle firmly because the whole cheek could be pressed against the butt stock.

The ideas in those first custom stocks for the Springfield didn't take any too well, however. The first Model 30 Remington rifles, for example, had a rather terrible stock with a rifle-butt plate and a thin fore end. The first Model 54 Winchester stock did not have enough pitch down. The butt plate was too small, the curve of the pistol grip wrongly placed.

Largely because of the squawks of the gun writers, the factories gradually improved their stocks. The later N.R.A. stock on the Model 54 Winchester was very good—not perfect, but a vast improvement over the original stock for the Model 54. The Remington Company put a most excellent stock on the Model 30-S and on the later 721. The stock on the present Model 722 is also good. Although the original stock on the Model 1920 was a very sad affair, that on the later Model 40 was excellent. Stocks on lever-action rifles have also been vastly improved. For use with iron sights, the stocks on the Model 71 Winchester and the Model 64 Deer Rifle are hard to beat, and so is the stock on the Model 99 Savage R and R-S. With scope sights the combs should be higher than they are, but the factory rifle must be stocked for use with iron sights. As it stands now, the average man with no marked peculiarities of build who shoots in the conventional manner will be pretty well fitted with most of the factory stocks.

The ideal stock simply puts the eye quickly into the line of sight and holds steady in any position. The ideal stock is also so pitched that recoil is minimized. Obviously, human beings differ a great deal in build and shooting habits and consequently no stock, however well designed, is perfect for everyone who shoots it. Really good design, however, is more important for the average man than the stock dimensions themselves in the way of length of pull and so on, because everyone can adapt himself to some extent to a stock.

As we have seen, the well-designed stock should have a comb high enough to support the cheek so that the eye will look right through the sights. This comb of proper height saves that split second when the whitetail buck jumps up and wastes no time in getting out of sight. That high comb is very important in accuracy because it gives a four-point suspension of the rifle—butt against the shoulder, cheek against the comb, right hand around the grip, left hand on the fore end. Actually, for most rifle shooting the right hand, shoulder, and cheek do most of the work. The rifle should be pulled firmly to the shoulder with the right hand against the pistol grip. It is always a mistake to try to pull the rifle back against the shoulder with the left hand. Except for swinging a rifle rapidly when shooting at running game, the fore end can simply lie against the heel of the left hand.

With this in mind we can see that the pistol grip should be well curved so the hand is in a natural, uncramped position and can exert the backward pressure to keep the butt firmly against the shoulder. The tendency is to make pistol grips too large. The average hand is best fitted with a pistol grip of about 4¾ inches in circumference and almost round but slightly oval in cross-section. The comb should be enough higher than the front part of the grip to keep the thumb out of the nose, and the base of the thumb should be firmly against the curve of the comb. The thumb should always be around the grip, by the way, as this is much more secure than having the thumb alongside the grip. The reason so many people shoot with the thumb alongside the grip is that they were trained with the poor stock of the old 1903

Springfield, which was much too short. When they tried to shoot with the thumb around the grip they were apt to get smacked in the snozzle.

The angle at which the butt plate is fitted on the butt is very important. This is called pitch and it is measured from the muzzle as shown in the illustration. The pitch should be such that the butt remains firm at the shoulder in any position, with no tendency to slip either up or down. Too little pitch tends to make the butt slip down below the armpit. Too much pitch down from the muzzle tends to make the butt slip up. There is nothing mysterious about pitch. Its whole purpose is to keep the rifle firm against the shoulder. The pitch down should be somewhere between 3 and 4½ inches, depending, of course, on the length of the barrel (as pitch is measured from the end of the barrel) and the straightness of the stock. Pitch that departs from these two figures is usually not satisfactory.

Drop is measured from the line of sights. Obviously the drop at comb and at heel that is perfect for iron sights is far too much for scope sights. The rifle that is to be used with both scope and iron sights will have to be stocked as a compromise. If the comb is too low the cheek is not supported, and this triangle of butt at the shoulder, right hand at the pistol grip, and cheek at the comb is broken up. If the comb is too high, so that the cheekbone has to be pressed hard against it to force the eye into the line of sight, the rifle becomes very unpleasant to shoot. If the recoil is heavy at all the cheek will be painfully bruised.

Ordinarily a drop from line of iron sights at comb of about 1⅝ to 1¾ inches is about right for the average man. Drop at heel should be around 1 inch more, or 2⅝ to 2¾.

For a rifle to be used only with scope sights the same figures apply. With the bolt-action rifle, however, to be used with scope sights only, the comb should be made as high as the withdrawal of the bolt will permit. I believe also that the rifle to be used with scope sights only should be "straighter," with less difference in drop between comb and heel. I like only ½ inch difference. That is a very straight stock, but it handles well for me. This straight stock means that even if the face isn't put at the same place each time, there isn't much difference in the actual drop as far as where the cheek goes. The straighter the stock also, the less the apparent recoil because the straight stock brings recoil back in a straight line instead of accentuating it as a crooked stock does. Some hunters have stocks made with Monte Carlo combs, which simply means that the comb goes back absolutely parallel for some inches and then drops off to give more drop at the heel. For my part I have never cared for the appearance of the Monte Carlo comb, although some prefer it.

A cheek piece not only improves the appearance of a modern rifle but aids in firm holding since the entire side of the face can be placed firmly against the stock. Some cheek pieces are more ornamental than useful. The one on the old super-grade Model 70 Winchester and the equally fine Winchester Model 52 sporter looks like a limp pancake wrapped around the comb. It is too thin to do any good. The cheek piece should be flat. It should be thick, projecting at the bottom of the stock about ½ to ⅝ of an inch. It should be of the Scheutzen type, which merges into the comb. If it is of the common English type it is no good for the stock crawler who thrusts his head as it puts a sharp edge right against the cheek.

In recent years there has been a tendency to make fore ends too large, heavy, and bulky, just as there was once a marked tendency to make them too small and skinny. The fore end should be more or less pear-shaped in cross-section, but even a perfectly round fore end is not bad. The pear-shaped fore end gives the hand a good grip if the rifle has to be swung rapidly at big game. A fore end shaped like this and about 1⅜ inches in diameter is very neat and also surprisingly adequate. Possibly a fore end of that type 1½ inches in diameter is a little better. Just now it is the fashion to put a black fore-end tip on a rifle. Sometimes these tips are made of some plastic like Bakelite, others of white plastic or ivory. The British, from whom we got this fashion, use East Indian buffalo horn and do a brisk trade in it. The best-looking fore-end tip is simply a round continuation of the fore end and not the snobble formerly seen on many rifles.

Most factory stocks are quite satisfactory for the average man if iron sights are used. If scope sights are to be used exclusively, all of them have too much drop at comb and heel. Right now the only remedy for the man who wants to get a factory rifle and use it exclusively with scope sights is to have a custom stock with a higher comb made. This is an expensive remedy although it is the only complete solution. It is also possible to get a lace-on cheek pad to raise the comb, but this is a makeshift and one that destroys the smart appearance of the rifle. With the continued growth in popularity of the scope sight, a factory probably will bring out two models of stocks—one for iron sights and one for scope sights only.

Lines of a stock are difficult to describe—almost as difficult to describe as the difference between the features of a beautiful woman and those of a homely one. In spite of this difficulty and the fact that the measurements of the features would be in small fractions of an inch, almost everyone knows this difference. It is the same way with stocks. The handsomest stocks are things of sweeping beauty. Equally well-fitted stocks may be bulky and ugly. The art of stock shape and design that combine beauty with utility is a very high one.

The average man is quite well fitted with a stock with a length of pull (or distance from the center of the trigger to the center of the butt plate) of from 13¼ to 13½ inches. The tendency on the part of the man who doesn't know much about stocks is to think he wants a longer stock than he ought to have. The short man will be very well off with a 13-inch stock and most men will be better fitted with a 13¼-inch stock if they plan to shoot the rifle in cold weather when they are bundled up in many layers of clothing. A boy or a woman can use a stock even shorter than 13 inches. As a matter of fact, a stock of 12¾ inches is not bad at all for a small woman. As we have seen, then, a man from 5 feet

6 inches to 5 feet 10 inches or so should have a stock of from 13¼ inches to 13½ inches. The six-footer can take a somewhat longer stock—usually 13⅝ to 13¾ inches—and the very tall man with exceedingly long arms can use a stock as long as 14 inches. On the whole we can say that because of the different methods of mounting and handling a gun the rifle stock should be from ½ to ¾ of an inch shorter than the shotgun stock, and of course it should have more pitch down.

The average American factory stock is made from plain American walnut with little figure in it. American walnut is good stock material although it is not the finest. The very best stock material is European walnut from trees of the thin-shell "English" variety. Wood of this type comes under various names, depending upon the locality from which it is presumed to have been imported—English, French, Italian, and Circassian. In years past the very finest walnut stock blanks have presumably come from the Circassian district of the Caucasus Mountains, but the bulk of the fine walnut used by the best makers in Germany, England, and the United States has come from the Rhone River section of France. Imported into the United States, even though they are duty-free, the best walnut blanks are quite expensive, costing from ten dollars for a rather plain one to as high as fifty dollars or even more for a superlatively figured one. European walnut has more contrast than American walnut. Its colors range from black to light yellow, with intermediate yellowish and reddish browns. It takes checking better and will hold much finer diamonds than American walnut.

Another excellent wood for stocks is maple. It is rather light in color, but if it is touched up with a blowtorch to increase the contrast—a process known as the Japanese "Suigui" finish—an ornate and complicated figure results. A well-marked wood known as Oregon myrtle is also used for gunstocks. So are apple, cherry, and mahogany, and in the Southwest even mesquite. But the finest of all gunstock materials is the thin-shelled European variety of walnut. In the past few years many English walnut groves in California have been cut down. Much of the wood has been sliced very thin to be used as veneer for furniture, but a good deal of it has been made into gunstocks, and some of them are as fine as the finest that have ever come out of Europe.

Good checkering on the rifle stock adds greatly both to beauty and to utility. On factory stocks checkering runs from 14 to 18 lines to the inch. Much of it is sloppy, carelessly done, fuzzy. Fine custom stocks made of hard, fine wood are generally checkered 24 to 26 lines to the inch. Some crack stockers like Al Biesen of Spokane, Washington, recess their checkering patterns about $\frac{1}{16}$ inch. The effect is very handsome. Right now there is a fad for French-skip or "basket-weave" checkering. I do not care for it. Fine, precise checkering with small diamonds filed up sharp and uniform is generally an indication of the class of a stock.

Since the war some pretty terrible-looking stocks, both factory and custom-made, have come on the market. Many of the stock shapes are bizarre and there has been a fad to inlay them with contrasting wood, ivory, mother-of-pearl and to carve them with portraits of moose that look like rats with horns, with scantily clad but well-endowed maidens, and slavering grizzlies. To me this is like the useless chrome, tail fins, and junk on mass-produced automobiles, and I want no part of it.

A fine custom stock costs money, as the making of a custom stock is handwork and handwork takes time. Before the war it was possible to get a fine custom stock for about $75 plus the cost of wood and fittings, and in those days a stock blank of good French walnut cost about $10 and the very finest about $25. A stock job the late Alvin Linden did for me back in the middle 1930's cost me, all told, I believe, about $85. Now a good custom stocker will charge from $200 to $275, or even more for a complete stock if he furnishes wood and fittings. To inlet, shape, finish, and checker a stock takes about a week's steady work. A fair French walnut blank costs at least $50.

There have never been more than a handful of really fine

stock-makers in this country. The firm of Griffin & Howe, the Holland & Holland of the United States, has employed some excellent stockers and has turned out some beautiful rifles. Most of their workmen have been from the Old World. Many of the old-time American stockers have gone to the land where all wood is hard, well figured, and cuts clean. Adolph Minar has been dead almost thirty years. Alvin Linden died during the war, Bob Owen about 1956. What has happened to Bob Hutton and John Wright I cannot say. Like John Dubiel, also dead, they were English. August Pachmayr is very old, and so is Tom Shelhamer.

However, members of a new generation of American stock-makers are doing the finest stock work in the world, far better than anything I have seen come out of England or the Continent since the war. Alvin Biesen of Spokane, Washington, is a meticulous and uncompromising stocker in the classic tradition. His stocks for big-game rifles are superbly inletted, beautifully shaped, flawlessly checkered. He likewise does fine shotgun stocks. Leonard Mews of Appleton, Wisconsin, is another superb stocker. He departs more from the classic tradition than does Biesen, since he once stocked for Weatherby and got the California virus in his blood. Lenard Brownell of Sheridan, Wyoming, is yet another top hand who stocks in the classic manner.

Anyone planning to make his own stock or go more deeply into the subject can do no better than to buy Alvin Linden's three booklets on stock-making. They are published by Thomas G. Samworth of Georgetown, South Carolina. Clyde Baker's book *Modern Gunsmithing*, although it came out thirty years ago, has excellent material on stock design. It is likewise a Samworth publication.

What Is Accuracy?

THE word *accuracy* means as many different things to different people as, let us say, those other very general words, *beauty* and *virtue*. One man has a rifle that he says is "accurate," meaning that now and then he actually hits something with it because the stock fits him fairly well and the recoil does not scare him to death. Another man is an experimenter and bench-rest shooter. To him a rifle is not accurate unless it will group ten shots into a one-inch circle at one hundred yards.

For varmint hunting, where the man behind the rifle will try to take the very small mark that is a crow or a prairie dog at 200 yards or more, accuracy is of prime importance. It is also important for the long-range big-game hunter who may have to knock over his antelope at four hundred yards. For big-game hunting at short and moderate ranges, gilt-edged accuracy is not important, because practically any sort of rifle is accurate enough for a deer, moose, or elk's vital areas at from twenty-five to a hundred and fifty yards.

There are various kinds of accuracy.

One is simply the ability of a given rifle and load to place the bullets in a small group at a given range. Old black-powder cartridges like the .32/40 and the .38/55 had this grouping ability in a superlative degree. Yet this ability merely to group does not give these rifles practical field accuracy for varmint shooting, let us say. Both have too curved a trajectory. At long and unknown ranges they are not *accurate* because one cannot hit with them. This is not the fault of the inherent *grouping* ability of the rifle and cartridge but of *too much departure of the bullet from the line of aim.* The cartridge with the curved trajectory, then, although it may have grouping ability, does not have practical hunting accuracy. In its broader aspects accuracy is not only the ability to shoot small groups at known ranges, but also the ability to hit at unknown ranges. Such a cartridge as the .38/55 is indeed a good grouper, but as far as practical field accuracy goes it cannot sit at the same table with such a cartridge as one of the fine .22 wildcats like the .22/.250, which has a very flat trajectory.

Surely another aspect of practical field accuracy is the ability of a bullet to buck wind. What avails it if a certain cartridge will group under ideal conditions into two inches at two hundred yards if a little puff of breeze will blow the bullet two or three inches out of the group! As far as results go, it is better to have a cartridge that will group into four inches at that distance and buck wind than to have one that will shoot into two inches on a still day and yet get blown off.

Still another aspect of accuracy is the ability of a rifle to shoot into the same group with various weights of bullets and charges and kinds of powder. Some rifles will shoot practically anything into a six-inch group at two hundred yards. Others, although they may shoot small groups with one particular brand and lot of ammunition, will shoot different brands and lots all over the paper.

Once upon a time I had a beautiful 7-mm. Mauser that illustrates many of the things I am trying to point out. It was really a good grouper and on a certain day with a certain load it could be depended upon to keep its shots in a bit less than two inches at one hundred yards. But if I changed brands of ammunition, even though I used the same weight of bullet at presumably the same velocity, the group enlarged greatly.

Furthermore, that was the darnedest rifle to change point of impact that I have ever seen. It never shot in the same place on two consecutive days. Under ideal conditions that rifle would group, but was it accurate? I'll say it wasn't!

For the moment let us discard all aspects of accuracy except the ability to group, which, as we have seen, is only part of the picture. In this respect accuracy is only another word for uniformity, and the more uniform the ammunition is, the more accurate it is.

Ideally, each bullet should weigh exactly the same and should be of exactly the same diameter. Each jacket should be of the same degree of hardness. Points and bases should be perfect. The hardened and enthusiastic group shooters weigh and spin each bullet they use to see that they are uniform and they segregate bullets according to weight into different lots. Many sporting bullets will vary as much as 2.5 grains plus or minus. In other words, a bullet that is listed as weighing 150 grains may weigh 147.5 grains or 152.5 grains. One would naturally expect some variation in accuracy between the two extremes.

Not only should the bullets be uniform, but the powder charges also. Powder measures, whether those used by the handloader or by the loading companies, will vary from ½ to 2½ grains in the charges they throw with the coarsest-grained powders like Hi-Vel No. 2 and No. 4350. These variations will of course make a difference in point of impact, particularly at the longer ranges, and good match ammunition should have each powder charge individually weighed.

Cases also differ in thickness and therefore in powder capacity from lot to lot and from make to make. A given power charge will give greater pressure and higher velocity in a small case than in a large one; and this variation will show up on the target. Those wanting the smallest groups weigh cases and segregate them according to weight, because in the same caliber the heavier the case, the thicker the brass and the smaller the capacity.

The tension of the bullet in the neck also has an important bearing on accuracy and uniformity. Match ammunition is rigorously tested for uniformity of bullet pull. A certain number of bullets from each thousand loads is pulled. If the pull is not uniform, the whole lot will be demoted down to cooking ammunition.

As cases are fired, the necks stretch and lengthen, and some flow and thicken. If a man tries to shoot minimum groups with a mixed lot of cases, some of which have been fired once and some twenty times, he is going to be disappointed.

As we have seen, this business of getting accurate and *uniform* ammunition alone is very important and enormously complicated. But accuracy just begins there.

The bore itself should be straight and uniform, with no high and low spots. The famous "star-gauged" barrels turned out at the Springfield arsenal were simply barrels that had been measured with a special gauge and that came within a predetermined standard of uniformity. The action should lock the cartridge up tight and uniformly and center the bullet in the leade.

The barrel should be straight so that as it heats up it will not begin to unkink and "walk" the group. It should be of such a contour and weight that it vibrates uniformly with slight variations of bullet weight and powder charge.

It is of enormous importance that the barrel and action be bedded correctly in the stock, with the recoil shoulder of the receiver snug and true against its recess in the stock. A warping stock, which will warp against the fore end, then away, bear against the left side of the barrel, then the right, will mean a constantly shifting point of impact from day to day.

The question is often asked if a light barrel can be as accurate as a heavy one. The answer is that barrel weight is just one of many factors affecting accuracy. A good uniform and straight *light* barrel will outshoot a poor heavy barrel. It is true, however, that the heavier a barrel is within reason, the less sensitive it is to poor bedding and to variations in loads because it vibrates less violently. It is also true that the rifle with a heavy barrel is less sensitive to variations in sling tension and methods of holding.

Nevertheless, a light job with a good barrel will shoot right along with heavy rifles, especially for the first three or four shots.

For target work, where long strings of shots are fired and it is essential that the tenth shot won't land very far from the first one, the heavy barrel has it all over the light one. For big-game hunting, where it is seldom that more than three shots are fired at an animal, but where a rifle is often carried in a day many miles over the roughest of country, the light rifle will acquit itself nicely. The same thing is true of the varmint rifle. If the rifle is to be carried for long distances, as in Western coyote and jackrabbit hunting, the light rifle is the thing, just as long as it is accurate. On the other hand, the Eastern woodchuck and crow hunter who does most of his shooting out of a car can have a heavier rifle built.

For many years there has been a controversy between rifle-men whether a barrel should "float" or not—in other words, whether it should be free of the fore end, so the fore end does not touch at any point. Probably the heavy barrel had best be left free-floating, and the barrels of most target rifles are so made.

However, the light barrel should be bedded so that the barrel touches the barrel channel for about an inch forward of the receiver and is then freed up to a point just back of the fore end. There the fore end should bear against the barrel with a slight upward pressure of four or five pounds. I have yet to see a free-floating light barrel that shot particularly well, whereas many light rifles with barrels bedded as I have described will shoot like a house afire.

Some gunsmiths bed the barrel snug the entire length of the fore end with this same upward pressure. This seems to work out very nicely, particularly if the wood has no tendency to warp hard against the stock. If the fore end bears against the barrel, it is of primary importance that the stock should have the wood so cut that the grain is diagonal with the barrel and does not have the tendency to warp hard.

Good Bedding Is an Extremely Important Factor in Accuracy. Some cartridges are more accurate than others. Sometimes this is because a certain cartridge may not be particularly popular and not many pains are taken with it, whereas another cartridge may be made to much more rigid specifications. The .220 Winchester Swift cartridge, for example, is made to very rigid specifications, and that is one of the reasons why it is so accurate. The .32 Winchester Special is purely a deer cartridge. It is not held to such rigid specifications and hence does not give particularly good accuracy.

Once upon a time the .30/06 cartridge was the leader in the big-game hunting and target field and great pains were taken with .30/06 ammunition. In recent years, however, fewer pains seem to be taken with .30/06 ammunition, and ordinary factory loads are not so accurate as formerly.

Some cartridges are *inherently* more accurate than others. It has been my observation that the cartridges in which the bore has been brought down to a much smaller diameter than the body usually show pretty good accuracy. Furthermore, they seem to put various powder charges and bullet weights, all things being equal, into a better group than cartridges in which bore and body are more nearly the same size. Add to this a fairly sharp shoulder and the result is usually an inherently accurate cartridge.

There are certain cartridges that seem to have "balance," where bore capacity and powder capacity are about right. The .270 will usually shoot a bit better than the equivalent .30/06. The .30/06 case is under .30-caliber bore capacity, whereas the .270 bore is about right for the case of the .30/06 capacity. The .250/3000 and the .257 Roberts are about right in the relationship of bore and powder capacity, but the .250 is an easier cartridge to work out good loads for than the .257, probably because it is more nearly exactly right in bore capacity.

Anyone who has done much handloading knows that some combinations of powder charge and bullet just naturally make more accurate loads than others, probably because of the cleaner and more uniform burning of powder. Some experts believe that the one most important factor in accuracy is the *correct charge of the correct powder.*

Let us take the .270, for instance. A good many years ago I tried out different powders and different charges with the Winchester 130-grain pointed expanding bullet. I soon decided that No. 3031 powder was hopeless. It seems to be too quick burning for best results in the .270 case. I also decided that No. 4320, although good, was not quite good enough. No. 4350 shot like nobody's business with the 150- and 160-grain bullets, but it did not close those groups up as much as I'd like to see with the 130-grain. No. 4064 gave me good results from the first. I loaded 48, 48.5, 49, 49.5, 50, 50.5, and 51 grains, and of all the loads my best groups were obtained with 49.5 grains of No. 4064. That load shoots well in any .270 I have ever tried it in, so evidently No. 4064 is the right bullet powder for the .270.

As a rule slightly better accuracy is obtained when the bullets are seated so they almost touch the lands of the rifling. I have always got better results with this method than when the bullet is seated so it is jammed hard into the rifling and better than when the bullet has to make a jump to engage the lands.

On the other hand, the free-bored rifles of Roy Weatherby, California gunmaker, give fine accuracy, and I have seen .220 Swifts with all the rifling gone four or five inches up the barrel that still have good accuracy.

The best rifle in the world won't shoot unless the correct rate of twist is employed in the barrel. The longer a bullet is, the more rapid the twist that is needed to stabilize it. The shorter the bullet, the slower the twist. The higher the velocity, the slower the twist can be.

The ideal twist or pitch of rifling should be just enough to stabilize the bullets at the longest ranges at which they will be shot. If the twist is too slow and the bullet spins too slowly, the bullet will tumble or keyhole in the target. If the bullet is over-stabilized the accuracy is poor.

The .30/06 has a standard twist of one turn in ten inches because it was desired to stabilize bullets to one thousand yards. Actually a pitch of 1–12 will usually result in better accuracy and is sufficient to stabilize even the long 220-grain bullets over game ranges. The 100-grain .270 bullet at 3,540 is enormously overstabilized with the standard 1/10 twist, and for the .270 the best all-around twist is 1–12. It will stabilize even the 150-grain factory load. A .300 Magnum will give excellent accuracy with a twist of 1–14, and the Swift or Varminter with 1–16 or 1–14. For the 100-grain bullet alone in the .270 the 1–14 twist is best.

But all this talk of accuracy is of no avail unless the sights are such as to enable the man behind the rifle to *see*. Put a big gold bead on an open rear sight on the finest, most accurate rifle in the world, and a group of 4 inches at one hundred yards is a good one. Put a good peep sight and a blackened blade front sight on the same rifle, and the group will be cut down to 2½ inches or so because the error of aim is less. Take the same rifle and put a 2-x hunting scope with crosshair reticule on it, and the group will be about 2 inches. A four-power scope will reduce the error of aim by half, an eight-power will halve it again. In small-bore shooting, where the boys who win keep all their shots in the 2-inch 10 ring at one hundred yards with most of them in the 1-inch X-ring, scopes of ten, fifteen, and even twenty power are used.

Accuracy, then, is a combination of many things—of bullet, case, and powder charge, of barrel, of stock, of sights—of so many things that it would take two walruses to think of them.

CHAPTER X

Iron Sights

IRON sights have taken many and often exceedingly fanciful forms. Actually very few people understand the principles that operate in the use of the sight, as shown by the fact that some of the worst sights are the most popular.

There are two types of iron sights—the open sight and the aperture or peep sight. The open iron sight has to be a considerable distance from the eye, or approximately one third of the way down the barrel. The peep sight has to be relatively close to the eye. Sometimes the peep is mounted on the tang of the rifle. Sometimes it is attached to the receiver and sometimes to the cocking piece of a bolt-action rifle.

The ordinary front sight is a bead of some kind—gold, ivory, or red plastic; but for military and target use the front sight is usually a sturdy steel blade, flat on top.

The earliest rear sights were simply pieces of metal with notches cut in them so the front sight could be aligned in the notch. This type of open sight is still found on the majority of rifles as they leave the factory. A sight of this sort is cheap and easy to make, requiring little labor or material. It is the sight with which most people do their first shooting. The ordinary open rear sight may have either a *V* notch or a *U* notch. It usually has crude steps for elevation. Sometimes the *V's* are quite narrow. Sometimes they are wide and shallow. Sometimes these sights have white diamonds or triangles which presumably direct the eye to the middle of the *V*. The British are very fond of a shallow *V* rear sight with a thin platinum line. Usually British rifles come with what is known as the express rear sight, with a whole battery of leaves of various heights for various ranges from 100 to 400 or 500 yards. A favorite open sight in America for those who do not know much about sights is the strange contraption known as the Rocky Mountain rear sight. In this two big ears jut far up above the sighting *V*. Those ears do nothing except to blot out the light and obscure the target. It is a strange thing that many people feel that if a sight is easy to use, it probably isn't any good, and the more difficult it is to see through a rear sight, the better it is. The Rocky Mountain buckhorn is undoubtedly the most fantastically bad rear sight ever designed. Second honors for the poorest sight go to the semi-buckhorn, which differs only in degree.

The best type of open rear sight is the very shallow *V* such as the sights seen on British double rifles. Another good type of open rear sight is simply a flat bar with a white triangle forming the aiming point. The most accurate type of open rear sight is like the one used on the old 1903 Springfield. It is the "patridge" where the square post can be seen in a square *U* notch, and aim is taken with the flat front blade on the level with the top of the sight, and space is seen between the sides of the square *U*. Both horizontal and vertical aim can be nicely controlled with a sight of this type, and rather small groups can be shot with it. The fastest of all open sights is the shallow *V*. The British, who have had more experience shooting large and dangerous game in Africa and India than any other people, swear that these sights are faster for close range work than any other. Whether that is a fact or simply the famous British conservatism, I do not know.

Open sights have decided disadvantages. In the first place the use of the open sight is asking the eye to focus on three places at once—on the rear sight from eighteen to twenty inches from the eye, on the front sight, thirty-six inches or so from the eye, and on the game, which is anywhere from ten to several hundred yards from the eye. It requires no genius to know that this is an impossible feat. Young eyes with great powers of accommodation can make a pretty fair stab at it. Middle-aged eyes which have lost their powers of accommodation find it impossible. There comes a time in the life of every man when the rear sight begins to fuzz up and he says: "I can't cut them as fine as I used to." Then he must go to the aperture type of rear sight or to a scope.

The open rear sight also has a very bad fault in that it has a tendency to make the hunter shoot high under conditions of poor light or excitement. With quick shooting it is almost impossible not to shoot high, and the open sight is to blame for that ancient adage: "Always hold low on deer." There is nothing in particular about a deer that causes one to shoot high, but there is about the ordinary open sight. When the hunter is excited he does not draw the front bead down as fine as he does when shooting at a target. As a result the bullet goes over the deer's back. This tendency of the rear sight to make the maintaining of elevation difficult is a bad one. In poor light it is difficult to see the front bead when it is brought clear down into the bottom of the notch because the deeper the notch and the sharper the *V*, the poorer the light at the bottom. The hunter, then, won't draw down fine enough, because he wants to *see* that front sight and he shoots over. Couple all this with the fact that the ordinary rear sight is only crudely adjustable and one can see that it is no bargain.

A great many people act under the assumption that the rifle they receive from the factory is correctly sighted in for them. Sometimes it is, but most times it isn't, as no one can do an exact job of sighting a rifle in for anyone else, particularly with open sights. Rifles shoot to various points of impact with various brands of ammunition and weights of bullets. Different people have different ways of holding and pointing. One man may like a fine bead; another may habitually draw a coarse bead. Consequently a sight should be adjustable and every man should sight his rifle in for himself. With the ordinary open sight the notches on the elevation steps have a value of from four to six inches per hundred yards or range or from eight to twelve inches at two hundred yards. Windage is obtainable only by knocking the base of the rear sight over in the slot. As can be seen, this is a very crude method of adjustment and it is seldom that a rifle can be sighted in with ordinary rear sights right on the nose.

Probably the best use for the open rear sight is as an auxiliary sight to be left on a rifle that is mounted with a scope, as other sights are so much better.

Aperture Sights

Optically the aperture sight is far superior to the open rear sight. It is designed on the optical principle that the eye naturally centers the front sight at the point of strongest light, which is always in the middle of the peep. To use an aperture sight correctly, one should ignore the rear sight entirely and instead look *through* it, put the front sight on what one wants to hit, and squeeze the trigger. The aperture sight should be seen completely out of focus as a hazy and shadowy rim. One should not attempt to center the bead within it. The eye does that naturally and instinctively. As we have seen, the aperture sight is by far the best type of iron sight for the middle-aged man because he does not have to focus on it as he does on the open rear sight. His powers of accommodation are enough so that he can bring the front sight and the game into fairly sharp focus by simply seeing them *through* the rear sight.

Beginners with aperture sights always make two mistakes. In the first place they are appalled when they discover how much they can see through a rear aperture of this size. They can see the world, they think, and all that is in it. Used as they are to the difficulties of the ordinary open rear sight they think that this will never do. As a consequence they want to screw in one of the little target disks to cut down the field and block out the light. That is what I wanted to do myself. I had to experiment and argue with myself before I could bring myself to take out the target disks when hunting. Those target disks have their place. They sharpen the field slightly and the rifleman can make a slightly smaller group with them on a black and white target than with a large aperture. This difference, however, is not so great as one would believe. I have tried it on a target with a .30/06 Springfield with a Lyman 48 receiver sight and I found I could shoot about 2½-inch groups from a rest with the largest aperture and a blackened front sight. With the smallest target aperture I could improve that group on an average of only ¼ or ½ inch. On game this would not make the slightest difference, as anyone can see.

The earliest types of aperture sights were the tang peeps, with the sight mounted on the tang of the rifle and close to the eye. A sight so located is very fast and effective. Aperture sights have also been mounted on the cocking piece of bolt-action rifles. They are also close to the eye and fast. The tang peep can be used on a rifle of the .30/30–.25/35 class where recoil is not severe, but it is dangerous to mount a sight on the tang of a rifle of considerable recoil, particularly with a short stock, as on uphill shots the sight is dangerously close to the eye. Some years ago the hunting wife of a famous rifleman took a shot at a goat that was uphill from her, with a short-stocked rifle with a tang peep. The sight drove into her eye, and her eye had to be removed.

Most of the newer peep sights are of the receiver type. They are a little too far from the eye to be ideal, but they are safe and effective. Sights of this sort are the famous Lyman 48 series and the equally famous Redfield Model 70 series. Cheaper sights of this type are the Redfield 102 series and the Lyman 57 series. All of these receiver sights are adjustable for both windage and elevation. The price is moderate, and excellent shooting, both at game and on the target range, can be done with them. The more expensive sights of this type are adjustable in either ¼, ½, or one minute of angle. As we shall see in the chapter on sighting in, this is a priceless boon.

FRONT SIGHTS

Various materials in various forms have been used in the manufacture of front sights. The most widely used is a copper alloy, which the trade calls gold; another, bone, which is called ivory; still another favorite material is red plastic. Front sights for hunting are usually in the form of round beads. Sometimes they have a flat face turned toward the shooter. Sometimes they come to a point. Any front sight has a tendency to shoot away from the light because the light forms a false center on the bead. This is more noticeable in the case of the gold bead than with front sights of other materials, but it is present with any front sight. A few days before I wrote this I was shooting a .375 Magnum at two hundred yards. With an unblackened gold bead front sight and an aperture rear sight the group was forming about six inches to the right of the center of the target away from the light. I took a match and blackened the front sight. The next group formed about as far to the left.

In shooting big game at moderate ranges this tendency to shoot away from the light would ordinarily not cause a miss. It will, however, cause many misses on small game and lower scores on the target.

For all its faults, the gold bead is probably the best front sight. It is more durable and it will take quite a beating before it gets knocked off. It can be blackened with a match or with burning camphor for target use. The ivory or red plastic beads will not stand the flame of a match. They are much more fragile, and those I have had are always breaking off. Under some lights the red bead shows up poorly, appearing almost black. The flat-topped steel blade can be used for game shooting in the Far West and in regions of good light, but in dark woods and on overcast days it cannot be picked up quickly. Once it was customary to cut dovetail slots in the barrels of rifles for both front and rear sights. It has been found that that is not a good practice, as the slots cause the barrels to vibrate excessively and erratically and these slotted barrels give relatively poor accuracy. Now sights are put on the barrels with bands or mounted on integral ramps. The fanciest type of front sight is the ramp base, which is either integral with the barrel, put on with a band, or sweated on.

Actually the iron sight is for no purpose as good as the scope sight, but the iron sight is stronger than the scope sight, and iron sights can be used in fog and rain and snow, which would put the scope sight out of business.

CHAPTER XI

Telescopic Sights

IT IS not generally realized, but the telescopic sight has been in use in the United States for a great many years. In the American Civil War, Union snipers were armed with telescope-sighted rifles and it is a minor bit of history that a sniper so equipped killed a Confederate general a mile away after elaborate calculations of wind, temperature, barometer, and so on. Telescope-sighted rifles were used by those expert shots with their heavy single-shot rifles who exterminated the buffalo on the great plains in the 1870's and '80's.

It was not until after World War I, however, that the telescopic sight became popular in the United States or even satisfactory for general hunting. Indeed, when the first World War broke out, the American army was without a practical sniper's scope, and so few ordnance officers knew anything about the function of telescopic sights that the Warner & Swasey prismatic scope which was adopted was one of the most terrible turkeys ever designed. The only practical sniping scopes made and used during the war of 1914–18 were in the hands of the Germans and were the product of the great German optical industry of which the firms of Zeiss and Hensoldt are leaders.

Before the first World War the few scopes that were seen were usually of the target type and most of them were in the hands of Scheutzen target men. Early scopes of this type were the Stevens, the Malcolm, the Winchester A-5, and the Seidel.

During the 1920's however, the scope began to gain some popularity, largely because of the publicity given scope sights by such men as Townsend Whelen writing in *Outdoor Life*, Paul Curtis writing in *Field & Stream*, E. C. Crossman in various periodicals. The demand for good target scopes led to fine ones being brought out by the Lyman Gun Sight Corporation, Fecker, and Unertl. The first hunting scopes were imported from Germany and mounted with various American mounts, but before long good American scopes were being produced—the Noske, the Weaver, and others. Within a few years there were many thousands of scopes on big-game rifles and tens of thousands of small, inexpensive scopes on .22's. A scope is almost a *must* on the target range, and even shotguns have been equipped with telescopic sights.

The Advantages of the Telescopic Sight. There are many advantages that accrue to the user of a scope sight. It is fundamental that *no one can shoot any better than he can see* and the scope enables the rifleman to see better. Shots that are completely impossible with iron sights become commonplace with a scope. The difference is not so marked as it might seem on the target range. The target shooter uses a dead-black target, a square-topped dead-black front sight, which gives good definition with a six-o'clock hold against the black bull. He uses a small aperture peep. In game shooting the scope has tremendous advantages because the poorer the light conditions are, the better the scope shows up in comparison with any iron sight.

The *magnification* of the scope, which many consider all-important, is just one of the scope's many assets. Magnification reduces the normal error of aim that all of us have. Let us say that the normal error of aim of an individual is two inches at one hundred yards, with iron sights. By that we mean that this particular individual with the particular sights he is using is unable to tell if he is holding one inch to the right or one inch to the left, one inch high or one inch low. Thousands of experiments have proved that this error of aim exists. A rifle is put in a rest of some sort. Then the bull's-eye is moved around until the aimer declares it lines up perfectly with the sights. Then a pencil mark is made exactly in the center of the bull. It is surprising how large the triangle made by these three "shots" often is. A two-power scope will cut this error of aim in half; a four-power scope will cut it to one fourth, and so on. Scopes as high as twenty-power are being used in small-bore matches, the most highly competitive of all target shooting, and the reason for this is the desire to cut the error aim to an absolute minimum. As we shall shortly see, however, this business of magnification, for many purposes, can be greatly overdone.

Perhaps even more important than magnification is the fact that the telescopic sight puts everything in the same optical plane. With open sights the eye is given an impossible task—to focus at once on the rear sight, about eighteen inches from the eye, on the front sight, about thirty inches from the eye, and on the game or target, about a hundred yards, let us say, from the eye. The task can be done fairly well by young flexible eyes. It cannot be done at all by old or middle-aged, inflexible eyes. The peep sight makes it easier on the inflexible eye, as the user simply looks *through* the peep at the front sight, which he places against the target on the game. The front sight and the target then are relatively but not absolutely in the same focus. A suitable scope correctly adjusted to the eye will make the middle-aged man see like a boy again.

Another great advantage of the scope is a by-product of magnification and light-gathering power. With a scope it will become far more apparent that that "buck" is really a doe, or the bear by that rotten log is another sportsman looking for a lost cartridge. The scope enables the man without binoculars to size up a good head far better than he could with the naked eye. With a scope he is much less likely to shoot the wrong animal or to shoot a human being. Furthermore, when he shoots he can place his shots with much greater efficiency. The scope gathers light, and under poor conditions the field of view in the scope is much brighter than it is with the unaided eye. Game can be shot with a good scope and a suitable reticule early in the morning or late in the evening, when game is often afoot and when accurate shooting would be impossible with any iron sight.

Because scopes have so often been associated with the target range, many believe the scope to be slow. As a matter of fact, a suitable hunting scope with a wide field is one of the fastest of all sights.

The scope has its disadvantages as well, but, to me at least, they are relatively minor. The scope is necessarily more expensive than iron sights. The scope is also somewhat more fragile, although not nearly so fragile as might be believed. The scope can be put out of commission by rain or fog. This too, however, is something that has been greatly exaggerated. I have hunted with scope-sighted big-game rifles from the deserts of Mexico to the subarctic of the Yukon, during which time I have made hundreds of shots with scope-sighted rifles that I could not possibly have made with any iron sights. Only on a few occasions have I ever had a scope-sighted rifle put out of commission by rough use or by weather.

What a Scope Is.   The telescope sight is simply one form of what is known as a Galilean or terrestrial telescope, which consists of a metal tube of seamless steel or aluminum tubing and uses a number of lenses. The front lens is known as the objective. It picks up the picture and passes it back within the tube. The picture, however, is upside down. The next lens, within the tube, is known as the inverter; it turns the picture right side up once more and passes it on to the lens into which one looks, which is known as the ocular lens. Lenses, of course, vary in size and formula. The best lenses are compound achromatic lenses made of two kinds of glass cemented together and corrected for color and for spherical aberration. The best lenses give fields of view that are clear, sharp, and bright to the edges of the field. Through them colors are seen naturally. Poor lenses will show straight lines as being curved. They will have color fringe and at the edges of the field one can see practically every color in the spectrum. Through them colors do not look clear and natural.

The telescope sight must be much more strongly constructed than the ordinary telescope because it has to stand the shock of the recoil. The scope must also have a *reticule* or *graticule* to aim by. Because of the recoil, one obviously cannot jam one's eye right up against the ocular and consequently the scope must form the picture at some distance from the eye—usually from two to six inches. There must be some provision for moving either the scope itself or the reticule to make it coincide with the bore of the rifle so that the bullet will strike where the reticule rests. When this is done, the rifle is said to be "sighted in."

Let us now examine some terms used in connection with telescopic sights. One is "field of view." That simply means how much one can see when looking through the scope. It is usually stated in terms of feet at 100 yards. If it is said that the field of view is 30 feet at 100 yards it means that the man looking through the scope can see a circle with a diameter of 30 feet. Some hunting scopes like the Weaver K-2.5 and the Lyman Alaskan have fields of view of around 40 feet per 100 yards of range. A relatively wide field of view is exceedingly important for the big-game scope to be used in woods or brushy country, because one should be able to see the game instantly when the rifle is snapped to the shoulder. On the other hand, one can use a very small field of view with a target scope because the target remains stationary and doesn't jump over a log and disappear.

The field of view of a scope is determined by the power and by the diameter of the ocular lens. A $\frac{7}{8}$-inch (22 mm.) ocular such as was popular on pre-war scopes like the Zeiss or Hensoldt gave a field of around 30 feet at 100 yards when the magnification was $2\frac{1}{4}$ or $\frac{1}{2}$-X. At 1-X the field is doubled. At 4- to $4\frac{1}{2}$-X the field is cut in half. There isn't any way to get around it. On the other hand, if the power is cut in half, the field of view is doubled. If a scope-maker claims a larger field with that power, he is not telling the truth either about the field or about the power. If a 30-foot field is wanted with a 4-power scope, then the diameter of the ocular lens must be increased. There isn't any way out of it. For instance, the famous Zeiss 4-X Zielvier scope, which for many years was the finest 4-X scope in the world and is still one of the best, has a field of view of something over 30 feet at 100 yards, but the ocular lens has a diameter of approximately 1⅜ inches. As a matter of fact, long experience has proved that a field of view of about 30 feet per 100 yards is enough even for fast shooting in the woods. That field can be obtained with a straight tube scope which can be mounted very low. As a consequence, the enlarged oculars on such scopes as the Lyman Alaskan, the Weaver K-2.5, and the Norman-Ford Texan are of doubtful value in spite of the fact that all these scopes give fields of around 40 feet. I happen to prefer the low mount and the fit it gives to the extra field of view.

The relative brightness of the scope is determined by several factors. The kind of optical glass used in the lenses, the formula by which they are ground, and whether the lenses are coated or not—all these points are important. Everything else being equal, however, the brightness is largely dependent upon the size of the objective or front lens. The larger the objective, the more light is let in, just as the larger a window is, the more light it lets in. A ⅞-inch objective such as is found in the Noske, the Lyman Alaskan, or the G-88 is entirely satisfactory with a 2½-X scope and will produce a good bright glass. When the power is boosted, however, the light is cut down in relation to the increase of power. It is for this reason that a 4-X glass must have a large objective. It is also the reason that target scopes of high power have those large objectives and that binoculars to be used in poor light conditions must have large objectives.

If the power is increased without enlarging the objective, the result is a scope with poor definition, or the ability to distinguish detail. Let us suppose that you are hunting without binoculars. You see a black lump in the distance and you think it may be a bear. Let us say that your scope has high power but poor definition. Then you will simply see a larger black lump, still without form or detail. On the other hand, if your scope has good definition you will be able to determine detail and see whether this lump is a bear or a log. The best target scopes can spot bullet holes at one hundred yards, and under good conditions a highly corrected 4-X hunting scope can do the same thing.

Another term often used is "latitude of eye relief." Eye relief is said to be "critical" or "non-critical." Considerable latitude of eye relief is exceedingly important in a hunting scope, and in the best hunting scopes a working, satisfactory field of view can be obtained with a scope anywhere from two to five inches from the eye. With a target-type scope to be used on stationary objects this latitude is not nearly so important, because again the target stays put. But if you try to use a scope with a critical eye relief on running game, you will come to grief. Your eye has to be exactly in the right place or else the whole field will black out and you will lose sight of the game. All of the good modern hunting scopes have considerable latitude, but every scope has a point at which the full field is obtained. With most German scopes this is three inches from the eye. With most American scopes it is obtained at a slightly greater distance. For a scope on a fixed mount, at least three inches is necessary because of the danger of recoil.

Every scope should make provision for focusing. Various optical systems do this by various means. One of the commonest is to screw the eyepiece containing the ocular lens in or out and then lock it with a knurled ring or a set screw, a system used in Weaver, Lyman, Redfield, and other big-game scopes. Another system is to screw the objective in or out, which is used by the Lyman and Unertl target scope. Still another method of focus is to move the inverter lens, which is used with the Fecker target scope and some foreign big-game scopes.

To focus a scope, one should increase the focal length until things look fuzzy and then shorten it by screwing in with the typical eyepiece focusing until the letters on a sign at 100 or 150 yards are sharp, black, and clear. Focus slightly on the long side does not hurt the eye. Focus slightly on the short side will cause eyestrain.

The lowest-power scopes have universal focus, which means that anything viewed through such a scope from twenty-five yards to infinity is in workable focus. The high-power target scopes do not have this feature and must be focused every time for the shorter ranges. An 8-X scope, for example, focused at twenty-five yards will give severe eyestrain if used at one hundred yards.

The subject of parallax is one that causes a good deal of confusion. The term simply means that the reticule is not properly located in the focus of the lens. The result is that if parallax is present a scope can be rested on something with the hands not touching it; then when the head is moved back and forth and up and down the reticule will move against the target. As can be easily seen, this will result in inaccuracy because unless the eye is in exactly the same position for every shot, the point of aim each time will be different. With the cross-hair reticule a little parallax can usually be detected in one hair or the other as they do not lie exactly in the same optical plane. If they are adjusted as a good compromise, however, the parallax will usually be so slight as to cause absolutely no trouble.

As a usual thing, parallax is removed at the factory, but not always.

A scope that will show no parallax whatsoever at one hundred yards and up will, nevertheless, show parallax at a short distance. Friends of mine have practically knocked themselves out because they tested new scopes for parallax by training them on something within the room and then found parallax.

Some scopes have no provision for the removal of parallax and have to be returned to the factory. The Noske scope, however, has this provision, and parallax can be removed by turning the front lens in and out. With the Weaver scopes the screws holding the reticule housing can be loosened and moved until parallax disappears.

The Kinds of Scopes. Scopes are designed for various purposes. Although the classifications overlap to some extent, we will divide telescope sights here into big-game scopes, target scopes, varmint scopes, and scopes for the .22 rim-fire cartridges.

Choosing the proper kind of scope is very important. An 8 or 10-X target scope, large, bulky, and mounted on relatively fragile mounts, would be almost worse than nothing for hunting whitetail deer in the woods. The field of view is small, the illumination none too good under poor conditions, the eye relief critical. A 2½-power big-game scope would be almost useless on a small-bore target range in competition with scopes of higher power and ¼-minute precision target mounts. Likewise this same low-power hunting scope will leave much to be desired for use on varmints. Any scope is better than iron sights, but as compared with a scope made especially for varmint hunting, it would come off a poor second best.

Much criticism of the scope sight comes from men who have tried to use the wrong scope.

Several years ago a friend of mine had a Lyman 5-A target scope put on a .30/06 rifle. He felt he would be all fixed up for deer hunting. He went out, jumped a big buck up within thirty yards. He threw the rifle to his shoulder, and because of the small field of view and critical eye relief he could not even see the deer through the scope. He went back immediately to the use of iron sights and ever since has been a mortal enemy of scope sights in general.

I get many letters from shooters who want to put the light, small, neat big-game scopes on varmint rifles. The man who does so simply cannot hit small objects at long range because a 2½-X scope does not have the magnification and definition to enable him to do so. I will discuss the types of scopes in detail in the remainder of this chapter.

Big-Game Scopes. The scope sight to be used on a big-game rifle should ideally be small, light, and rugged. It should be mounted as low as possible to give a line of sight not much higher than that of iron sights. It should be mounted with strong mounts because the hunting rifle often has to take some rather rough treatment. It is highly important that the field of view of the hunting scope be relatively large—at least 30 feet per 100 yards of range if it is ever to be used in brush and woods. The scope should have great light-gathering power and the resulting brightness because big game is often shot early in the morning and very late in the afternoon. It is also shot in cloudy and overcast weather and often in heavy woods where the light is pretty well blotted out. Because the big-game hunter has to shoot fast the eye relief should be non-critical.

Fine micrometer adjustments are not important with a big-game scope because the best practice with a big-game rifle is to sight the rifle in for one particular load and then to leave it. It makes no difference on big game if the rifle is shooting an inch to the right at 200 yards or even an inch to the right at 100 yards, but such a rifle would enormously handicap the prairie-dog or woodchuck hunter or the target shot.

The first successful big-game scopes used in the United States were the German Zeiss Zielklein 2½-X and the Hensoldt Zielklein of 2¾-X. Both of these were straight-tube scopes with the body of the scope ⅞ inch in diameter. The portion of the scope containing the ocular lens is slightly larger and is threaded for adjustment of focus. These scopes can be mounted very low. They are bright, optically excellent, and in every way satisfactory. Back in the early 1920's they were imported in great numbers from Germany and mounted usually with the Noske, Redfield, or Griffin & Howe mounts. Both of these scopes have adjustments for elevation only, and hence windage must be within the mount itself.

In those early days most gunsmiths were reluctant to tackle a real bolt-handle alteration where the bolt handle is cut off and welded back on at a lower angle. As a consequence those scopes had to be mounted high to clear the uplift of the bolt handle.

Along in the later 1920's, R. Noske, of San Carlos, California, who pioneered the first successful side mount for scopes, brought out a 2½-X scope with a .22-mm. tube (⅞-inch) and an enlarged ocular lens ground to give an eye relief so long that the scope could be mounted ahead of the unaltered bolt handles of Winchester Model 54 Springfield and Mauser rifles. This plainly showed how great an advantage it was to mount a scope as low as possible so the shooter's cheek could be firm against the comb. This scope also pioneered the way in that both windage and elevation were in the tube, and the mount did not need to be complicated by a windage feature. Since that time almost all American scopes have been made with windage.

Following the Noske, one of the first successful big-game scopes to come out was the Weaver 330, which had a ¾-inch tube and was consequently smaller than the Noske or the German scopes. Optically, however, the 330 was and is excellent. The field of view is over 30 feet at 100 yards. Although Weaver advertised 2¾-X, the power was in reality about 2. It was Bill Weaver who put scopes on tens of thousands of American rifles because he sold the good little 330 complete with a simple and satisfactory, though homely, "T" side mount, for $27.50. Prior to that time getting a hunting scope mounted on a rifle cost around $75. The mounting charge was from $7.50 to $10, and such mounts as the Neidner and Griffin & Howe cost $30. The first attempt of the Lyman Gun Sight Corporation to bring out a practical hunting scope resulted in a failure known as the Stag. It was too heavy, too bulky, mounted too high. When the Lyman Alaskan 2½-X came out, however, it was one of the world's fine scopes. Externally it resembles the Noske with a 22-mm. tube and enlarged eyepiece. In fact, any mount made for the Lyman Alaskan can be used with the Noske. The Alaskan was at first made with an aluminum tube, but the tubes were soft. They dented and bent, so it was equipped with a steel tube. John Unertl of target-telescope fame also brought out a 2½-X scope similar to the Alaskan and the Noske, but no great numbers of them were distributed.

The Weaver 330 served to introduce many riflemen to the use of the hunting scope sight. It served satisfactorily and honorably in World War II as a sniper's scope on special 1903 Springfield rifles. When the war was over and Weaver tooled up to get back to peacetime production, he decided to bring out a better scope. The result is the K-2.5. It was one of the most brilliant scopes ever made anywhere. It has a 1-inch tube with the larger objectives lens and for a scope of only 2½-X a 1-inch objective is enough to give great brilliance. The optical system is excellent. The field of view of approximately 40 feet at 100 yards is tremendous, the reticule adjustment system is superior to that of the old 330. Some may object to the K-2.5 on the ground that it is unnecessarily bulky with its enlarged ocular and 1-inch tube. It is a fact that it cannot be mounted as low and give as low a line of sight as a scope with a smaller straight tube. Nevertheless it is a very fine and effective scope.

The early Noske, Zeiss, and Hensoldt 2½-X scopes all had ⅞ (22 mm.) tubes, and so did the excellent but now obsolete Lyman Alaskan. The Weaver 300 and 440 scopes, also obsolete, had ¾-inch tubes, and the moderate-priced Weaver J-2.5 and J-4 scopes and the inexpensive Weaver G-series scopes for .22 rifles still use this small tube diameter. Right after the war, Weaver set the fashion by increasing his tube diameter on the K-series scopes to 1 inch. Other manufacturers followed his lead, and today most hunting scopes are so made. The Redfield scopes, which have had a checkered career and which have appeared under the Stith, Kollmorgen, and finally Redfield names, were for years made with 26-mm. tubes, an odd size and one that complicated the problem of mount rings. However, as this is written, in late 1961, I understand that the plan is to go to 1-inch rings in 1962. Most Japanese and German scopes made for the American market have 1-inch rings so they can be adapted to American mounts, but a few still use the odd-size 26½ mm. tube.

Because the American market is by far the world's largest for telescope sights, American manufacturers have been enabled to invest heavily in expensive precision machinery for scope manufacture. American scopes are the best in the world, and the only scopes comparable to them are foreign scopes made for American importers to American specifications. The field is fiercely competitive, and scope prices have not risen much since the war. In about 1946, Weaver set a price of around $45 for his excellent K-4 scope, and although the K-4 has undergone several modifications and improvements, the price has remained the same. Other dealers have not been able to sell scopes in quantity at prices much higher than those set by Weaver.

Many scopes are imported from Japan at cut-rate prices. Some are junk, poor optically, erratic in adjustment, flimsy. Some Japanese scopes are, on the other hand, quite good. British scopes and mounts are expensive and old-fashioned, although, like most British goods, they are sound enough. Actually the London custom-rifle makers generally use German scopes. The scopes turned out in Germany and Austria range all the way from superb to fair.

Today all of the good hunting scopes have similar specifications. As we have seen, the use of the 1-inch tube is just about universal on the high-quality hunting scopes. Most have similar eye relief and are generally usable at from 3 to 5 inches from the eye. All have similar fields of view. The good 2½-X scopes, for example, have fields that run from 40 to 45 feet at 100 yards. The 4-X scopes have fields of around 30 and the 6-X scopes of around 20.

A case can be made for scopes with fixed reticules equipped with mounts adjustable for windage and elevation. However, the American scope buyer has expressed a preference for scopes internally adjustable for windage and elevation. Most American scopes are so adjustable, with graduated dials marked in minutes of angle and protected against dust and moisture with screw-on caps.

Since the war, all American quality scopes have been made with coated optics which aid in the transmission of light by cutting down on reflection and which have done away with the old bugaboo of the scope user—shooting in the direction of the sun.

Before the war, the favorite power for the hunting scope was 2½. The famous Zeiss and Hensoldt Zielkleins were of that power, and so were the 330 Weaver and the Lyman Alaskan. The 2½ is still the best bet for woods shooting, where a wide field is more important than definition. I have used scopes of that power extensively and I am convinced that they will do about as well as any for ALL big-game shooting, including shots up to 250 to 300 yards on mountain game. After all, a deer, a caribou, a goat, an elk, or a moose is a large animal, and one does not need high power for shot placement except at the most extreme ranges. The 2½-X scope also has the advantage of eye relief less critical than that of the scope of higher power.

An interesting scope that has never been very popular is the 1-X made by Weaver and called the K-1. It has no power whatsoever and the field merges with the outside air. It is very fast and has been used on rifles for brush shooting and on repeating shotguns used with slugs for deer hunting. It is also used on single-barrel shotguns (pumps and autoloaders) for skeet and wing shooting. With such a sight, the shotgun can be "sighted in" to place the center of the pattern wherever the shotgunner wants it.

For years I argued with Bill Weaver that the most useful all-around power for the scope to be used purely for big-game hunting and in the open as well as in the woods would be a full 3-X.

He finally brought out the K-3, and it has sold so well that Leupold and Lyman both make 3-X scopes in competition. The 3-X gives a little less field than the 2½, more than the 4-X, a bit less definition than the 4-X, but more field. It is an excellent compromise. I have a pair of .375 Magnum rifles fitted with 3-X scopes.

Since the war, the best selling scope has been the 4-X. This is the best power for plains and mountain big-game hunting. It is also best for varmints generally shot on the run, such as jack rabbits and coyotes. It is usable even on small varmints like woodchucks up to about 150 yards. I do not consider the 4-X to be ideal for brush shooting, but for this it will do. For the mountain rifle, the 4-X is the thing, and on a large animal a good scope of this power gives definition sufficient for good holding to 400 and 500 yards.

A 6-X scope is a compromise. It is a bit lacking in field for running shots at big game, particularly in the woods, and is lacking in power for long shots at small varmints. However, a 6-X will get out about all there is in such cartridges as the .22 Hornet, the .218 Bee, and the .222 Remington.

Telescope sights of the hunting type and of 8 and 10-X, such as the Weaver K-8 and K-10 and the Lyman All-American scopes of that power, are strictly varmint scopes. There has been a considerable shift to hunting-type, internally adjustable scopes of such power from the externally adjustable target-type scopes.

An increasingly hot item on the American scope market is the variable-power scope. The idea is not new, as the German optical firm of Zeiss made scopes of changing power back in the 1930's. The first American variable power was the now obsolete Weaver K V, which could be shifted in power from about 3 to 5-X. I understand that the K V didn't go over too well, as scope buyers were not content with a choice of *two* powers: they wanted *many* powers.

In my position as a practicing gun-editor, I get thousands of letters a year from readers seeking advice on the purchase of rifles, scopes, and various equipment. A high proportion say they want a variable-power scope on a hinged mount so that the scope can be swung out of the way for the use of iron sights. This, of course, is beginner stuff. To the innocent hunter this sounds like more for the money. Our bright-eyed boy imagines himself looking at his game judiciously, then deciding whether he is to use scope or iron sights, then, if he is to use a scope, selecting the right power and letting the game have it.

The whole idea is full of seductive and voluptuous appeal. With one purchase, the boys reason, they are fixed up with a scope for the woods, for the mountains, for varmints. However, there are some serious holes in the proposition. Variable-power scopes are more complicated than scopes of fixed power. They are at their optical best at only one power. Most serious criticism of all is that with most of them the reticule becomes apparently larger with higher power, smaller with lower power. If a scope is variable in power from 3 to 9-X for example, the cross wires are usually about right at 4 or 5-X, far too coarse at 9-X, far too fine at 3-X. Most lads who buy variable-power scopes set them about mid-range and leave them that way. However, Bausch & Lomb has whipped the problem after a fashion by the use of a tapered "cross-wire" reticule which is etched on glass. In his new variable, Weaver uses a trick reticule, which consists of one fine and two coarse cross-wires. At high power, aim is taken with the intersection of the fine cross-wires. At low power, the whole combination is used.

Weatherby imports excellent variable-power scopes made in Germany to his specifications. Bausch & Lomb makes two—one of the hunting type and one of target type. Both must be used on adjustable mounts. Bushnell and Stoeger import variable-power scopes from abroad, Stoeger brings in variables from Europe, Weaver and Leupold make variables which have sold well. Redfield came on the market in 1962 with a variable power with the reticule in the eyepiece. It remains the same apparent size at all powers—a real breakthrough in variable powers.

The Target Scopes. As we have seen, magnification is far more important than field in the target scope. High magnification cuts down the error of aim, and in competitive shooting every possible means to close up a group must be used if the shooter is to be in the money. Since the target stays put, it can be kept in a relatively small field. The field of view of the 8-power Lyman Target Spot is only 14 feet at 100 yards and the field of view of the 10-power Target Spot is only 12 feet.

Target-type scopes slide in the mount. As a rifle recoils, the scope tends to stay still and it must be pulled back for each shot in a rifle of heavy recoil. Because of this the eye relief can be much shorter than in the big-game scope and also much more critical. The eye relief of the Target Spot is only 1 ¾ inches. With a big-game scope on a rigid mount this short eye relief would be dangerous and on uphill shots the shooter would eventually get smacked in the eye.

In the Unertl target scopes power up to 14-X can be obtained —and in that case the field at 100 yards is only 6 feet. For practical purposes the Lyman, Unertl, and Fecker target scopes all give just about the same results. All are quite long, from 20 to 24 inches in length. All are optically good. Choosing between them is a matter of personal preference.

None of these target scopes has either windage or elevation in the tube. All are mounted with blocks on the barrel or on the barrel and receiver ring. The mountings are in two pieces. They fit on the blocks with female dovetails and are clamped by thumbscrews. When the screws are loosened they can be quickly removed and replaced without any change in point of impact.

The rear portion of the mount is adjustable for windage and elevation and marked with ½- or ¼-minute clicks. There should be exactly 7.2 inches between the front and rear mounts.

These fine adjustments are necessary for target shooting. A man has to stay in the 10 ring, which at 50 feet on the official small-bore target measures only .15 inch, .335 inch at 25 yards, and 2 inches at 100 yards. At the greater distance many a match

is settled by the number of X's—and the X ring measures only
1 inch.

These target scopes of around 8- and 10-X are often used for
varmint shooting by those hunters who specialize in long-range
work with high-velocity rifles of small bore. They are practical,
however, only for shooting at sitting woodchucks, perched
hawks and crows, etc., because of the small field of view. Further, the focus is not universal, and ideally they should be re-
focused every time the range is changed.

Varmint Scopes. The successful varmint hunter has to do
much finer shooting than the big-game hunter. A crow is a very
small mark, measuring only about 2½ by 5 inches. A full-grown
woodchuck or a rock chuck will measure only about 9 by 14
inches. The antelope jackrabbit of the Southwest, one of the
largest of the American jackrabbits, will measure about 5 by 10.
The average prairie dog doesn't measure more than about 2 by
5. These marks are small, hard to see, and hard to hit. Although
a big-game scope is certainly better than iron sights for this
work, it is by no means ideal. More power, enabling the hunter
to see better, is indicated. About 4-X is the minimum for the
successful varmint scope. I am inclined to believe that 6-X is
better. Over 6-X makes refocusing necessary. The field of view
is cut down further and consequently I would not advise a scope
of the higher power for use on varmints only.

The varmint scope should also be susceptible to fine adjustments. A rifle that averages shooting off an inch or two or even
a little more at 100 yards certainly does not cause anyone to
miss big game, but a rifle shooting off that much will cause a man
to miss a prairie dog every time. Because varmints are often in
high grass and weeds or against hillsides not very different in
color from the animals themselves, a scope with relatively good
gathering power and fine definition is needed.

This takes in a lot of territory. One gains magnification at the
sacrifice of field and illumination—and field at the sacrifice of

magnification. Consequently any varmint scope must to some extent be a compromise.

For the hunting of prairie dogs, woodchucks, crows, and hawks, about as good a scope as one can get is one like the 6-X Lyman Junior Target Spot. With its precision target mounts it enables the shooter to sight in very exactly. It is pretty well in focus from 50 yards to infinity and the 6-X has a field of view of about 16 feet at 100 yards. With a fine cross-hair reticule I have found that from a good steady prone position one can kill crows and prairie dogs regularly to about 150 yards. The Junior Target Spot is not quite so heavy as the Target Spots, with their larger objective. It is a very neat and satisfactory scope. Another good little scope for varmints is the Fecker 4-X small-game scope with precision mounts and the Fecker ¾-inch target scope in either 4.5-X or 6-X.

A good deal of Western varmint shooting is entirely different from the conventional woodchuck and crow shooting familiar to Eastern hunters. One of the most interesting of all Western varmints is the jackrabbit. He seldom stays put long, and although he is often shot sitting, he is usually about to jump up and dash away. He makes a relatively large mark and one that duplicates on a small scale any type of big-game hunting. He can be picked off at long range across the canyon as he squats half asleep in the shadow of a bush or he can be shot as he bounds through the grass at short range. The Western coyote is also an animal that often has to be shot on the run. This tendency of Western varmints to pick up and leave the country in a hurry makes an entirely different type of scope necessary—one with universal focus and a wide field of view. Many Western varmint hunters simply use their regular big-game rifles with 2½-X hunting scopes. Because of the low magnification they are not very satisfactory. They are fine for shooting running jackrabbits or running coyotes to 100 or even to 150 yards, but beyond that distance one simply cannot see well enough with them.

It is typical of Western varmint shooters that they start with the 2½-X scopes. They usually wind up by getting scopes of about 4-X with fields of view of around 30 feet at about 100 yards of range. Scopes like the Zeiss Zielvier and the new Weaver K-4 are very satisfactory for shooting of this type. If someone pinned me down, I would prefer the K-4 to the Zeiss because with the internal adjustments for ¼-minute clicks of both windage and elevation it is far easier to sight in exactly. The varmint hunter is usually also a handloader who likes to fool around with various combinations of powder, primer, and so on. He needs a scope that will enable him to adjust for the different points of impact these loads will give.

Small-Game Scopes. The varmint hunter shoots animals that are not edible. He uses bullets traveling at high velocity that tear the animal up badly, disintegrate when they strike the ground, and do not ricochet. The small-game hunter, on the other hand, uses the .22 rim-fire cartridge since he wants to save the game for the table. The small-game hunter does his shooting within 100 yards. He has to hit very small marks which are often in deep shade and partially concealed by grass, leaves, and twigs. He needs a scope with a reasonably wide field, magnification of about 3 power and clear and bright. On the other hand, he does not need long eye relief because there is no danger of the tube being driven back into his eye by recoil.

The conventional big-game scope of about 2½-X does quite well for this shooting although the magnification could be greater. One of the greatest disadvantages to using the big-game scope on a .22 is the expense. All of them are built very strong and the strength increases the expense of construction. As this is written, Weaver has just brought out his S2-5, an excellent little scope optically, which will sell for $22.50. It is not a bad scope for a big-game rifle and is ideal for a .22 small-game rifle. At least two other manufacturers have scheduled for production good 3- and 4-power scopes that will cost, complete with mount, about $30, which will be good optically and should answer this real need. The old Weaver 29-S was a good inexpensive little scope of this class. From what I can hear, the new scopes will be even better.

In the past some very poor scopes have been put on .22 rifles on the theory that practically anything would do for a .22. Some of them were optically very sad. The mounts were fragile and any blow would change the point of impact. On some of them the eye relief was so critical that a movement of the head a quarter of an inch one way or the other would blot the field out. Although those scopes made many people interested in better ones, they also served to prejudice many against scopes of all kinds. Small-game shooting with a .22 is precision work and deserves a good scope. The head of a squirrel at forty yards is a small mark and cannot be struck regularly unless the scope can be adjusted exactly and unless the optics are good enough so that the head can be seen clearly and precision aim taken.

Reticules for the Scope Sight. The mind of man has run riot when it comes to thinking up reticules for the scope. The Germans particularly have brought out some very fantastic jobs—combinations of bars, cross-hairs, and dots. The reticule should be as simple as possible so as not to clutter up the field of view with miscellaneous hardware. It should concentrate the attention at the point of aim. It should be easily seen under the conditions in which it is used and one should be able to take exact aim with it.

The three best types of reticule are the cross-hair or cross-wire, the post, and the dot. Cross-hairs are usually defined as fine, medium fine, medium, and coarse. If the hairs are of the proper thickness the cross-hair is a very fine reticule that can be used for practically any kind of hunting or shooting. A very fine hair can be used for small-bore shooting—one that should enable the shooter to quarter the 10 ring. For varmint shooting, the hair should be wider and for big-game shooting still wider. For all-around big-game hunting the hairs should subtend about 1 inch per 100 yards of range. One can see, however, that such a hair wouldn't be much good for a crow at 200 yards, because the hair would just about cover the crow. Let us say, then, that for small-bore target shooting the fine hair should be chosen, for most varmint shooting the medium-fine hair, and for big-game shooting the medium hair. The coarse cross-hair blots out too much game even for long-range big-game shooting and should never be chosen. The medium cross-hair used in such a scope as the Weaver K-4 can be seen even in very poor light with a bright scope, and nothing is to be gained by getting a coarser hair, whereas a good deal is to be lost.

Particularly those who don't know much about it believe that the cross-hair is only for target shooting. Actually the cross-hair is one of the very best of all reticules. It is a particularly helpful reticule to use for running shooting and big game on the plains or across canyons, as the horizontal cross-hair can be dragged along the body of the game animal and correct elevation can be maintained. Then when the vertical cross-hair is a proper distance ahead, the rifle can be touched off. I myself prefer the cross-hair to the post for the shooting of running game because of this. I have used cross-hair reticules under all conditions for big-game shooting and have found them satisfactory *if* the hair or wire is of proper width. I have even killed animals silhouetted against the skyline when it was so dark that I could not see the intersection of the cross-hairs. Because of the proportion of the cross, however, it was easy to tell where the intersection was, even though it could not be seen.

Another most excellent reticule is the dot. As made by Captain T. K. Lee of Birmingham, Alabama, the dot is suspended on cross-hairs made of spider web, so thin that it is difficult to see them, and the dot appears to float. For small-bore shooting on rifles with scopes of considerable power, the dot can be made as small as ¾ inch so it can be centered within the X ring. For a 4-X varmint or big-game scope, a dot subtending about 2½ or 3 minutes of angle is about right. The tendency of almost all beginners with a dot reticule is to order it too small. Some have even ordered 1-minute dots for 2½-power big-game scopes and then have been disappointed when they could not see them. For the conventional big-game scope a dot subtending 4 minutes of angle is just about right. My experience has shown me that a dot of this size can be seen practically anywhere and under any conditions, whereas a smaller dot cannot.

Either the dot or the cross-hair can be held over the long shots without blotting out the game. The dot has the added advantage of being usable to judge distance by comparing it with the depth of the animal's body from the top of his shoulder to the bottom of his chest. An antelope, let us say, measures from 14 to 16 inches through the body. Suppose that the dot almost but not quite covers the antelope. You know then that the antelope is about 300 yards away. A bighorn ram or large mule deer is 22 to 24 inches through the body. Suppose a 4-minute dot appears to cover approximately half the width of such an animal's body; we then know that the animal is right around 300 yards away. If it covered the whole body it would be evident that the animal was between 500 and 600 yards away.

On several occasions the use of the dot has enabled me to tell the range rather exactly and to make a hit where without it I should have missed.

The post either with or without a vertical cross-hair is an exceedingly popular reticule. The Germans have made sharp-pointed picket posts, but these are not to be recommended, because the sharp point tends to fade out in poor light and a group fired with such a reticule will tend to string up and down. For woods hunting at fast jumping whitetail deer in poor light a most excellent reticule is the flat-topped post with a top subtending about 6 minutes of angle. Such a reticule is the one to use if light conditions are going to be very poor. It can be seen as long as anything can be seen through the scope. Such a post, however, isn't much good for long-range shooting because it blots out too much game and makes hold-over difficult. A better compromise is a tapered flat-top post with a flat portion subtending about 3 minutes of angle. The horizontal cross-hair often used in connection with a post has only one useful function: to tell the rifleman if he is canting his rifle or not. Actually the cross-hair is seldom noticed when hunting. My old Springfield, which I have carried all over North America, is equipped with a Zeiss 2½-X Zielklein scope with a post and horizontal cross-hair. Actually I can't remember ever seeing the cross-hair at all when I was hunting big game.

CHAPTER XII

Mounting the Scope

THE first mounts for hunting scopes were all designed with the notion that the scope should be an auxiliary sight. Not only were the mounts built so they could be put on and taken off in a few seconds, but they were also built so that iron sights could be used while the scope was on the rifle.

Back thirty and forty years ago, people simply didn't trust telescope sights. What disturbed them, I am convinced, was the fact that scopes had glass in them. They pictured all the lenses in a scope flying into bits at the slightest bump.

Nothing sounds more sensible than having a scope so mounted that the hunter can switch to iron sights. I thought so when I bought my first scope-sighted hunting rifle. It was a beautiful little 7-mm. Mauser. It had a Lyman 1-A peep on the cocking piece and a ramp front sight. The scope was a big 4-X German Gerard. The mount was the usual German quick-detachable deal utilizing bases screwed to receiver bridge and ring. It was tunneled so that iron sights could be used *under* the scope.

It was, sad to say, a lousy mount. The hooked leg by which the detachable portion of the mount was affixed to the base on the receiver ring was not hardened. The scope was heavy and way up in the air. The result was that the soft metal of the hooked leg got battered. The scope wobbled, and about the best I could do with the rifle was an 8-inch group at 100 yards. With iron sights the rifle was satisfactorily accurate. Even if the mount

[147]

had been strong enough, it would have been difficult to shoot the rifle accurately because the scope was mounted so high that I had no contact with my cheek against the comb and could not hold the rifle steady.

In due course I mustered up enough courage to try to depend on a glass sight alone. I had Bill Sukalle of Phoenix, Arizona, put a Noske 2½-X scope on a Noske side mount on a .270 as low as possible and with the eyepiece on the scope ahead of the bolt lift. I have carried that rifle on foot and on horseback from Sonora to the Yukon, in rain, sleet, and snow, at 125° above on an August sheep hunt in Sonora and 10° below in the Yukon, at sea level and at 12,000 feet above. The outfit has never failed me and I have never needed auxiliary sights.

Most generally used mounts are those affixed to the top of the receiver—either the bridge type with the one-piece base of the famous Redfield Junior or the similar Buehler or the two-piece mounts like the Tilden, the two-piece Redfield, or the Buehler. Williams, Lyman, Weaver, Leupold-Stevens, and other outfits make top mounts.

The many advantages of these top mounts made them popular. In the first place, they are cheap and easy to mount, as most factory rifles are now drilled and tapped for them. They have dummy screws in the receiver, and all the rifle owner has to do is to remove the dummy screws, then select the right base or bases, and screw them to the receiver. Because of the ease of mounting, I'd make a guess that at least 90 per cent of all scope mounts in use in this country are of the top-mount type and utilize the holes drilled in the receiver.

There are various types of top mounts. Some have no provision at all for any adjustment or have adjustment only for windage. Those that adjust for windage by opposing screws in the bases are the Redfield, Tilden, and Buehler. Some top mounts have adjustments for both windage and elevation and are designed to be used with scopes that are not internally adjustable. One such mount is the familiar and relatively fragile one used with target scopes. Among fully adjustable mounts are the Bausch & Lomb, the Leupold Adjusto, the Buehler Micro Dial. There are others.

Generally speaking, the American shooting public has expressed preference for internally adjustable scopes and solid, simple mounts affixed to the top of the receiver. Those who manufacture and sell mounts with double adjustments emphasize the fact that such mounts make possible simpler and stronger scopes with no moving parts inside. To me the choice has always seemed to be between a simple mount and a fairly complicated scope or a simple scope and a complicated mount. Take your pick.

For a good many years now I have had no trouble at all with scopes. I cannot say that, however, about mounts. Most of them are still too complicated. They have too many parts, too many screws that can work loose. When a hunting rifle is used on a trip where there is constant jiggling—in a hunting car on an African safari or a pack trip in the Rockies—the hunter should constantly check his mount screws for any looseness. Otherwise he is in for some rude surprises.

No hunter should go on a long trip without a screwdriver that fits the screws in his scope mount, and he should go over the mount and check the screws every two or three days. If Allen screws are used in the mount, he should by all means have the proper wrenches in his kit. Unfortunately, as I once found out, Allen wrenches are hard to come by in the middle of the African veldt.

But I am no engineer and have no plans to design a mount. Maybe it is just as well. Some of the doggonedest mounts I have ever seen have been those dreamed up by mechanical engineers who were not rifle nuts, who tackled the problem cold, and who looked upon all existing mounts as the work of witless savages. The ideal mount would be almost as strong as the receiver itself, and the fewer parts and screws it has the better.

Like the variable power scope, the mount one can quickly take off or move out of the way sounds like more for the money.

There are two ways the quick switch can be accomplished. One is by the use of the side-bracket mount. The other is by the use of the swing-type mount which allows the scope to be swung aside so iron sights can be used. Right now this is a very hot item and a very high proportion of my correspondents contemplating the purchase of their first scopes and mounts want variable-power scopes on swing mounts.

The swing mount was introduced by Frank Pachmayr of Los Angeles before the last war. Now mounts by which the scope can be swung out of the way on hinges are also made by Weaver and by Redfield. Many have used them with perfect satisfaction.

One disadvantage of most swing mounts is that they are top-mounted and the bases on the receiver interfere with the normal line of iron sights. Special high iron sights must be used to clear the base portions. Receiver sights, the best of all iron sights, cannot be used because the bases interfere with their mounting. Pachmayr furnishes his Lo-Swing mount in both top-mounted and side-mounted versions, and normal iron sights can be used with the side mount. Theoretically at least, these hinged mounts are not as strong as other types. Practically, they seem to get by.

My favorite type of mount if both iron and scope sights are to be available is the side-bracket type. With it the base is screwed and pinned and simply screwed to the side of the receiver. This is the fixed portion of the mount. The scope is on a removable side bracket, generally fitted to the base with a dovetail and held tight to it by various means.

Side mounts are not nearly as popular as top mounts. They are not so easy to mount. Holes have to be drilled and tapped in the side of the receiver and great care must be taken in lining the holes up exactly right. Generally the gunsmith or dealer by whom a top mount is furnished will mount it free or for $2 or so. A scope mount can be attached and the scope bore-sighted in a half hour or less. Not so the side mount. To mount one properly takes about a half day's work by a good gunsmith and a mounting charge of $10 to $20 is generally made. Not only is mounting expensive, but unless the stock wood alongside the receiver is left thick, the effect is not too handsome. However, if plenty of wood is left on the stock and only the top of the base shows, the appearance of the base left on the rifle is not bad. Good features of the side-bracket mount are that when the scope and the detachable portion are removed, the top of the receiver is left clear for iron sights of normal height. Likewise, because the receiver ring and bridge are uncluttered, a receiver sight can be used.

Side mounts, besides the Pachmayr Lo-Swing, which has already been mentioned, are made by Jaeger, Weaver, and Williams. Top mounts cannot be used on rifles with split receiver bridges. Then the side mount is the answer. Offset side mounts are also a necessity on top-ejecting rifles like the Winchester Model 94.

The side mount with which I have had the most experience is the Griffin & Howe. To me it is an excellent bet for a rifle that is to be used on dangerous game in heavy brush where the hunter might have to stop a charge at a few yards and wants to use iron sights. It is also excellent if the rifle is apt to be used in rain and wet brush, as is generally the case when the hunter is after the giant Alaska brown bear. The G & H mount is an extremely reliable one. The base is both pinned and screwed to the receiver, and the scope can be taken off and put back on innumerable times without changing the point of impact. The base of a Lyman No. 48 receiver sight can be left on and when the scope is removed the slide can be slipped in, and the hunter is all set.

Another advantage of the side mount is that the scope can be taken off for shipment. When I sent a .375 and a .30/06 to Africa in 1959, I took the scopes off and carried them in my luggage and shipped the rifles to Nairobi by air freight. When I hooked scopes and rifles up again, they were both right on the button.

[151]

The hunter who takes only one rifle on a long trip away from gunsmiths isn't too dumb if he has iron sights to fall back on in case something should happen to the scope. It doesn't happen often, but the scope could fog up, get stepped on by a horse, be badly bumped.

I wouldn't pick a side mount for a rifle that is to be carried a great deal in a saddle scabbard. Most leave considerable over-hang, and the front part of the scope can wedge into a too-tight scabbard and bend the aluminum-alloy arms of the mount. I missed a nice buck one time because that had happened to my side-mounted .30/06. For rough use in a saddle scabbard, the all-steel Tilden top mount is a dandy and one that has never given me the slightest trouble.

If there are no complications, a handy man with a screwdriver can easily install a top mount on a rifle tapped and drilled for it. However, sometimes there are complications. The receiver may be higher or lower than it is supposed to be. The screw holes may be put in cockeyed. The barrel of the rifle may be out of alignment with the receiver. In some cases, or so I have been told, the objective lens of the scope may be out of line and then the scope looks off toward the Finnegan place. Any of these things call for a shimming job to line up scope and bore, and a gunsmith has the skill and tools to do it.

However, if all goes well, the installation of a top-mounted scope on a rifle drilled and tapped for it is a breeze. All one has to do is to remove the dummy screws, then dip the screws hold-ing the base to the receiver in shellac or even in linseed oil. They should then be turned up tight with a screwdriver that fits the slots. Next, one should take a hammer, tap the butt of the screw-driver lightly, and tighten the screws once more. The screws are now tight and should stay put.

The scope should then be put into the rings and placed on the base portion of the mount. The eyepiece of the scope should be positioned far enough ahead so that recoil won't drive it back into the eyebrow in any shooting position. Some foreign scopes have only 2½ to 3 inches of eye relief, and this short critical eye relief has resulted in injury to many people.

Most American big-game scopes of from 2½ to 4-X have longer and less critical eye relief, and an adequate field of view is obtained at from 4 to 6 inches from the eye. Scopes of power higher than 4 generally have less eye relief than scopes of lower power and should not be used on rifles of heavy recoil. Distance of ocular lens from the eye can be arrived at by sliding the scope back and forth in the rings. When the distance from the eye is decided on and the crosswires are on an even keel, the rings can be tightened.

As we have said, the screws holding the base of the mount to the receiver should be dipped in shellac. Dipping the other screws in linseed oil slows up their tendency to get loose and back out. On mounts using opposing windage screws such as the Redfield Junior and the Buehler, I dip the left-hand windage screw in linseed and leave the right screw clean. Then I check for looseness, when I am on a trip, by tightening up the right-hand screw with a coin. It isn't too difficult to twist the head off a Redfield Junior windage screw with a large screwdriver, so, for safety's sake, a coin should always be used for tightening.

The last step is to focus the newly mounted scope. I like to train one on a lettered sign about 150 yards away. I back the eyepiece out (counter-clockwise) until the letters are fuzzy, then turn in (clockwise) until the letters are instantly sharp. Focus on the slightly long side gives no eyestrain, but focus on the short side does. The crosswires should be instantly sharp. If they look fuzzy or you see two of them, the focus is not correct.

The scope can then be lined up by bore-sighting. One way to do this is to put the rifle with the bolt removed in a vice, in a cardboard box with V's cut in it, or on sandbags so it can be held steady. Then the scope should be adjusted so that at 50 yards or so the intersection of the crosswires, top of post, or whatever aiming device is used, rests on the center of the bull while the bull is seen in the exact center of the bore.

Bore-sighting is no substitute for sighting in. It simply assures that the first shot will be somewhere on the target. For proper sight adjustment there is no substitute for *shooting*.

Very often I do not bore-sight at all when I put a scope on a rifle. Instead I simply take the rifle out, put up a 100-yard small-bore target at 25 yards, then sit down, and shoot. At that distance a scope would have to be cockeyed indeed not to put the first shot on the target somewhere. I then adjust the scope to put the bullet in the center of the bull. With a scope-sighted big-game rifle so adjusted, the bullet is generally approximately 1 inch high at 50 yards, 3 inches high at 100 yards, on aim at anywhere between 175 and 275 yards, depending on the velocity.

However, the scope-sighted rifle should be checked by shooting at 100 yards, and the sighting refined so that the center of the group is 3 inches high. Any error made at 25 yards is multiplied by 4 at 100 yards, by 8 at 200, and by 12 at 300.

Today's riflemen are lucky to have available so many good scope mounts. They are cheap, strong, easy to put on. Generally all the sight a rifleman will need under hunting conditions is a modern, rugged, waterproof scope on one of the light strong mounts now available. Conditions might arise when the hunter would want to be able to switch to iron sights, but chances are overwhelmingly against it.

THE FUTURE OF SCOPE MOUNTING

There are still undoubtedly more hunting rifles in the United States that are equipped with iron sights than rifles equipped with scopes. The old Winchester Model 94 has sold about 2,500,-000, and probably 2,000,000 of these are still in relatively usable condition. By that I mean that if a cartridge is put in the chamber and the rifle is fired, it will make a noise and the shooter will retain his head. Most such rifles are still equipped with iron sights—probably the original sights put on at the factory. Many of these have never been sighted in, unless one calls shooting at a white rock at some undetermined range sighting in. Such rifles are not suited to scope mounting and not many wear scopes.

To this add the vast number of old military rifles that have found their way into the hands of casual deer hunters—old .30/40 Krags, pre-1917 Springfields, old Model 93 and 95 Mausers, 6.5 Mannlicher Carcanos, primitive Model 91 Argentine and Belgian 7.65 Mausers, Swiss Schmidt-Rubin. Most of these weird rifles are not scope-mounted, and indeed putting scopes on these old rifles would be like endowing a 10-dollar horse with a 200-dollar saddle.

But the majority of good, new American sporting rifles are quickly scope-mounted. Probably 90 per cent of the Winchester Model 70, Savage Model 110, and Remington Model 700 rifles have scopes mounted within a year after they are purchased. The man who buys a really expensive rifle like a Weatherby, a Browning, or a custom job by Griffin & Howe, Biesen, or Brownell usually orders the scope and mount at the same time that he orders the rifle.

Consequently, since most of the expensive rifles—not only the bolt-action jobs I have mentioned but the pump, lever, and automatic weapons—are quickly scope-mounted, the next logical step is to incorporate at least part of the scope mount into the receiver. Some of the Finnish Sako rifles and some of the Czech Mausers already have integral dovetails milled into receiver ring and receiver bridge. These are in effect the fixed portion of the scope mount, and the detachable portion, along with the scope, is quickly put on. Something like this should be done with quality American-made sporters.

CHAPTER XIII

Selecting the Rifle

MANY different factors are to be considered in buying a rifle, either new or second-hand. The use to which the rifle is to be put, who is to use it, and the cost and availability of ammunition are highly important. No matter how finely finished a particular rifle is, it is a poor buy if the ammunition for it is obsolete or may become obsolete before the life of the rifle is over. A rifle is a poor buy if it is too heavy for the person who is to use it or if the recoil and muzzle blast are so excessive that the man behind it never feels comfortable in shooting it. Any rifle is a poor buy if replacement parts are unobtainable. A rifle is no bargain, either, if it is chambered for a cartridge unsuited for its purpose.

More .22 rifles of one kind or another are sold than all other rifles put together. Most people learn to shoot with a .22, and the .22 is usually the first purchase. There are many different types of .22's, from light little single-shots through bolt actions, pumps, and automatics to the heavy super-accurate heavy-barreled target rifles that are used in highly competitive small-bore shooting. Probably the best buy for a young boy to learn on is one of the many little bolt-action single-shot rifles. The boy with the single-shot is taught by necessity to conserve his shots. He doesn't have more cartridges in reserve if he misses with his first. He always knows when it is loaded and when it isn't. Usually, but not always, these .22 single-shots are somewhat lighter and smaller than the more expensive rifles and more nearly fit a child. The young boy nearly always gives his first rifle a pretty bad beating, and in two or three years of use it has a pretty beaten-up appearance. Of the repeaters I would consider a bolt-action clip-loading rifle to be the next best bet and the .22 semi-automatic by far the poorest for the boy.

The common variety of .22 is a sort of family affair that everyone shoots. It is used by the young son of the family for small-game hunting, by others for informal target shooting or "plinking"—breaking bottles, rolling tin cans, perhaps for some aerial shooting. Hair-splitting accuracy is not needed for such a rifle. Any of the pump-action .22's do nicely for this, and if the people who use it are careful, a semiautomatic will do. The bolt-action .22 is also suitable and somewhat more foolproof, but it does not give the speed of fire of the automatic or the pump.

A great many people get an enormous amount of pleasure out of hunting small game with the .22 rifle—squirrels, cottontail rabbits, and even jackrabbits and prairie dogs. In the north woods a good .22 has kept many a trapper and big-game hunter in grouse. For laying down a barrage on a scampering cottontail the .22 semiautomatic has no equal. Actually for most small-game hunting these little semiautomatics are almost perfect instruments. They are made by various concerns in various weights and styles of stocks. Savage, Remington, Winchester, Mossberg, and Marlin all turn them out. They are seen at their best in the Winchester Model 63 and the Remington Model 241, which of course are a great deal more expensive. Fitted with a good aperture sight, or even better a good scope of about 2½-X, these little semiautomatics are beautiful all-around .22's and deadly on running small game.

For the very finest accuracy the better bolt-action .22 rifles are in a class by themselves. The best accuracy is needed when the .22 rim-fire is used on varmints or on squirrels. The man who wants to take a prairie dog at one hundred yards or hit a squirrel at fifty when only the top of the head is showing over a limb had better get one of the more precisely and carefully built bolt-action .22's.

Standouts are, for boys, the rather light Winchester Model 250 lever, and for adults the Remington 513-T. Both are nicely constructed rifles with exceedingly accurate barrels. They are just about as accurate light .22 rifles as one can get. The de-luxe .22 sporter of them all was the famous Winchester Model 52 in the sporting form. It had the famous Model 52 Winchester target action, a beautifully designed and finished stock, and a handsomely tapered barrel. The rub was that the Model 52 sporter cost important money—more than most people would care to put into a .22 rifle of any sort. It is no longer made. Roy Weatherby will soon announce a .22 sporter for his line, however.

Some men simply like to shoot a .22 to give themselves practice in the off season so they will be more efficient when the big-game season rolls around. Such men should always choose a .22 with an action similar to that on their big-game rifle. The man who uses a pump shotgun and a Remington pump-action big-game rifle would be foolish to buy any other type of .22 than a pump. Likewise the man who likes the lever action and wants some preseason practice should get himself a Marlin Model 39-A, which at the present time is the only lever-action .22 rifle on the market. The man who hunts with a bolt action will find plenty of .22 bolt-action rifles to choose from, and some of the heavier models do not weigh such a great deal less than the light bolt-action big-game rifle.

Many factors go into the selection of the rifle for big-game hunting. It is unwise to be undergunned, and also unwise to be greatly overgunned. The man who is going to hunt nothing larger than deer or the ordinary small black bear of the Eastern woods is foolish to equip himself with a .300 Magnum, for example. Likewise the man who has to hunt in open canyon country where many shots will be taken at long range would be handicapped greatly by selecting a .30/30. The small man who doesn't get much exercise is foolish to plan to lug around a ten-pound rifle. In the chapters on the deer rifle and on the various cartridges I have gone rather thoroughly into this business of selection. Let it be said here, however, that no rifle is much good if it is tiring and burdensome to carry or if ammunition is not readily available. For ordinary deer hunting the rifle should be as light as possible and yet chambered for a cartridge of adequate power. In the Eastern woods shots tend to be quick and at close range. There is no need for hairsplitting accuracy. For that reason lightness and handiness are two factors that the purchaser of the deer rifle should consider. Too much writing about rifles is done by men who do a lot of shooting on the target range but spend too little time in the woods. The average deer hunter is not an expert rifleman nor a very good shot. He needs a rifle easy to operate fast and one that is easy to carry. He simply isn't a good enough shot to take advantage of hairsplitting accuracy. The lever-action or the pump is the best bet for the casual deer hunter. The lighter such a rifle is, all things considered, the better. With their excellent stocks and relatively light weight such lever-actions as the Winchester Model 88 and the 99 Savage are hard to beat. The Remington 742 pump is a fine rifle, particularly for the man who is used to the pump-action shotgun. The lightweight Savage Model 99-F is most excellent because of the ratio of power to weight. With its short barrel, short stock, and good dimensions it is a wise choice particularly for the young boy or the woman who would find a heavier rifle burdensome.

In many instances a rifleman will want to use the same weapon on deer and on varmints. In that case his choice will be altogether different from that for hunting deer alone. Then he will want high velocity, flat trajectory, and great accuracy. He will usually have to put up with more weight. If he is a handloader he will want a bolt action. In such a case fine all-around cartridges are the .243 and the .244, although a handloader can use the .270 very nicely as an all-around deer and varmint caliber.

In the Western states antelope and elk are often on the open list as well as mule, whitetail, and blacktail deer. Elk require a more powerful cartridge than does any deer, and more often than not the antelope must be taken at long range. For such hunting the man with the ordinary deer rifle, which does perfectly for the Eastern woods, is very greatly handicapped. He can do fairly well for such hunting with the .308 W.C.F. cartridge in the Model 99 Savage, the Model 88 Winchester or Model 742 Remington semiautomatic, and also with the Remington Model 760 pump X. For the most part, however, he is better off with a bolt action than with anything else. As we have seen, the bolt action will hold higher pressures and more powerful cartridges than any other type of action. For the long ranges in the West and for animals that are relatively hard to kill like elk and moose, cartridges of considerable power like the .264, .30/06, or .270 are necessary.

The Custom-Made Rifle

As this is written, many thousands of rifles are being produced by various firms and individuals who specialize in rebarreling military actions and fitting them with stocks and sights. These firms call themselves custom rifle-makers. The best rifles they turn out are highly accurate jobs that are things of beauty. The poorer rifles, many of which are sold for high prices, are in every way inferior to factory-made bolt actions. There are all kinds and conditions of gunsmiths practicing their trade today.

There is plenty of reason to own a custom rifle. If a man wants a rifle lighter than ordinary because he finds a factory rifle in the caliber of his choice too heavy and burdensome to carry, he is justified in going to a custom maker. If he wants a rifle in some good wildcat caliber, a special barrel contour, or particularly fine wood, design, and lines to his own specifications, he is also justified in getting a custom rifle made up. Many people take great pleasure in the ownership of fine and handsome weapons that they have had a part in designing.

The man who wants a special rifle should not expect to get one at a price comparable to that charged for a factory job produced by mass-production methods. The factories are equipped to run stocks on a copying lathe. They are set up for mass production. They turn out thousands of rifles exactly alike. Consequently they can make them more cheaply than the small custom maker. These factory rifles are strong, accurate, reliable, well stock for the average man. They have the fault, however, of looking exactly like many thousands of other rifles. For utilitarian purposes there is no better rifle made in the world today than the bolt-action Model 70 Winchester, which is chambered for a large number of excellent high-intensity cartridges. Some rifle enthusiasts do not like the Winchester Model 70 stock in spite of the fact that it is generally well bedded and fits the average man well. Others do not like the way the barrel is contoured or the weight.

The man who simply wants finer wood and some engraving can have a special custom job done on a Model 70 at the Winchester factory. The custom rifle, however, will simply be a standard Winchester barrel and action that has been prettied up. Let us say that a man is going to start from scratch in having a rifle built up. He wants, let us say, a lightweight rifle with a 22-inch barrel. He wants good wood and he has his own notions about stock lines and shape. He can get a Model 1903 Springfield action or a good military or commercial Mauser action of the Model 98 type. He can have either of those actions altered to suit him. He can have, if he wishes, the floor plate hinged and a release button put in the trigger guard. He can have the bolt handle and safety altered for low scope mounting and the trigger guard streamlined. He can have a special lightweight 22-inch barrel fitted to any contour he wishes. He can have it engraved with any design or type of engraving that comes to his mind. He can have a fine trap buck plate or even a trap pistol-grip cap made and fitted. He can have a fine custom-built stock superbly inletted, shaped, and checkered, and made of fine and showy wood to any shape and dimensions he wants. All of this, however, is going to cost him plenty of money. Depending on the details, this custom rifle will cost him from two to five times as much as the equivalent factory rifle.

Custom rifles of almost any sort can be built by Griffin & Howe, 202 East Forty-fourth Street, New York City; P. O. Ackley; Roy Weatherby, 8823 Long Beach Boulevard, South Gate, California; Frank Pachmayr, 1220 South Grand Avenue, Los Angeles 15, California; Alvin Biesen, W. 2039 Sinto, Spokane, Washington; or Lenard Brownell, Sheridan, Wyoming.

Some craftsmen specialize in fine stocks and do no barrel and action work. Among them are, besides Biesen and Brownell, Thomas Shelhamer, Dowagiac, Michigan; Charles Golueke, 1721 South Roosevelt Street, Green Bay, Wisconsin.

The man who is skillful with his hands and has some knowledge of the use of tools can restock a rifle himself, and if he does a good job it will make him happy. He can obtain a rough turned and inletted blank from such firms as E. C. Bishop & Sons, Warsaw, Missouri, or Rienhardt Fajin, also of Warsaw. He can fit such a stock to a Model 98 Mauser, a 1903 Springfield, or a 1917 Enfield. He can end up with a practical and often handsome rifle that will compare favorably with a good factory bolt-action rifle at a considerable saving in money if he does not count the many weary hours he spends.

Let us not forget that the ordinary "custom-made" rifle that is sold for anything like the price charged for a factory-produced bolt-action rifle is usually not much of a bargain. Often these rifles are turned out by people who are long on ambition but short on skill and theory. The barrels are not straight, the chambering is sloppy, the trigger pull is out of this world, and the stock work is enough to make a man's blood run cold. The man who buys such a rifle should have it very thoroughly and carefully inspected by someone who knows rifles or else he is likely to get a lemon.

CHAPTER XIV

Rim-Fire Cartridges

IT IS paradoxical that rim-fire cartridges are at once a dying form of metallic cartridge and yet the most widely sold and widely used of all cartridges. In the larger calibers the rim-fire is gradually being dropped by the world's loading companies, but in the form of the various .22-caliber cartridges it is tremendously popular.

The rim-fire cartridge with the priming compound enclosed in the folded head of the case was the first really successful form of metallic cartridge. It did not take long, however, to show that for the larger calibers and higher pressures the rim-fire case was not ideal. Gradually the big-caliber rim-fires dropped out of the picture. The last remaining survivor was the .41 Swiss rim-fire, which was still being made when the United States got into World War II. It remained in demand because along in the late 1880's or early '90's, tens of thousands of old Swiss army rifles were dumped over here, where they were sold for a few dollars to those who needed a cheap firearm for close-range deer hunting.

Today a few .25 Stevens rim-fire cartridges are being loaded and also a few .32 Short and .32 Long cartridges. At the present time, however, no rifles are being made in those calibers and it is only a matter of time before those cartridges are obsolete. If the .25 Stevens were stepped up to high-velocity form and *if* a good accurate bolt-action rifle were brought out for it, it *might* regain some popularity, but the chances are against it.

As a consequence, a discussion of the rim-fires means a discussion of the .22's. The father of all of them is the little BB cap, which is still loaded in Europe but is no longer loaded here. It consists of a .22-caliber spherical ball weighing 18 grains driven along at a muzzle velocity of 780 f.p.s. from the force of the exploding primer compound *alone*. Its big brother the CB cap uses a conical bullet weighing 29 grains at a velocity of 720 f.p.s.

Before we go farther, we must bear in mind that all .22 rim-fire cartridges are named from their groove diameter rather than from their bore diameter, as is the usual practice. The bore diameter of the .22 barrel runs from .217 to .219 in .22 Short, Long, and Long Rifle. The only real .22's in the lot are the now obsolescent .22 W.R.F. and .22 Winchester Auto cartridges, which are used in barrels bored .220 and rifled .226.

While we are getting technical, the proper twist of rifling for the .22 Short is 1–24, for the .22 Long 1–20, and for the .22 Long Rifle 1–16. The compromise twist for tubular repeaters that will handle Shorts, Longs, or Long Rifles interchangeably is 1–17.

The .22 Short is one of the most useful cartridges ever invented. It is small, light, cheap, quiet, and accurate. It is a fine cartridge for gallery and indoor target shooting and for plinking around on tin cans and bottles. The .22 Long, on the other hand, is a pretty useless contraption. It uses the .22 Long Rifle case and the .22 Short bullet. The curious thing, though, is that the velocity of the .22 Long is no greater than that of the .22 Long Rifle, even with the lighter bullet. In reality it should be discontinued.

The .22 Long Rifle is one of the most highly developed, most accurate, and most widely used cartridges in the world. Every week many hundreds of .22 match shooters fire thousands of matches with it and each one will lie down with literally hundreds of dollars' worth of equipment scattered around him—a fine .22 heavy-barrel match rifle, a fine scope, a spotting scope, a shooting jacket and mitt. To get in the money he has to keep most of his shots in the 1-inch x-ring, and if he gets out of the

2-inch 10-ring he is out of luck. All the loading companies put out special match ammunition in this caliber—Winchester's EZYXS, Remington's Palma, and Western's Xpert. This ammunition is loaded to velocities of around 1150 f.p.s., by the way, instead of up to 1375 as with the high-speed stuff. The reason velocity is held down with match ammunition is that .22 bullets traveling well above the speed of sound are much more wind-sensitive.

As far as small-game hunting goes, the high-speed .22 cartridges that came out about 1931 add a great deal of killing power. They are made with brass instead of copper cases and they develop a good deal higher pressures than the old standard-velocity stuff. When these high-speed loads are given hollow-point bullets, however, they are much more deadly.

For small-game hunting, when anything but head shots are to be taken, the high-speed hollow-points should *always* be used. Really, the .22 solid bullets are pretty poor killers. I remember once when I was hunting ptarmigan, an arctic grouse about the size of a domestic pigeon, high above timber line in northern British Columbia, I had thought that the .22 Long Rifle high-velocity solid bullet should kill one of those birds with a body hit. I knocked over four birds, but got only one. Another time I shot a ruffed grouse through the body at forty-five or fifty yards. He fell, but when I went to pick him up I found feathers but no grouse. From then on I shot only at the neck and head and did not lose a single bird I hit.

A squirrel, which has a lot of vitality for its size, will carry off two or three solid bullets in the body. The man who likes squirrel hunting and isn't up to shooting the handsome little rodents in the head should use the high-velocity hollow-point loads by all means. The same applies to the cottontail.

The .22 rim-fire is only a small-game cartridge, even with the high-speed hollow-point bullet. It is a *small*-game cartridge— and I mean small. I know that someone will rise up and cry out that his Uncle Jake shot a bear with a .22. I know a chap who killed an Alaskan brown bear with a heart shot with one. I know of a Mexican who has killed a couple of bighorn rams with one, and many professional lion hunters use .22's to knock the big cats out of trees. Nevertheless, the .22 is *still* only a small-game cartridge. I have seen literally thousands of jackrabbits killed with .22's. Up to fifty yards the high-speed hollow-point will kill quickly with a lung shot. Beyond that distance it isn't so hot. With solid bullets it is under no circumstance a jackrabbit cartridge. It isn't even a fox or coyote cartridge. I have seen dozens of coyotes hit in the lungs with the high-speed, hollow-point stuff run off from a hundred yards to a half mile.

It is a poor wild-turkey cartridge, as dozens of turkey hunters found out in my native Arizona when the shotgun was barred from turkey hunting. From the reports I could get, about half the turkeys hit solidly in the body got away. It is a poor woodchuck cartridge for anything except short range shooting and head shots.

Primitive and callous men in the backwoods often use the .22 on deer, antelope, and even moose. They kill some, but for the most part they wound many more than they kill. Anyone who uses a .22 on big game is cruel or ignorant.

In the .22 field many developments have taken place in the last few years. Most important, undoubtedly, was the development of non-corrosive priming, which was pioneered by Remington with Kleanbore. Before that the .22 had a very short barrel life because potassium chlorate was used in the priming mixture. There was a lot of it in proportion to the powder charge. Oil did little or no good and a .22 barrel could rust out almost overnight. When rust-causing, moisture-attracting potassium chlorate was eliminated, however, the .22 became almost everlasting. The combination of the primer residue and the wax or grease of the bullet protects the bore from rust, and unless a rifle is to be stored for a long time, no cleaning whatsoever is necessary. I have left .22 rifle bores uncleaned literally for years without a speck of rust forming.

This holds true *only* if waxed or greased bullets and *not* copper-coated bullets, since bullets of this latter type, though not rust-causing, do not deposit the protective waxy or greasy coating.

It is absolutely unnecessary and even undesirable to do much cleaning of a .22 rim-fire rifle, as the rod can damage the delicate lands.

The use of dry wax bullets in the .22 has been an advance and it makes the outside lubricated .22 bullets much easier to handle. The greased bullets shoot beautifully and protect the bore indefinitely, but they pick up dirt, lint, and sand and cannot be carried loose in the pocket.

One note of warning must be sounded here about not cleaning a .22: a rifle used with different brands of cartridges with different types of non-corrosive priming should be cleaned, and thoroughly, as there is a possibility that the union of different chemicals may set up harmful reactions in the barrel.

It is distinctly a good idea *not* to use .22 Shorts in a handgun or rifle chambered for Shorts, Longs, or Long Rifles. In time the use of the shorter case will cause *erosion* in the chamber so the longer cartridge will not seat easily. Anyway, the excellent .22 Long Rifle cartridge is the best .22 rim-fire, and one should stick to it.

.22 Pressures

Not much has ever been published about the pressures developed by .22 rim-fire cartridges, but this is something the owner of an old .22 should keep in mind. Pressures for the ordinary low-speed or standard .22 run about 16,000 pounds per square inch. Pressures in the high-speed type run much higher—around 24,000 pounds—or as much as in the big old black-powder cartridges like the .45/70. This is the reason that the cases for the high-velocity .22 cartridges are made of *brass*, not copper. Brass has a much greater tensile strength—35,000 to 40,000 pounds per square inch instead of about 25,000 pounds for copper.

Because of these higher pressures developed in the hot variety of .22, this ammunition should very definitely not be used in old .22 rifles of doubtful ancestry and condition made before the advent of this high-pressure ammunition. Its continued use will develop excessive head space in old rifles with soft carbon-steel actions intended to handle nothing hotter than the old loading. Many rifles have excessive head space, and with the low-pressure ammunition the cases do not rupture. In a rifle with excessive head space, however, many ruptures will occur. The case will blow out just forward of the rim, with the result that gas will escape back into the shooter's face. Many eyes have been injured by this. Don't shoot high-velocity ammunition with brass cases in an old .22 rifle. Likewise do not shoot it in .22 revolvers unless the chambers have been countersunk to protect the head of the cartridge. Unprotected heads will blow out.

SIGHTING IN THE .22

Because of its relatively low velocity even in the "high-speed" load, the .22 is distinctly a short-range cartridge. Many have the notion that the addition of a telescopic sight to a .22 will make longer-range hits possible. It will not. The fault of the .22 is the curved trajectory.

When a standard-velocity .22 Long Rifle cartridge is fired in an iron-sighted rifle sighted to hit the point of aim at the usual distance of 50 yards, and aimed at an object 100 yards away, the bullet will drop 7 inches and at 125 yards 14 inches. The man who kills a chuck or a rabbit under those conditions at over 100 yards has to do some sharp figuring.

Using high-speed ammunition with the same sights and setting will flatten the trajectory a bit. At 100 yards the drop is 6 inches

RIM-FIRE RIFLE CARTRIDGES
HIGH VELOCITY

Cartridge	Bullet Weight Grains	Style	Velocity—Feet Per Second Muzzle	Velocity—Feet Per Second 100 Yards	Energy—Foot Pounds Muzzle	Energy—Foot Pounds 100 Yards	Mid-Range Trajectory In.—100 Yards
22 Short	.29	Lead	1125	920	81	54	4.3
22 Short	.27	Hollow Point	1155	920	80	54	4.2
22 Short "Rocket"	.15	Composition	1710	—	97	—	—
22 Long	.29	Lead	1240	965	99	60	3.8
22 Long Rifle	.40	Lead	1335	1045	158	97	3.3
22 Long Rifle	.36	Hollow Point	1365	1040	149	86	3.3
22 W.R.F. (Remington Special)	.45	Lead	1450	1110	210	123	2.7
22 W.R.F. Magnum	.40	Hollow Point	2000	—	—	—	—

STANDARD VELOCITY

Cartridge	Bullet Weight Grains	Style	Velocity—Feet Per Second Muzzle	Velocity—Feet Per Second 100 Yards	Energy—Foot Pounds Muzzle	Energy—Foot Pounds 100 Yards	Mid-Range Trajectory In.—100 Yards
22 Short	.29	Lead	1045	810	70	—	—
22 Short Gallery Special Spatter-Less	.29	Lead	1045	—	70	—	—
22 Short Spatter-Less	.29	Lead	1045	—	70	—	—
22 Short New & Improved Spatter-Less	.15	Composition	1710	—	97	—	—
22 Long Rifle	.40	Lead	1145	975	116	84	4.0
22 Winchester Automatic	.45	Lead	1055	930	111	86	4.6
22 Remington Autoloading	.45	Lead	920	—	84	—	5.5
25 Stevens	.67	Lead	1130	985	184	140	3.8
32 Short	.80	Lead	945	840	158	125	5.3
32 Long	.90	Lead	945	850	178	144	5.3

MATCH TYPE

Cartridge	Bullet Weight Grains	Style	Velocity—Feet Per Second Muzzle	Velocity—Feet Per Second 100 Yards	Energy—Foot Pounds Muzzle	Energy—Foot Pounds 100 Yards	Mid-Range Trajectory In.—100 Yards
22 Long Rifle	.40	Lead	1145	975	116	84	4.0
22 Long Rifle Mark II	.40	Lead	1145	975	116	84	4.0
22 Long Rifle EZXS	.40	Lead	1145	975	116	84	4.0
22 Long Rifle Mark III	.40	Lead	1105	970	108	84	4.1
22 Long Rifle L V EZXS	.40	Lead	1105	970	108	84	4.1

and at 125 yards 12 inches. The thing to do to get an apparently flatter trajectory is to sight in to put the bullet 1 inch high at 50 yards. With the standard-velocity ammunition and iron sights, the bullet will drop 5 inches at 100 yards and 11 inches at 125. This combination with the high-speed .22 Long Rifle cartridge will give a drop at those ranges of 3 and 8 inches.

The addition of a scope apparently flattens trajectory considerably because of the higher sight line. With a scope mounted 1½ inches above the line of bore and the .22 Long Rifle high-speed cartridge sighted to put the bullet 1 inch high at 50 yards, the bullet first crosses the line of sight at 20 yards. It hits 1 inch high at 50, crosses the line of sight the second time at 75, and hits 3 inches low at 100. But even with the scope the drop is 8 inches at 125, and the .22 is just no long-range rifle.

Actually, most people have no business shooting varmints with a .22. Something like the .22 Hornet is far superior.

The .22 Rim-fire Magnum

The .22 Winchester Rim-fire Magnum cartridge has been on the market since about 1960. It is a hopped-up rim-fire which probably gives pressures of around 34,000 p.s.i. in driving a 40-grain jacketed hollow-point bullet at a velocity of 2,000 feet per second. Ruger, Colt, and Smith & Wesson make revolvers for it, and Mossberg, Winchester, Marlin, and Savage turn out rifles in the caliber. Velocity in a 6½-inch revolver barrel is 1550.

However, all is not roses with the cartridge. Ammunition is expensive, $2.60 at retail for fifty, as compared to 90 cents for the .22 Long Rifle high-velocity ammunition. The accuracy has not been sensational, and some difficulty has been encountered with the cases blowing out at the rim. The .22 WRFM should be a pretty fair wild-turkey cartridge and a 125–150-yard varmint cartridge. It cannot, of course, be reloaded.

CHAPTER XV

Varmint Cartridges

ONE of the most interesting developments on the shooting scene since the end of the last war has been the enormous increase in the popularity of varmint hunting. Probably fifty enthusiasts are hunting varmints today for every one who hunted varmints prior to 1941. Tens of thousands of people who heretofore used rifles only in deer season or for a little plinking at tin cans or bottles during the summer months have now taken up shooting of varmints. As a consequence, they now fire hundreds of shots where they once fired dozens. "Varmints" are birds and animals which are considered pests or nuisances in civilization. For the most part there is no closed season on them because of the damage they do to domestic birds and animals and to crops and game. The woodchuck of the East is a favorite varmint to shoot at in the summer and so are its Western cousins the rock chuck, the hoary marmont, the prairie dog, and the ground squirrel. In the West the white-tailed, black-tailed, and antelope jack rabbits are leading varmints, and tens of thousands of them are shot annually.

The villainous crow is the leading bird in the varmint class, and harmful hawks and owls are legitimate game for the off-season hunter.

For the most part varmints are shot in settled localities off and on farms where domestic livestock ranges. Consequently, the varmint cartridge is a more or less specialized job. Ideally it should have a high velocity with a flat trajectory. Because varmints are for the most part small, the ideal varmint cartridge should give superlative accuracy. A deer rifle that will group into a one-foot circle at 100 yards will kill plenty of deer at the short ranges of the Eastern woods. The varmint rifle that gave no better accuracy would be utterly worthless. The best varmint cartridge will group into from ¾ inch to 1½ inches at 100 yards. The ideal varmint cartridge should have a bullet that is driven fast enough and is thinly constructed enough that it will disintegrate when it strikes the ground instead of ricocheting over the countryside and annoying the landowners. The ideal varmint cartridge should also have a light report. Many people who know nothing about rifles think that the danger of the rifle is in proportion to the noise it makes. In reality the quiet little .22 rimfire is one of the most dangerous of all calibers because the lead bullets are not driven fast enough to go to pieces when they hit the ground. They will ricochet over the countryside and may strike a house or wound a man half a mile or more away. On the other hand, the .30/06 used with the 110-grain bullet and the .270 used with the 100-grain bullet are among the safest rifles made because those light bullets are driven at high velocity and go to pieces on impact. Most landowners, however, cannot be told that. The heavy report of those rifles frightens them because they associate noise with danger.

Most people who begin to hunt varmints start with the .22 rim-fire and iron sights. They find that they can make hits pretty regularly up to 75 yards on animals the size of crows or prairie dogs and up to 100 yards on animals the size of jack rabbits and woodchucks. Their next step usually is to buy a telescope sight for the .22. They find that although they can see better they cannot extend the range much because of the roundhouse trajectory of the little rim-fire cartridge. They usually go to center-fire cartridges of some sort eventually. Thirty-five or forty years ago a favorite varmint cartridge was the .25/20, which is now just about dead. Nowadays the hunter of woodchucks usually ends up with a rather heavy rifle, often for some high-velocity cartridge like the .222 Remington, the .220 Winchester Swift, or the .243 Winchester. He will get a telescope sight of from 6 to 10 power and do most of his shooting prone with a sling or from some sort of a rest. The expert varmint hunters of America are the finest precision riflemen in the field. They can do things with a rifle that will astound the ordinary big-game hunter, and when these same varmint shots go after big game in open country they find the shooting, for the most part, ridiculously easy.

In the West, where the relatively large coyote is common, and where not only the coyote but also the jack rabbit must be shot on the run, the varmint hunters usually end up with somewhat lighter rifles than their Eastern brothers because they often have to walk long distances carrying their rifles. Since they have to shoot running game a good deal, they use scopes of from 4 to 6 power and of the hunting type rather than the target type. They also tend to use cartridges which can also be used for antelope and deer—the .243, the .270, even the .30/06.

THE .25/20 AND THE .32/20

Prior to the development of the .22 Hornet cartridge, the .25/20 and the .32/20 cartridges were among the leaders for varmints. In its day the .25/20 was a very fine little cartridge with practically no recoil and a light report. For those days the accuracy of the original loading of an 86-grain bullet with a velocity of about 1,450 foot-seconds was good. In later years the velocity of that bullet was stepped up to 1,710 foot-seconds and a 60-grain bullet at a velocity of 2,210 was loaded. Winchester, Marlin, Remington, and Savage rifles were chambered for the .25/20, and also for its twin, the .32/20. This sister cartridge of the .25/20 originally used a 100-grain lead bullet for a velocity of about 1,280. Later it was loaded with a 115-grain bullet with the same velocity, and still later a high velocity load gave that bullet 1,600. An 80-grain bullet was given 2,050.

Both the .25/20 and the .32/20 are dying, just as any cartridge dies when no rifles are made for it. However, both rifles remain highly useful for wild turkeys, as they kill them quite well with body shots and do not tear up much meat.

THE .22 HORNET

About 1931, the .22 Hornet, which was and is a very useful and satisfactory varmint cartridge, was developed. It is really a modernization of the old .22 Winchester center-fire black-powder cartridge, which at the time of the development of the Hornet was just about obsolete in the United States. Long ago the Germans took this old .22 Winchester center-fire cartridge and loaded it with smokeless powder and jacketed bullets. They called it the 5.6 x 35-R. Similar to our Hornet, it was used in little single-shot rifles and in three-barrel guns for varmint and small-game shooting.

In the United States the Hornet began as a wildcat. It was developed by the late Captain Grosvenor Wotkyns and by the government technicians at the Springfield arsenal in Massachusetts. They took the old .22 Winchester center-fire cases, loaded them with new powders, non-corrosive primers, and jacketed bullets of the .22 Velo-Dog revolver cartridge. They were amazed at the accuracy and velocity they got. There was a tremendous interest in the new cartridge and Winchester agreed to load it commercially. The first .22 Hornet rifles were altered and rechambered .22 Springfield rifles, but Winchester brought out a fine Hornet rifle in the Model 54, and also chambered the later Model 70 for it. Savage made the Model 23 and Model 19 bolt-action rifles for the cartridge, and also the Model 219 single shot. Winchester chambered the bolt-action Model 43 for it.

The .22 Hornet stirred up a great deal of interest in the hot-shot .22 center-fire. However, today it is pretty dead. Shooters wanted flatter trajectory and higher velocity and were willing to go to bigger cases. Gradually the .22 Hornet was driven out of the field and is now becoming slowly obsolete. The fine Winchester Model 70 is no longer chambered for the .22 Hornet. The only rifles being made for it today in the United States are the Savage Model 340 bolt action and Model 219 single shot.

Actually, for most purposes the .22 Hornet is an exceedingly satisfactory varmint cartridge. It is quiet, accurate, and flat-shooting enough for 150–175 yard shooting. That takes in about ninety per cent of all hits on varmints.

THE .218 BEE AND THE .219 ZIPPER

Following the development of the .22 Hornet, Winchester brought out two other .22 center-fire varmint cartridges which could be used in existing Winchester action. The .218 Bee was a fine little cartridge. As made by Winchester, the Bee has a bore diameter of .219 and a groove diameter of .224, whereas the Hornet has a bore diameter of .217 and a groove diameter of .222. Both rifles had a twist of one turn in 16 inches. The Bee uses a 46-grain bullet at a muzzle velocity of 2,860, or about 200 foot-seconds higher than the velocity of the Hornet.

The original Bee cartridge was simply a .25/20 repeater case necked down. The result was a short case with good powder capacity to give a light .22 bullet relatively high velocity. It was developed by Winchester to work through the short Model 92 lever action—the same action that was used for the .25/20 and the .32/20 cartridges. Winchester brought out a lever-action rifle for the Bee on this action, but it was never very popular. Accuracy was good enough but not outstanding and scopes mounted on this rifle had to be slightly offset to the left because of the top ejection. Winchester also made the Model 43, a light bolt-action, for the cartridge. Both rifles are now obsolete.

The cartridge itself is dying. Hardened varmint hunters wanted heavier rifles. They wanted rifles that would mount

[175]

scopes low and central over the bore and they wanted actions that would keep the cases from stretching. The Bee cartridge is still on the active list, but I doubt if it is long for this world, because no rifles are being made for it.

Winchester's .219 Zipper is another cartridge that is on the sick list. No rifles have been made for it for years. It was based on the .25/35 case and was designed to work through the Model 94 Winchester action. It came out in the now-obsolete Model 64, an adaptation of the Model 94. With its long, whippy barrel, and its two-piece stock, the Model 64 in .219 Zipper never gave good accuracy. There was nothing wrong with the cartridge. In good single-shots and bolt-actions, the Zipper shot well. At one time there was a fad for blowing out, or fire-forming the .219 case to a sharp-shouldered cartridge known as the ".219 Improved Zipper." This was used in single-shot rifles and was loaded to give velocity not far from those of the .22/250 or .220 Swift. However, since the war this wildcat has died because post-war .219 Zipper ammunition will not blow out successfully and gives a case loss of four out of five.

THE .220 SWIFT

An interesting phenomenon of the post-war world of varmint shooting is the relative decline of the .22 center-fire for varmint shooting. As we have seen, the .218 Bee, the .219 Zipper, and the .22 Hornet are dying. Even the .220 Swift seems on its last legs. As this is written in 1963, Winchester no longer chambers the standard Model 70 rifle for it. The Swift is available only in a special heavy-barrel varmint rifle. My guess is that the Swift may become obsolete in the next ten or fifteen years, and I suspect the Model 70 rifle may be discontinued for the cartridge before that.

Nevertheless, the .220 Swift was one of the most important cartridge developments in the last thirty years. Rifle enthusiasts used to speculate about velocities of 4,000 foot-seconds, and here all at once was an ultra-high-velocity cartridge that produced such a velocity. As originally loaded, the Swift produced 4,140 foot-seconds with a 48-grain bullet, and 3,720 with a 55-grain bullet. Over 300 yards the trajectory with the 48-grain bullet is only 3.5 inches. The Swift can be sighted in to hit the point of aim at 250 yards, and shots fired at 40, 100, 150, 200, and 250 yards, and the bullets will all be in the same small group. No one who has ever done much varmint shooting needs to be told what such a development means.

Like the Hornet, the Swift was originally the brain-child of Captain Grosvenor Wotkyns. As is not generally known, the original Wotkyns "Swift" was a .250/3000 case necked down to .22—about identical to the wildcat .22/250. When Winchester took over the development of the cartridge, it was decided to use the semi-rimmed 6 mm. Lee navy case shortened and necked down. Winchester chambered the Model 54 Winchester for the cartridge and gave it a 26-inch barrel. Actually Swift rifles have always been remarkably accurate and almost any Model 70 Winchesters I have seen for the cartridge will group into a minute of angle or less.

The early Swift had its troubles. Winchester found out that the nickel steel barrels on the Model 54 quickly gave up the ghost with the high pressures and stratospheric velocity. This led to the development by Winchester of chrome-molybdenum heat-treated barrels, which were later used in all Model 70 Winchester calibers. Eventually, though, to obtain long barrel life Winchester had to go to the so-called stainless steel barrels, which are actually a high-chrome iron, so rust-resistant, as well as erosion-resistant, that they cannot be blued. Instead they have to be iron-plated and the iron-plating blued.

When the Swift was first developed, enthusiasts simply had to try it out on big game. Much big game was killed with it, and killed very dead, but also much big game was lost. If the tiny bullet slipped through the rib cage and exploded in the lungs the animal was not long for this world. On the other hand, if the bullet struck a large bone it generally blew up. Hunters found it worthless for rear-end shots at animals, and gradually the fad of shooting big game with the Swift died out. At present the use of the Swift with its light bullets on big game, including deer, is now outlawed in many states.

As loaded today, the Swift is given only one bullet weight— a 48-grain soft-point at 4,110. Handloaders have made many attempts to load the Swift with heavier bullets to give greater killing power at long range and to make the cartridge less susceptible to crosswinds. The heaviest bullet that anyone has attempted to use is one weighing 65 grains. I doubt if they are made any longer, but at one time they could be given a velocity of about 3,550 foot-seconds with 40 grains of No. 4350 powder. Since the Swift is primarily a varmint cartridge, however, a bullet weighing about 50–55 grains is probably the best.

The Swift has a rather long, sloping shoulder, and as a consequence is not the most flexible of cartridges. It needs a somewhat sharper shoulder to burn the powder in the chamber instead of the barrel to cut down on throat erosion. Roy Weatherby, the riflemaker and experimenter of South Gate, California, blows out the Swift case to give it a sharper shoulder and less body taper. He calls the fire-formed cartridge the Weatherby Rocket and loads it with 46 grains of No. 4350 to give a 60-grain bullet 3,727, and with 44 grains of No. 4064 to give a 55-grain bullet 4,100. The Rocket, however, has not been as popular as some of the other Weatherby cartridges.

Despite the Swift's decline in popularity, I still consider it in many ways the best of all varmint cartridges. Accuracy is generally excellent, trajectory fantastically flat, and killing power adequate for jack rabbits and woodchucks as far as they can be hit. Furthermore, it is just about the safest of all cartridges because the light bullets at terrific velocity explode when they strike the ground and do not ricochet.

THE .22/250 OR "VARMINTER"

Probably the most popular wildcat cartridge ever designed is the cartridge variously known as the .22/250, or "Varminter." It is the original Wotkyns Swift, and most consider the case more efficient for burning powders than that of the Swift. The cartridge has been so popular and so satisfactory that at various times rifle manufacturers have considered bringing out factory rifles for it. In the spring of 1960, one factory was seriously considering making a .22/250 rifle if they could get one of the loading companies to bring out the ammunition. The .22/250 is simply the .250/3000 Savage case necked down but given a slightly steeper shoulder of 28°—rather than the 26° shoulder of the .250. Case forming is very simple. All one has to do is run .250/3000 cases through a full-length die and then load them up. No shortening, no trimming, no blowing out are necessary. The .22/250 is a very flexible cartridge and will handle almost any sensible charge of almost any powder and still give good accuracy as long as good bullets are used. The amount of powder used is not critical. I once saw a loader dunk five Varminter cases into a can of No. 4350, fill them to the mouths, then seat 55-grain bullets on top of the powder and go out and shoot a 1-inch group. The cartridge very quickly got a great reputation for accuracy and at one time held most of the bench-rest records. Since then it has been displaced by a wildcat known as the Wasp, and later by the newer .222 Remington.

The .22/250, like all .22 center-fire varmint cartridges, has suffered a decline in popularity, but since the middle thirties I imagine thousands of rifles have been chambered for the cartridge. I still have a .22/250, a very handsome one, built on a shortened Springfield action and then stocked by Al Biesen. For years my standard load has been a 50-grain bullet with 36.5 grains of No. 4320. Velocity is about 3,700 foot-seconds and the accuracy sensational and the barrel life long.

[179]

THE .222 REMINGTON AND .222 MAGNUM

One of the best and most accurate of all .22 varmint cartridges and the Queen of the May since it was developed is the .222 Remington. Unlike many other varmint cartridges, the .222 is based on no existing case. The case is new and specially designed. It is a small, rimless case which moves a 50-grain bullet along at the very respectable velocity of 3,200. It is a much flatter-shooting cartridge than the .22 Hornet, for example, since the mid-range trajectory over 300 yards is 7 inches, whereas that of the .22 Hornet is 13 inches. It is not as flat, though, as the .220 Swift, which has a mid-range trajectory over 300 yards of 3.8 inches. The .222, in spite of its name, takes bullets measuring .224, like the .220 Swift.

The .222 has many advantages. It gives sufficiently high velocity and flat trajectory for about ninety-five per cent of all varmint shooting and is definitely a 225-yard varmint cartridge. It is an exceedingly pleasant cartridge to shoot because of the light report and almost non-existent recoil. This mildness of the .222 is probably responsible for the fact that it is the most accurate cartridge in existence as far as bench-rest records go. Some of the groups that have been shot with a .222 with heavy special rifles are simply fantastic. Probably there are other cartridges inherently as accurate as the .222 but because of the lightness of report and recoil people can shoot the .222 better. Most people who reload for the .222 use between 17.5 and 19.5 grains of No. 4198 for velocities ranging from 2,978 to 3,210. However, the .222 can also be loaded with slower-burning powders. For example, 23 grains of No. 3031 gives the 50-grain bullet 3,272, and 25 grains of No. 4064 gives 3,273.

The running mate to the .222 is the .222 Remington Magnum, which has a longer case and will give higher velocity but which, for some reason, has never attained the popularity of its smaller brother. With the 50-grain bullet and 30 grains of No. 4320, the .222 Magnum will produce a velocity of 3,485, and with 28 grains of No. 4064, velocity is 3,458. The .222 Magnum was a development for an experimental military rifle.

The original rifle for the .222 was the Remington Model 722, but later Remington brought it out in the excellent Model 725. Winchester has never made a .222 rifle, but Savage manufactures the bolt-action Model 340 for it. Very handsome, light, and accurate .222 rifles are also made by Sako in Finland and imported into this country.

THE .250/3000 AND THE .257 ROBERTS

In the last few years, the .25 caliber cartridges have been on the decline and rifles are no longer made for the .25/35, the .250/3000, or the .257. The .250/3000 and the .257, in spite of the fact that they are growing obsolete, are both excellent cartridges for varmint shooting and for game up to the size of deer, sheep, or antelope.

The .250/3000 came out for the Model 99 Savage rifle in 1914, and for over forty years has borne a fine reputation for accuracy. It is based on the .30/06 case, shortened and necked down to .25 caliber. With its 26-degree shoulder it was one of the original sharp-shoulder cartridges. The original loading gave an 87-grain bullet 3,000 f.p.s., and this light bullet always shot well in the heavier-barreled models of the Model 99 Savage with the 1–14 twist. Later, a 100-grain bullet at about 2,800 was loaded.

Besides the various Model 99 Savages chambered for the cartridge, Winchester for a time chambered the Model 54 and Model 70 bolt-action rifles for it, and Savage chambered the Model 1920, Model 40, and Model 45 bolt-action rifles for it. Many excellent .250/3000 sporting rifles were built in Germany by Mauser Werke on the short Mauser "K" action. The same action was used by custom gunsmiths like Hoffman and Griffin & Howe back in the 1920's and 1930's for many lightweight sporters in .250/3000.

However, after World War II, interest in the cartridge began to lag. The .250 was dropped from the line of Model 70 Winchesters, and by 1961, sales of the .250/3000 in the Savage Model 99 had declined to such an extent that Savage for the first time in over forty years ceased making rifles in that caliber. Its place seemed to have been taken by the .243 Winchester—of which more later.

Another good .25 caliber cartridge which is in the process of going down the drain is the .257 Roberts. It was first introduced in 1934 and was based on a similar wildcat made by necking down the 7 mm. case to .25 caliber. Incidentally, headspace and shoulder angle are the same for the .257 and the 7 mm. Remington chambered the Model 30 bolt-action rifle for the .257, and after the war made rifles in the bolt action Model 722 for it, as well as some pump-action rifles in Model 760. Winchester made Model 54 and Model 70 bolt-action rifles for it.

The .257 got some bad breaks. For one thing, the original bullet was round-nosed and the cartridge was given a short over-all length. As a consequence, factory rifles for it had magazines so short that to work through them the Spitzer bullet had to be seated deep in the case. The bullet then had to take a considerable jump before it engaged the rifling. Moreover, the ballistics of the .257 were standardized back in 1934 with the then new No. 3031 powder, which turned out to be too fast-burning to be efficient in the .257 case. Standard factory ballistics give the 100-grain bullet at 2,900 and a 117-grain bullet, 2,650. These figures can be considerably improved by judicious handloading. With 45 grains of No. 4350, the 100-grain bullet will travel along about 3,100, and with 49 grains of No. 4831 it can be given about 3,200 with permissible pressures. The 117-grain and 120-grain bullets can be loaded to 2,860 with 45 grains of No. 4831, or 2,800 with 42 grains of No. 4350.

For many years the .257 was my favorite coyote and jack-rabbit cartridge with the 100-grain bullet loaded up to between 3,000 and 3,100. This load was absolutely deadly on coyotes to 300 yards, about as far away as I have ever shot one.

I have seen my wife and sons' .257 kill in the neighborhood of fifty deer, antelope, and javelinas, and I can't remember one that ever got away. With the 117-grain full-metal jacketed bullet loaded to about 2,200 it is an excellent wild-turkey cartridge. The cartridge gives light recoil and muzzle blast along with good accuracy, and I know of no better combination cartridge for varmints, deer, sheep, antelope, and game of that class. Although the cartridge will eventually become obsolete, it will probably be loaded for quite a few more years, and it is well worth getting a custom-made rifle for it.

Both the .25 Remington and the .25/35 were used for varmints extensively before the .22 center-fires came along. Both were fair-enough cartridges, but it isn't worth discussing them here because they are quite dead.

OTHER .25 CALIBER VARMINT CARTRIDGES

Varmint-hunting enthusiasts, particularly woodchuck hunters, have been playing with .25 calibers for many years. An early wildcat varmint cartridge which is now pretty dead was the .25 Krag—the .30/40 Krag case necked to .25. It was used in rebarreled Krag rifles and in rifles made on various single-shot actions.

Today the liveliest of the .25 caliber varmint cartridges is the .25/06. It is a very old cartridge, as it was originally developed before World War I by the Neidner Arms Company of Dowagiac, Michigan, a pioneering custom rifle-making firm. It was the .30/06 case necked to .25 caliber and was known by various names—the .25 Neidner, the .25 Whelen, the .25 High Power. Now, however, the name .25/06 is the one most widely used.

For years the .25/06 was much over-bore capacity—which means that it could hold more of any existing powder than it could burn efficiently. Velocities produced by it with such powders as No. 15½ and No. 17½ (both tin-incorporated powders now obsolete) were not a great deal superior to those produced by the smaller .250/3000 Savage case.

But the .25/06 came into its own with the development of slow-burning powders such as No. 4350 and No. 4831. The .25/06 will produce, with the 87-grain bullet, a velocity of 3,520 with 61 grains of No. 4831 and 3,448 with 56 grains of No. 4350.

With the ballistically better 100-grain bullet, 60 grains of No. 4831 gives 3,323 and 55 grains of No. 4350 gives 3,328. With the 117- and 120-grain bullets, the .25/06 is an excellent open-country mule-deer, antelope, and sheep cartridge. With 57 grains of No. 4831, either bullet will roll along at a bit over 3,100, and 52 grains of No. 4350 will produce about 3,050. Trajectory is flat, and these good bullets buck wind nicely.

Most other .25 caliber wildcats are now pretty dead.

THE .243 AND THE .244

Several new center-fire cartridges have been introduced since the end of World War II. Some have been conspicuously successful. Others have fallen on their faces. The two most conspicuously successful of the new cartridges are the .222, developed by Remington, and the .243, developed by Winchester.

The .243 and its less successful rival, the .244 Remington, are both 6 mm.'s. There is nothing new about the .240 or 6-mm. business. The 6-mm. Lee Navy cartridge was used by the U.S. Navy about the time the army was using the .30/40 Krag. The ancient British rifle-making firm of Holland & Holland of London has made for at least twenty-five years rifles for a cartridge known as the .240 Apex on a small belted case with a head-size like the .30/06, and about 1954 it brought out what it calls the

.244 H. & H. Magnum, the .375 case necked to .24 and loaded to a claimed 3500 f.p.s. with some variety of very slow-burning machine gunpowder behind a 100-grain bullet.

In this country the father of the 6-mm. calibers was Fred Huntington, who is a gun nut, an experimenter, and a maker of dies and loading tools in Oroville, California. He necked down the .257 Roberts case to .24 caliber, sharpened the shoulder, and had considerable success with it.

Hearing of the wildcat, Remington decided to bring out its version commercially for the Model 722 Remington rifle. It introduced the cartridge with two bullet weights—a 75-grain bullet at 3,500 and a 90-grain bullet at 3,200. Because Remington thought of the cartridge as exclusively a varmint cartridge, the barrels were given a 1–12 twist since experiments showed that the slow twist with light bullets gave slightly better accuracy. The .244 had two strikes against it. For one thing, the Model 722 rifle in which it was introduced was heavy for a sporter, light for a rifle to be used exclusively for long-range varmint shooting. For another, the 1–12 twist would not stabilize spitzer (sharp-pointed) 100-grain bullets. Many prospective purchasers wanted to use a 6 mm. for deer and antelope, so they shied away. Another thing the rifle fanciers did not like was that the Model 722 rifles for the .244 Remington were given a short magazine. Spitzer bullets had to be seated deep in the case and took a jump before they engaged the rifling.

The .244 sold so poorly that Remington dropped the manufacture of rifles bearing the name. Instead, the cartridge was rechristened the 6 mm. Remington, loaded with a 100-gr. bullet. Rifles for the 6 mm. have a 1–10 twist, but will handle .244 ammunition.

Actually, I prefer the .244 to the .243. I like the shape of the case better. The powder capacity is greater. The 26-degree shoulder is more adapted to the use of slow-burning powders than the 20-degree shoulder of the .243.

I had Al Biesen, the famous Spokane, Washington, gunsmith,

[185]

make me a .244 Remington with a 1–10 twist barrel on a Model 1912 Mauser action for the 7-mm. cartridge. He fitted a Leupold 8-X Mountaineer scope and stocked it superbly in French walnut. The rifle shoots beautifully with 48 grains of No. 4831 and any good 90-grain bullet. I seldom shoot a group from a bench rest with it that goes over one inch, and many are in the neighborhood of ½ inch. I have shot many rockchucks with it at 300 yards and over. For all practical purposes it is about as effective as the .25/06, with less blast and recoil.

The race between Remington and Winchester to bring out a 6 mm. ended in a dead heat. Winchester brought it out not long before the first rifles for the .308 cartridge and was about to produce the Model 88 Winchester lever action. They were thinking of necking the .308 case down to .25, but decided the new .24 caliber might have more novelty appeal.

So they announced the .243 first in the Winchester Model 70 Featherweight rifle. All of these rifles that I shot gave excellent accuracy, and Winchester apparently took great pains with both rifle and ammunition. Winchester loaded a 100-grain bullet at an advertised velocity of 3,070 feet per second and a 75-grain bullet at 3,500. The barrels had a twist of 1–10.

The velocities for the .243 are taken in a 26-inch barrel and are considerably less in the 22-inch barrels of the Model 70 Featherweight and the Model 88. On the chronograph to which I have access, factory 100-grain loads turn up about 2,920 in the shorter barrels and the 75-grain bullets about 3,220.

However, the .243 has been a roaring success. Savage chambers the Model 99 lever-action and Model 110 bolt-action rifles for it. The Finnish firm of Sako makes bolt-action rifles for it, and Remington now chambers for it as well as the 6 mm.

In my opinion, the .243 has been greatly overpraised. I consider it inferior not only to the .244–6 mm. Remington, but to the .250/3000 Savage cartridge which it drove from the Savage line. The handloader can get higher velocities with the same pressures in the .244 Remington case. In the .243 case, for example, the maximum load with the 90-grain bullet in the .243 is 47 grains of No. 4831 for 3,076 in a 22-inch barrel, whereas the .244 will handle 50 grains for over 100 foot-seconds higher velocity.

As a matter of fact, both the 6-mm. cartridges were greatly overpraised when they came out, and for all-around use on deer and varmints I'd prefer the old .250/3000 to the .243 and the .257 Roberts to the .244. The reason, of course, is that heavier bullets can be used in the .25 calibers, and 90- and 100-grain bullets used in the 6 mms. are a bit light for the larger game, even light for brush hunting of deer.

An Evaluation of Varmint Cartridges

Varmint hunters are among the nuttiest of rifle nuts, and as long as there are rifle nuts running loose, they will continue to play with strange and wonderful rifles and cartridges. I can use the term "nut" because I have been one myself since, at the age of five, I got hooked on my first Daisy air gun.

To the rifle nut, the perfect rifle and the perfect cartridge are always just over the horizon. The rifle nut is continually experimenting with new cartridges, either factory or wildcat, and with new rifles. His labors have resulted in some very good cartridges, and as we have seen, the varmint nuts have fathered many that have gone into factory production—the .22 Hornet, the .220 Swift, the .257 Roberts, the .244 Remington. They have also fathered some pretty weird turkeys, most of which, happily, are now gone and forgotten. Many of their wildcats have been good enough, but no better than factory cartridges. Others have been pretty bad—freakish in design, over-bore capacity, high of pressure, short of barrel life. The wildcat cartridges that have filled a useful place have survived, but most have not. Of the crop, probably the best are the .22/250, and the .25/06, and there is some possibility that at least one of these may yet see factory production.

About ninety per cent of all varmint shooters are probably better off with the .222 Remington than with any other cartridge. The .222 has just about killed off its rivals in the .22 center-fire field. It is accurate, relatively inexpensive to reload, mild of recoil and muzzle blast, and it will kill varmints up to the size of jack rabbits and woodchucks as well as any other cartridge to 225–250 yards. In addition, some very good rifles are available for it—the Model 700 Remington, the Model 340 Savage, the B.S.A., and the beautifully made little Finnish Sako. With a bit of tuning up, all these rifles will give satisfactory accuracy.

For shooting at the longer ranges, a very good choice is the Swift, a cartridge which should not be allowed to die. On a still day the Swift is the easiest cartridge I have ever used to hit with at ranges of over 200 yards.

For windy days and for larger varmints such as coyotes, a caliber larger than .22 is called for. There is no doubt but that the popular .243 is a good cartridge, but it must be remembered that the published velocity and trajectory figures have been arrived at with a 26-inch barrel—and not with the popular 22-inch barrel of the Winchester Model 70 Featherweight. The 6 mm–.244 is just as accurate and a better cartridge to reload. A good custom-made .244 is an excellent investment for anyone.

A decade or so ago I was in touch with two groups of long-range varmint shooters, one in southern Colorado and another in northern Washington and southern British Columbia. All shot rockchucks and hoary marmots at long range in areas where there was considerable wind. After much experimenting, many members of both schools decided that the most satisfactory cartridge for the conditions under which they shot was the .270 Winchester. Some used the 100- and 110-grain bullets, but a surprising number of them came to the conclusion that the .270

was at its best in windy country with the 130-grain bullet loaded to between 3,100 and 3,200.

I have probably killed thousands of black-tailed and antelope jack rabbits in Arizona with the .270, and well over a hundred coyotes. But this is a very specialized type of varmint shooting. Much of it is on the run and ranges are seldom over 250 yards. The shooting is done with sporter-weight rifles and scopes of from 4 to 6 power. With any bullet the .270 is a deadly killer on coyotes, as a hit almost anywhere will generally kill a coyote in his tracks.

This jack-rabbit and coyote shooting is not long-range precision varmint hunting, but taking chucks at 300–400 yards definitely is. For this work my feeling is that the recoil and blast of the .270 handicap the shooter greatly. Most of us hate to admit it, but we are all sensitive to recoil and blast to some extent, and the less a rifle kicks and the less the noise it makes, the better most of us shoot it. That is one reason that the mild little .222 holds most of the bench-rest records. I know that with a very accurate .270 equipped with a 10-power scope I used to miss shots I should have made. The only conclusion I could come to was that every now and then I was flinching.

The same criticism applies to a somewhat lesser degree to the .25/06 or to the .270's ballistic twin brother, the .280 Remington. All of them belt the shooter a bit too much when fired in unorthodox positions and make a bit too much noise for the finest precision shooting. About as good a combination of flat trajectory, good accuracy, ability to buck wind, and reasonably moderate recoil that I know of is the .244 Remington with a 90-grain bullet rolling along at well over 3,200.

WEIGHT AND THE VARMINT RIFLE

There are two kinds of varmint hunters. One type does most of his hunting by cruising about in an automobile and either shooting from inside the car or over the hood. At most he carries his rifle only a short distance. Weight does not make much difference to a chap of this sort. If his rifle and scope weigh twelve or thirteen pounds, he doesn't mind. It is true that heavy rifles with massive barrels will shoot smaller 10-shot groups than will light rifles. It is also true that they generally maintain their point of impact better from day to day and from month to month than will light rifles.

However, these heavy jobs are murder to carry for long distances and they seldom shoot much smaller 3-shot groups than will rather light rifles with good, carefully bedded barrels. No one ever has a chance to shoot a 10-shot group on a woodchuck —or even a 5-shot group. For the varmint rifle (or, for that matter, any rifle to be used for field shooting), the criterion should be the 3-shot group.

One of the most accurate rifles I have ever owned was an 8¼-pound .25/06. Two other very accurate light jobs are my .222, a Sako barreled action stocked by Lenard Brownell, and a .244 custom made for me by Al Biesen on a 7 mm. Mauser action. Either will put the first three shots out of a cold barrel into about ¾ inch. When more shots are fired, the groups open up, but it is seldom that one fires a chuck rifle often enough to get the barrel hot.

The active hunter, the chap who likes to put his binoculars around his neck, pick up his rifle, and walk, should use a light rifle. He'll find that when he has it tuned up he will do about as well as he would have with a heavy one.

SIGHTING IN THE VARMINT RIFLE

The big-game rifle is generally sighted in to put the bullet about three inches above line of sight at 100 yards. This means that a cartridge with a velocity of about 2,700 feet per second, such as the 180-grain bullet in the .30/06, will be at point of aim with iron sights at 200 yards and at 225 with the higher line of scope sights.

A three-inch rise of trajectory is not very successful with a varmint rifle, however, for with a rifle so sighted there will be too many misses at mid-range. A chuck lying on a rock to sun himself doesn't offer much vertical leeway, and if the hunter's rifle is striking three inches high at the range at which the shot is taken, and the hunter forgets to hold into the rock below the chuck, he'll miss.

It is my practice, to sight in my varmint rifles, to put their bullets 1½ inches high at 100 yards. So sighted, the .22 Hornet puts the bullet at point of aim at 150 yards, is 1½ inches low at 175 and about 4 inches low at 200. It is about a 175-yard varmint cartridge. The .222 so sighted is on at 200. It is certainly a 225-yard varmint cartridge, and if you stretch it, kills can be made very neatly at 250.

With the 100-grain bullet, the .270 so sighted is at point of aim at 225, only one inch low at 250, and 4 inches low at 300. The same trajectory applies to the light fast bullets at 3,400–3,500 in the .243 and .244.

The flattest of all is the Swift (or the .22/250 with suitable loads), for when the 50–55 grain Swift bullets at velocities approaching 4,000 feet per second are 1½ inches high at 100 yards, they are flat on at 300. However, they rise 3 inches at 200, and unless some care is exercised, it is easy to shoot over a resting chuck at that range.

The .280 Remington and the .284 Winchester, excellent big-game calibers both, can also double very nicely as varmint cartridges if suitable bullets are used and if the rifles are mounted with scopes of adequate definition. Both cartridges are factory loaded with 125-grain bullets at velocities of between 3,100 and 3,200, depending on barrel length. These travel in a very flat trajectory and give good accuracy in tuned-up rifles. Excellent

VARMINT CARTRIDGE BALLISTICS

Cartridge	Wt. Grs.	Velocity—Ft. per Sec.				Energy—Ft. Lbs.				Mid-Range Trajectory		
		Muzzle	100 Yds.	200 Yds.	300 Yds.	Muzzle	100 Yds.	200 Yds.	300 Yds.	100 Yds.	200 Yds.	300 Yds.
218 Bee............	46	2860	2160	1610	1200	835	475	265	145	0.7	3.8	11.5
219 Zipper.........	56	3110	2440	1940	1550	1200	740	465	300	0.6	2.9	8.3
22 Hornet..........	45	2690	2030	1510	1150	720	410	230	130	0.8	4.3	13.0
22 Hornet..........	46	2690	2030	1510	1150	740	420	235	135	0.8	4.3	13.0
243 Winchester.....	80	3500	3080	2720	2410	2180	1690	1320	1030	0.4	1.8	4.7
243 Winchester.....	100	3070	2790	2540	2320	2090	1730	1430	1190	0.5	2.2	5.5
244 Remington Hi-Speed.....	75	3500	3070	2660	2290	2040	1570	1180	875	0.4	1.9	4.9
244 Remington Hi-Speed.....	90	3200	2850	2530	2230	2050	1630	1200	995	0.5	2.1	5.5
220 Swift..........	48	4110	3490	2930	2440	1800	1300	915	635	0.3	1.4	3.8
222 Remington......	50	3200	2660	2170	1750	1140	785	520	340	0.5	2.5	7.0
222 Remington Magnum......	55	3300	2800	2340	1930	1330	955	670	455	0.5	2.3	6.1
250 Savage.........	87	3030	2660	2330	2060	1770	1370	1050	820	0.6	2.5	6.4
250 Savage.........	100	2820	2410	2070	1770	1760	1290	950	695	0.6	3.0	7.7
257 Roberts........	87	3200	2840	2500	2190	1980	1560	1210	925	0.5	2.2	5.7
257 Roberts........	100	2900	2540	2210	1920	1870	1430	1080	820	0.6	2.7	7.0
270 Winchester.....	100	3580	3160	2770	2400	2840	2210	1700	1280	0.4	1.7	4.5
270 Winchester.....	130	3140	2850	2580	2320	2840	2340	1920	1550	0.5	2.1	5.3
280 Remington......	125	3140	2840	2550	2280	2740	2240	1800	1440	0.5	2.2	5.5

These figures are for a line of scope sight about 1½ inches above the line of bore. A higher line of sight will, of course, flatten the trajectory to some extent.

varmint bullets for either caliber are the 120-grain Sierra spitzer and the 130-grain Speer, likewise a spitzer. With about 54 grains of No. 4350 in the .284 and 56 grains of the same powder in the .280 Remington, these bullets can be driven at around 3,150 in a 22-inch barrel.

Rifles and Cartridges for Deer

NEARLY all American hunters dream of going after the enormous moose, the lordly bighorn sheep, the truculent grizzly bear; but most of them are fated to do their hunting for the more esoteric species in the pages of the sporting magazines. When they do hunt big game, they go after deer—whitetails in the East, Columbian blacktails on the Pacific coast, and mule deer in the Rocky Mountain states.

By far the most important North American big-game animal is the whitetail. He is found from Maine to Florida, from Wisconsin to Mexico. He gets along with civilization better than any other large game animal. The old and populous state of Pennsylvania affords some of the best whitetail hunting in the Union. Once almost exterminated in New England, deer have made an amazing come-back, and I have seen them in the outskirts of that commuters' haven, Westport, Connecticut. In many areas the whitetail is more numerous probably than when Columbus discovered America, and if it weren't for him big-game hunting would be a dead letter over the greater part of the United States.

Every year hundreds of thousands of hunters go out after whitetails with everything from 20-gauge shotguns to .300 Magnums. Some get their bucks, some do not. Tens of thousands of deer are hit and lost. Other thousands of deer are claimed by hunters who do not kill them.

In the West, most mule-deer hunting is at fairly long-range, and the scope-sighted rifle with high velocity and flat trajectory comes into its own. In other words, the deer rifle is also a sheep and antelope rifle. The whitetail country of the East, however, is for the most part heavily wooded and shots are short. Further, because the country is wooded and brushy, the bullet often has to get through twigs and limbs before it hits the game. Deer hunting on public land is likely to be a rat-race these days, with the woods full of hunters, many of them excitable, inexperienced heels. A man who shoots a buck and has it run for a hundred yards before it falls is liable to find another hunter has claimed it.

So let us see what sort of rifle our whitetail hunter needs. In the first place, the good whitetail rifle should be light and fast-handling like an upland shotgun. It should come to the shoulder fast and line up *instantly*. The deer hunter doesn't have to get his shot off with hairsplitting accuracy, but he has to get it off *fast!*

Let us take a typical shot at a whitetail buck. Our hunter has been toiling through the woods for several hours. He is leg-weary, arm-weary, and discouraged. So far he has not seen a deer, and he is about convinced that there aren't any. But he keeps on—decides to cross a little valley and try another ridge. Halfway up he hears, over to his right and above him, the rustle of leaves and then the pound of hoofs. Looking up, he sees a great white tail held high and jaunty, a flash of gray-brown hide, and a beautiful crown of brown antlers, which, to his excited mind, look large enough to hang the family wash on. Swiftly he throws his rifle up. For one shaky instant he tries to steady himself and to align his sights. His finger jerks the trigger, the rifle booms, and the buck disappears over the ridge. Frightened, yet hopeful, he runs to the top. No buck, no blood—only fresh earth and disturbed leaves where the animal has run. His buck has departed for good.

It may sound like heresy, but the sportsman ought to pay more attention to the fit of his deer rifle than he does to that of his long-range rifle. With time you can adapt yourself to almost any rifle stock, but time is something you seldom have in deer hunting. If anything, the ideal deer rifle ought to be a trifle light in the muzzle, as a gun of that sort handles faster on moving game. The muzzle-heavy piece, fine for deliberate long-range shots, is an abomination for fast-jumping whitetails. The barrel should be relatively short. I prefer twenty to twenty-two inches for a lever-action and twenty-one or twenty-two for a bolt-action, because of the longer receiver. Besides being light and handy, the short-barreled rifle is less likely to snag or hit the brush and make noise.

Before you buy your deer rifle, practice throwing it up. See if you can align its sights as swiftly as you can point a shotgun. If you can't, try another gun, or have the stock altered to fit you. Pitch—the angle of the butt plate—makes all the difference in the world when it comes to speed of fire. So does the length of the stock. A recoil pad, properly put on, can solve both difficulties in a factory-built gun. For instance, I changed a .348 Winchester lever-action, which had a bit too much pitch and a stock a little too short for a rangy person, into one of the fastest-handling rifles I have ever seen, by the simple expedient of changing the stock length and the pitch with a rubber recoil pad. If you have a gun stocked to fit you, be sure that the drop at butt is made just a bit less than you think you need. You'll like it and you'll find your rifle faster in the woods. Try to get a good, full forearm so you'll have something to grab hold of and swing the rifle by. No matter what the target shots tell you, *that left hand is all-important* in the woods just as it is with the shotgun, since it is what you swing and point the piece with in shots at deer.

Most deer rifles are equipped with open sights, which, for fast shooting at relatively short range, aren't bad—*if* they are good open sights. The best employ the shallow V, or simply a rear sight in the form of a segment of a circle, with the center marked by a white line, like the rear sight of the obsolete Savage Model 99-T. With either of these rear sights, there is little tendency for the hunter to overshoot. And overshooting has been the bane of hunters since men have sought deer with rifles.

Among the worst of all possible sights for quick shooting are those with the sharply angled V. And here is the reason: Anyone with good eyes, shooting deliberately, can do very well with open sights. Running game, however, is something else. The shots are almost always hurried, and nine times out of ten the hunter will not pull his front bead down "fine" into the V before he touches her off. As a result he overshoots.

The old adage of deer hunters—"Always hold low on a deer" —proves my point. There is nothing about deer that makes a man shoot high. But they are hunted in the fall and winter, often on overcast days, and in the woods. The light isn't any too good. As a consequence, the bottom of a sharp V is hard to see. The hunter pulls it down so-so, shoots—and misses.

Even worse than the ordinary sharply angled V's are the so-called Rocky Mountain rear sights, which are undoubtedly the damnedest sights ever invented. Their big horns, looming up, do nothing but cut out the landscape and the game, and dim the light that comes through. A worse sight for deer hunting cannot be imagined.

The best iron sights for deer hunting, particularly for a man who no longer sees as well as in his salad days, are the various types of peep sights. The ones mounted on the tang of lever-action rifles and on the cocking piece of bolt-actions are the fastest, since they are closest to the eye. Receiver sights like those made by Lyman, Redfield, and Marble are not quite so fast since they are farther from the eye. In any case, the widest aperture is the best, as the secret of using the peep sight in hunting is to look *through* it, slap the front bead on what you're going to shoot, and fire! For hunting, the various little gadgets one turns up or screws into peep sights for target work had better be left at home or thrown away. They simply cut out light and slow down shooting—rob the peep sight of its virtues. With a peep, a man can forget the "always hold low on a deer" stuff.

A low-mounted scope of low power, from 2¼ to 2¾, does very well on a deer rifle. It is about as fast as a good peep, and its light-gathering power often comes in handy late in the afternoon and early in the morning, or when the game is in deep shade. For woods-country hunting, however, the scope is not the necessity it is for long-range open-country shooting. It is handy, but it is no particular hardship to get along without one.

Many authorities recommend automatics for deer. I don't like them particularly. In the first place, some automatics necessarily have to contain so much machinery that they are neither light nor handy. In the second place I think they are bad psychologically. If you have five or six shots at your instant disposal, you are frequently tempted to cut loose. If you miss with the first, you think you'll get your deer with the second, the third, the fourth. As a consequence, the user of the automatic all too often fills the air with lead and hits nothing.

Your first shot is the important one. Nearly always it is the best, and if you miss with it you probably won't hit with subsequent ones. In deer hunting, speed of getting into action is all-important. Speed of fire is secondary. Make that first shot count and you'll bring home the bacon. Miss with it and you're sunk in the majority of cases. In mountain and plains hunting for mule deer, sheep, goats, and antelope you will often have time to empty a whole magazine. In woods hunting you seldom get that chance.

A light bolt-action rifle is excellent for deer, but if I were choosing a weapon for the brush hunting of deer alone, I would pick a lever, pump, or automatic. The lever is faster for the second shot and the pump or automatic faster still. The Savage Model 99's in the lighter versions and the Winchester Model 88's are excellently stocked and balanced for deer and so is the Marlin Model 336. The light, handy bolt-action Remington Model 700 and the Winchester Model 70 Featherweights are likewise very good. Those who shoot pump shotguns will feel at home with the Remington Model 760 pump in various calibers. Remington and Winchester bolt-action rifles used to be too heavy and a bit long of barrel for brush hunting, but the new models have been lightened up and now weigh around six and a half to seven pounds without scope.

A brush rifle of mine used to be a lightweight 7 x 57 on a Mauser action. It weighed only seven pounds with a Lyman 1-A cocking piece rear sight. It handled like a flash.

The market is full of rifles about right for deer hunting in the woods—bolt-action, pump, lever-action, and automatic. One would have to go far to find a better brush rifle than the Remington Model 742 or the Winchester Model 100 automatics chambered for the .308 cartridge. Fit either of these with a good telescope sight of from 2½ to 3 power, use a 180-grain soft-point bullet, sight in to put that bullet about two inches high at 100 yards, practice on moving targets, so that you can bring up the rifle swiftly, get on the target without dawdling, and your deer is in the bag!

The deer hunter should select his cartridge as carefully as he chooses his rifle, remembering that he will shoot hastily at moving game often screened by brush, and that more often than not he will hit in non-vital areas. He should also remember that he will often hunt in country where someone else is likely to claim his buck unless he puts it down at once. Finally, he should choose a bullet that will plow right on through his deer, producing plenty of blood to trail by.

What sort of cartridge does all this mean? The best will send a fairly heavy, round-nosed bullet along at medium velocity. Any bullet made will be deflected by brush, but a blunt, heavy one stays in the same line of flight somewhat better than the light, sharp-pointed missiles that travel at high speeds. Furthermore, most of the light, fast bullets are designed to open properly at from 200 to 300 yards. At shorter ranges many of them blow up, giving little penetration. The big, blunt bullets plow on through the game.

Many fine deer bullets have come out in recent years, bullets that will expand properly at almost any distance. The Remington Core-Lokt line is excellent, and so are the Winchester–Western

Silvertips and various custom bullets. All have non-disintegrating bases, which assure adequate penetration and a good blood trail.

Don't let anyone tell you that the blood trail is not important in woods hunting. Animals are hard to track over stony ground, and even in soft going other animals often run across their tracks and obscure them. Some years ago I shot a whitetail buck with an 87-grain .250 Savage bullet. The animal fell, got up, and was out of sight in an instant. I tried to trail it. There was no blood and the country there was almost solid rock. I searched for several hours and then, as it was growing dark, I went back to camp. Bright and early next morning I was out on a point watching. Presently the buzzards began to drop and guided me to my buck. The bullet had hit pretty far back, penetrated to the lungs, and blown up completely. The deer had run a quarter of a mile and fallen dead. Though the body cavity must have contained almost a gallon of blood, there was not a drop anywhere on the trail. I saved the head, but the meat was ruined. If I had used a heavier bullet I would have found my deer within fifteen minutes.

The deer hunter buying a new rifle should look for more power than he thinks he needs, for the very good reason that in most deer country the well-placed shot is the exception and not the rule. It is easy to place a shot on a standing buck at close range, but under modern conditions few bucks are standing. On the contrary, they are usually jumping over down timber or getting behind brush or in general getting the heck away.

The ancient .44/40's and .38/55's are pretty good deer cartridges at close range. In the hands of good shots the Winchester .30/30 and the Remington .30 series are entirely adequate. The old black-powder rifles of the .45/70 class are poison, though they are now out of style. The .25 Remington and the .25/35 are good for a fine shot, but light for a dub. The heavy, soft-nosed bullets—like those furnished for the .30/06, Krag, and 7-mm. Mauser—are deadly. Just right are the .35 Remington, the .348 Winchester, and the .300 Savage with the 180-grain bullet. All have plenty of bullet weight, sufficient velocity, and worlds of destructive power. Furthermore, the rifles made for them—the Remington pumps, the Savage and Winchester lever-actions—are fast-handling and quickly reloaded.

In the brush the deer hunter needs lightness, handiness, and a slug that plows on through game without undue expansion at close range. With such a rifle and such bullets the deer hunter will boost his chances for bringing home a buck just about twenty-five per cent.

The .30/30 and Cartridges of its Class. The most popular deer cartridge in the United States and in the world is the .30/30 Winchester. To give some notion as to its popularity, over 2,500,000 Model 94 Winchesters have been manufactured and sold. They are in use all over North America and, for that matter, all over the world. Various other Winchester rifles of other models, like the Model 64, have been made. The Model 99 Savage rifles once were chambered for the .30/30 cartridge, and the Marlin rifles still are. Bolt-action rifles in the Model 40 and 45 Savage and the Model 54 Winchester have been made for the .30/30. Even today Savage makes an inexpensive single-shot rifle for the .30/30, and also turns out an inexpensive little bolt-action carbine for it. The .30 Remington rimless cartridge is simply a rimless version of the .30/30. Let it be said here, however, that those two cartridges are absolutely not interchangeable in spite of the fact that some believe they are, and .30 Remington rimless cartridges have actually been turned out with head stamps reading ".30–30 Remington."

The .30/30 is certainly the leading sporting cartridge of Mexico. Tens of thousands of beaten-up old .30/30 rifles occupy the place of honor in lonely Mexican ranch houses, and the .30/30 carbine was used as a military rifle during the Mexican revolution.

In the Canadian north the .30/30 cartridge is by far the most popular and ammunition in this caliber can be obtained at any one of the hundreds of trading posts. The Germans chambered single shot and combination guns for the .30/30, and in Europe the .30/30 is known as the 7.62 x 52R.

More deer have been killed with a .30/30 than with any other cartridge, and the .30/30 ammunition is the best seller of all big-bore center-fire cartridges manufactured. So popular is the cartridge that the high-power rifle and .30/30 have practically become synonymous. I have answered dozens of letters from men who have written in to *Outdoor Life* under the impression that the United States army rifle was the ".30/30 Springfield." The .30/30 led a tremendous revolution in its day. It was the cartridge that dethroned the big black-powder cartridges that had won the West and incidentally had killed off a good deal of the West's game. Those big charcoal-burning cartridges (many of which are now completely forgotten) threw heavy lead bullets at a velocity of from 1,200 to 1,500 foot-seconds. Among the survivors was the .44/40, which was the .30/30 of its day. It used a 200-grain bullet at about 1,300 foot-seconds, and over 200 yards the bullet rose 17½ inches. That was the great deer cartridge of the eighties and nineties. The great elk and grizzly cartridge was the .45/70 with a 405-grain bullet at about 1,300, or a 500-grain bullet at about 1,200 foot-seconds. Over 200 yards that bullet climbed 14 inches to reach the height of its trajectory. Even the faster .45/90 had a trajectory of over 200 yards of 11 inches.

When the .30/30 first came out it was loaded with a 165-grain bullet at a velocity of about 1,900 foot-seconds. The 200-yard trajectory was only about 5 inches. The cartridges were small, light, and easy to carry. The cartridge killed just about as well as most of the black-powder cartridges and it was far easier to hit with. Here was a 200-yard rifle, whereas the black-powder cartridges were only about 125-yard cartridges. In the space of a few years the .30/30 was ruling the roost, and even the old-timers were abandoning their old charcoal-burners.

Now the ballistics of the .30/30 have been stepped up. The 170-grain bullet is given 2,200 foot-seconds with a muzzle energy of 1,830 foot-pounds and with a 4.5-inch trajectory rifle over 200 yards. With iron sights the .30/30 can be sighted in to hit the point of aim at 175 yards. The bullet will rise three inches at 100 yards and fall two inches at 200 yards. That gives a good working trajectory to a little over 200 yards. This is the sight setting that should be used for whatever shots are to be taken over 150 yards, and is probably the best sight setting for all-around use because even in heavily wooded country the hunter will occasionally get a long shot across a lake or a clearing.

With its good killing power, its fair velocity, and its light recoil, the .30/30 is still an adequate deer cartridge for most conditions under which deer are shot in America, *if* the man behind it does his stuff. The .30/30 will also do for moose and elk if the animals are taken at reasonable ranges and if the man behind the rifle is a good shot and gets his bullets in the chest area. Tens of thousands of moose have been killed in Canada by .30/30's and will continue to be. Plenty of grizzlies have been killed by .30/30's.

On the other hand, the .30/30 is used by a great many once-a-year hunters who are not very good shots and who are highly excitable. They take chance shots at running deer in the Eastern woods. In the West they try long shots across deep canyons at deer. In the hands of these once-a-year hunters who have bought a .30/30 because that is the only rifle they have ever heard of, the .30/30 is not an adequate or satisfactory caliber. I believe the combination of this medium power in the hands of so many thousands of poor hunters is responsible for the fact that the .30/30 probably wounds more game annually than any other caliber.

In the West, anyway, one seldom sees a .30/30 in the hands of a good shot who knows rifles these days. The good shots will be armed with scope-sighted .30/06's, .270's, or even .257's. The bum shots will have some old moth-eaten .30/30, .30/40 Krag, or something of the sort. They will be able to tell you how they killed a running deer at 600 yards, and most of them have no notion of how far they would have to hold over with the .30/30 to make a hit at that distance.

With well-placed shots the .30/30 kills deer well. With well-placed shots on unexcited animals the .30/30 will also take care of moose and elk. With a poorly placed shot from a .30/30 a deer will run all day. The .30/30 with its low velocity does not have a shocking power to anchor game in its tracks. Many years ago I was hunting mule deer in northern Arizona with a .30/30 when suddenly I saw a big buck walk across a little opening and start feeding with his head and chest behind a tree. I was excited and instead of waiting for him to step out from behind the tree, I shot him squarely amidships. The buck went off and I missed him as he flashed through the trees. I finally killed him, but I had to track him four or five miles before doing so. Just as a contrast, the first deer I killed with a .270 was hit under very similar circumstances in exactly the same place. That buck went down as if a house had fallen on him, and when I got up to him his eyes were glazed in death. I have killed about two dozen deer with a 130-grain .270 bullet and the 150-grain .30/06 bullet at their much higher velocities which would have got off to die if they had been struck in the same place by a bullet from a rifle of the .30/30 class.

It would be interesting to find out just what percentage of the deer hit with .30/30, particularly in the West, where the ranges are long, escape to die. I fear that it would be a shockingly high percentage.

In the Eastern woods, where shots are shorter and the velocity is still relatively high, the .30/30 is a better killer, but even for the East there are better calibers for the man buying his first rifle.

In my native state of Arizona the use of the .30/30 has been outlawed on elk because of the great number of elk that escaped wounded as long as rifles of the .30/30 class were allowed. A scared elk is a very hard animal to kill, particularly when he is running and when the man behind the rifle has a nice case of elk fever.

The best bullet for the .30/30 is the standard 170-grain, and of all the bullets, I believe the most effective, on deer anyway, is the old-fashioned soft-point because the velocity of the .30/30 is not high enough to open up some of the other types of bullets effectively. At various times the .30/30 bullet weighing 110 grains and driven at a velocity of 2,700 feet have been loaded, as well as 150-grain bullets at about 2,500 feet. Neither is as effective as the old 170-grain, and the short blunt 110-grain loses its velocity so rapidly that it is much inferior to the 170-grain even at 100 yards. The average .30/30-owner is not an expert, and he is wonderfully short on theory. Many of those buying such light bullets never target their rifles in with them and don't discover for a long long time that they are far off even at moderate ranges. Most .30/30 rifles with their light barrels slotted for the rear sight are highly sensitive to changes in powder-burning characteristics and bullet weight.

Other Cartridges of the .30/30 Class. As we have seen, the .30 Remington rimless is only a slightly different .30/30, with identical ballistics of the 170-grain bullet at 2,200 foot-seconds. What can be said of the .30/30 can also be said of the .30 Remington. The .303 Savage is simply a .30/30 load with a somewhat heavier bullet at a lower velocity, in this case the 190-grain bullet at 1,960. I have never used a .303 Savage, but those who have tell me that it is a little more effective on big game like elk and moose than the .30/30 because that heavier bullet at lower velocity penetrates more deeply. Some hunters believe that the .32 Winchester Special is superior to the .30/30. I cannot see any logical reason why it should be. It uses a 170-grain bullet of a slightly greater diameter at a slightly higher velocity of 2,260. Ballistically the .32 Special and the .30/30 are almost as alike as two peas in a pod, and again the .32 Remington automatic cartridge is simply a rimless version of the .32 Special. The .32/40 was a great old cartridge in its day, but it is pretty much of a dead number nowadays. It was a great target cartridge in the black-powder days, and it has killed many a deer, but with its 165-grain bullet at 1,440 foot-seconds it is very inferior ballistically even to the .30/30.

The .300 Savage. One of the finest of all deer cartridges, and one that is really quite an effective all-around cartridge, is the .300 Savage, which was developed right after the first World War by the Savage Arms Corporation. The .300 had to be made short to work through the short Model 99 Savage lever action. It is the .30/06 case shortened and given a sharper shoulder. With a 150-grain bullet it will practically duplicate the original .30/06 loading of the 150-grain bullet at 2,700 foot-seconds. With a 180-grain bullet it gets a velocity of 2,380. The heaviest bullet ever loaded in the .300 was the 200-grain bullet load at one time by Peters for a velocity of 2,200.

From the reports that I get on the .300, it is by far the most effective with the 150-grain bullet at its relatively high velocity. With anything like a well-placed shot it is a one-shot killer on deer. Even with a rather poorly placed shot the .300 will ordinarily anchor deer so that the hunter can come up and finish him off. The development of the .300 was an exceedingly shrewd move on the part of the Savage people because it gave a cartridge with bolt-action ballistics that could be used in the popular lever-action to which so many hunters were wedded.

The .300 has been especially popular in the Western states, where so many of even the most conservative hunters want higher velocity and flatter trajectory than can be got with rifles of the .30/30 class. Throughout the West the Model 99 Savage in the .300 has been a best seller for a good many years. Back about 1941 more .300 Savage rifles were used on an Arizona antelope hunt than rifles of any other caliber. As a matter of fact, the .30/30, which for so many years was the favorite Western caliber, came out in third place.

Some of the best shooting I ever saw done was with a .300

Savage in the hands of an old-timer I knew who at that time was outfitting hunting parties into northern Sonora. He was an exceedingly skillful shot of the "practical" variety and he was also a lucky one. I once saw him nail four bucks running along the side of a canyon in as many shots with that .300 and every one of them was hit right through the lungs. The .300 is not the most accurate of cartridges, and I wouldn't select one for use at the longest ranges. With a 150-grain bullet it becomes, however, a good 250-yard rifle. With a scope sight most .300's will group into around three inches at 100 yards and will stay in a ten-inch circle at 250.

The Model 99 ejects at the side, and it is an excellent action on which to mount a scope. The .300 is well worth putting a 2½X scope on, and there are many good mounts for it—the Redfield Junior and the Buehler, both bridge mounts, for example. Either can be quickly installed by anyone who can handle a screwdriver. Those who want access to open iron sights as well as scope should use a side mount such as the Griffin & Howe.

The scope-sighted .300 Savage can be sighted in to hit the point of aim at 200 yards. In that case, with a 150-grain bullet, the bullet first crosses the line of sight at 25 yards. At 100 yards it is about 2¾ inches high, at 150 yards 2 inches high, at 200 yards right on the nose, and at 250 yards about 5 inches low. With the slower 180-grain bullet the rifle should be sighted in to hit the point of aim at 175 yards. In that case the bullet will strike about 2¾ inches high at 100 yards and about 3 inches low at 200 yards.

The .300 Savage cartridges is not a gun nut's cartridge. Because the 99 action does not lock up near the head of the case, there is always some stretching of cases, and usually a case that has been fired cannot be put back in the chamber and the breachblock closed up. Because of the sharp shoulder on the case, it is difficult to full-length resize, and handloading simply does not pay off.

For the great majority of hunters, however, the .300 is a most excellent bet. The cartridges are much better killers than those of the .30/30 class, and the ammunition is widely distributed. Although it is primarily a deer cartridge, it will take care of any North American big game in the hands of a good shot.

The .348 and the .358 Winchester. The .348 Winchester was an excellent and powerful woods cartridge for deer, moose, bear, or just about anything. The cartridge, a souped-up .33 Winchester cartridge, was used in a modernized version of the old Model 1886 Winchester rifle, which was long known as the slickest and smoothest lever-action rifle Winchester ever made. The bullet diameter of the .348 is actually .348, as against .338 for the old .33 W.C.F. Velocity with the 200-grain bullet in the .33 was 2,180, but with the .348 it was 2,530 at the muzzle and the energy 2,840 foot-pounds. A 250-grain bullet at 2,350 is also loaded, and with this the energy is 3,060. Because of the tubular magazine of the Model 71, the only rifle ever chambered regularly for the .348, the bullets had to be flat-pointed, as the end of the bullet rested on the primer of the cartridge ahead in the magazine. Consequently, there was never much excuse for the 150-grain .348 bullet loaded to 2,890, for it lost its ambition with great speed because of its flat point and poor sectional density.

The Model 71 rifle for the .348 was the old Model 86 given some goat glands by the use of modern alloy steel. It is a grand rifle but was never very popular because it ejected its fired cases straight up and if a scope were mounted it had to be offset. It was a rifle out of tune with the times and became obsolete about 1957.

In bringing out the .358 W.C.F. cartridge, Winchester's idea was to produce a cartridge for a modern lever-action rifle which would not use a tubular magazine, would mount a scope low, and would have a breech bolt that would lock at the head. The rifle was the Model 88. The cartridge that was supposed to take the place of the rimmed .348 was the smaller, rimless .358. It produces about the same ballistics as the .348-A 200-grain bullet at 2,530 foot-seconds with 2,840 foot-pounds of energy and a 250-grain bullet at 2,250 with energy of 2,810. Pressures are, of course, much higher than with the .348. However, the Model 88, with its front-locking breech bolt, is much stronger than the Model 71. It is my understanding that pressures for the .348 run about 40,000 p.s.i., whereas those for the .358 run around 50,000.

The first rifle chambered for the .358 was the Winchester Model 70 Featherweight, a rifle that weighs between six and a half to seven pounds. The venture was not entirely successful. With a cartridge of the power of the .358, the recoil was unpleasant in a rifle that light. In addition, the slight shoulder on the .358 case was not sufficient to hold the headspace against the blow of the bolt-action firing pin. The Model 70's in .358 were recalled.

Later the Model 88 Winchester and the Model 99 Savage rifles were both chambered for the .358, a logical development since the .358 is simply the .308 case necked up to .35. Once in an article I described the ideal woods cartridge. When the .358 came out, it was very much like this ideal of mine. But for some reason the good .358 has never gone over. Why this should be will forever remain one of the many mysteries of the gun world.

The .35 Remington. Another very fine deer cartridge and one that can be used in a pinch on any North American big game is the .35 Remington rimless. It uses a 200-grain bullet at a muzzle velocity of 2,200 foot-seconds. Because of the large diameter of the big heavy bullet, it kills much better than cartridges of the .30/30 class. In fact, it can be said that the .35 Remington is usually a one-shot killer on deer. It is also entirely adequate for any North American big game if the shots are well and carefully placed. For really tough animals like grizzly and brown bear, however, I would say that the .35 Remington is on the light side, and no one but a cool and expert shot should hunt big bear with it.

A good many rifles have been made for the .35 Remington— the Remington pump-action Models 14 and 141, the semiautomatic Model 8, and Model 81, the Winchester Model 70, a

Stevens lever-action that was made prior to World War I, and also the old Standard rifle, which was made in either pump or semiautomatic. Currently, the Marlin Model 336 lever-action rifle and the Remington Model 760 pump-action are chambered for the cartridge. Before the last war Griffin & Howe, New York, made rifles on short Mauser actions for the cartridge.

The best thing to do with the .35 Remington is to sight in with iron sights to hit the point of aim at 150 yards. Then the bullet strikes about 1¾ inches high at 50 yards, about 2¼ inches high at 100 yards, on the nose at 150 yards, and 5 inches low at 200.

Particularly for the man who is used to the pump-action shotgun, the Model 760 Remington pump-action big-game rifle is an excellent bet for deer. The action, of course, is a very fast one, and combined with that excellent .35 Remington cartridge it is poisonous in the woods. Surprisingly enough those Remington pumps are highly accurate and will almost always shoot into two inches or less at 100 yards. Since the 760 ejects at the side, it is suitable for scope mounting.

The only defect in the 760 is that it is a very complicated action and one that has a tendency to freeze solid in bitterly cold weather if there is any oil whatever left in the action. The thing to do is to clean the action out thoroughly with gasoline and then lubricate with powdered graphite.

Old Black-Powder Deer Cartridges. There are a good many old black-powder rifles still floating around that will do for deer at short ranges. Of all of the dozens of black-powder cartridges, however, only a few have survived. One is the .38/40, which uses a 180-grain bullet at a velocity of 1,310 foot-seconds with a muzzle energy of 658 foot-pounds. The other is the .44/40 with a 200-grain bullet at a velocity of 1,300 and a muzzle energy of 650 foot-pounds. At one time those cartridges were favorites for deer. In the hands of the most skillful and careful shots they will still do. I think now, however, that a deer hunter owes himself a better rifle. Neither cartridge has the excess of powder

DEER-CARTRIDGE BALLISTICS

Cartridge	Wt. Grs.	Velocity—Ft. per Sec.				Energy—Ft. Lbs.				Mid-Range Trajectory		
		Muzzle	100 Yds.	200 Yds.	300 Yds.	Muzzle	100 Yds.	200 Yds.	300 Yds.	100 Yds.	200 Yds.	300 Yds.
30-30 Winchester...150		2410	2020	1700	1430	1930	1360	960	680	0.9	4.2	11.0
30-30 Winchester...170		2220	1890	1630	1410	1860	1350	1000	750	1.2	4.6	12.5
300 Savage........150		2670	2390	2130	1890	2370	1900	1510	1190	0.7	3.0	7.6
300 Savage........180		2370	2160	1960	1770	2240	1860	1530	1250	0.9	3.7	9.2
303 British.......215		2180	1900	1660	1460	2270	1720	1310	1020	1.1	4.9	12.5
308 Winchester....110		3340	2810	2340	1920	2730	1930	1340	900	0.5	2.2	6.0
308 Winchester....150		2860	2570	2300	2050	2730	2200	1760	1400	0.6	2.6	6.5
308 Winchester....180		2610	2390	2170	1970	2720	2280	1870	1540	0.8	3.1	7.4
308 Winchester....200		2450	2210	1980	1170	2670	2170	1750	1400	0.8	3.6	9.0
32 Winchester Special......170		2280	1870	1560	1330	1960	1320	920	665	1.0	4.8	13.0
348 Winchester....150		2890	2460	2060	1710	2780	2020	1410	975	0.6	2.9	7.9
348 Winchester....200		2530	2140	1820	1570	2840	2030	1470	1090	0.8	3.8	10.0
348 Winchester....250		2350	1970	1660	1410	3060	2150	1530	1100	0.9	4.4	11.5
35 Remington......150		2400	1960	1580	1280	1920	1280	835	545	0.9	4.6	13.0
35 Remington Express......200		2210	1830	1540	1310	2170	1490	1050	760	1.1	5.2	14.0
358 Winchester....200		2530	2210	1910	1640	2840	2160	1610	1190	0.8	3.6	9.4
358 Winchester....250		2250	2010	1780	1570	2810	2230	1760	1370	1.0	4.4	11.0

to use under modern hunting conditions. Each is a great wounder unless the shot is well placed.

A far better cartridge than either of those is the .38/55 with its 255-grain bullet at 1,320 and its muzzle energy of 985 foot-pounds. I have never used a .38/55, but those who have done so say that up to 100 yards it is a very effective cartridge. Again, however, the more modern cartridges, like the .35 Winchester, the .300 Savage, the .348, would be far better in every respect.

CHAPTER XVII

The All-Around Rifle

AS WE have seen, the Eastern whitetail deer is not a particularly large animal and is usually shot at short range. Most whitetail hunters do not need particularly powerful rifles—or rifles delivering the finest accuracy.

The rifle to be used for *all* American game should be quite different from the more or less specialized woods rifle. Western mule deer are often shot at long range. In the semi-open mountain and canyon country of most of the Western states a 300-yard shot at deer is far from uncommon, and now and then it is possible for a hunter to get an unhurried standing shot at deer even farther off. The little Arizona whitetail, which I hunt a great deal, is also long-range game, and I am sure that I have shot more whitetails at well *over* 200 yards than I have under that distance. Actually, as I look back, I believe my average shot at those little whitetails runs around 300 yards—the longest *average* shooting I have got at any American big game.

Antelope are almost always found in wide-open plains country, where a 200-yard shot is a relatively short one, and the antelope hunter needs a flat-shooting, *accurate* rifle if he is not to be handicapped. Elk are large animals, very tenacious of life, and in certain sections of their range they are found, during the early part of the hunting season, in open country above and just below timber line, where the success of a long shot may mean the difference between success and failure.

Where sheep and goats are hunted, the long shot comes so often that the hunter should be prepared for it, and often both animals have to be killed in their tracks or they will fall and ruin their horns.

In the Canadian Rockies the hunter is never quite sure what sort of game he is going to run into. He may go out for a goat and come in with a grizzly—or decide he is going to hunt caribou and instead knock over the grandpa of all the bull moose in the country.

For all this shooting, the answer is what is known as the all-around rifle—a weapon with a flat trajectory that will make judgment of range easier, with first-rate accuracy so that the long, correctly held shot will be in a vital area, with plenty of power so that a killing or disabling blow is struck 'way out at 300 yards where the game is.

All sorts of rifles have been used as all-around rifles. Good, cool shots with .25/35's and .30/30's have killed all American game. The late Charles Sheldon, the authority on the northern Stone, Fannin, and Dall sheep, killed everything on this continent, including many grizzly and brown bears, with the relatively light 6.5-mm. Mannlicher, using a 160-grain bullet at about 2,100 foot-seconds velocity. Eugene Jacquot, the Yukon outfitter, has shot everything in that great game country with a .250/3000 Savage.

Nevertheless, the man buying a rifle for Western open-country shooting where shots average long and where the animals often run large should get a reasonably powerful, accurate, flat-shooting rifle. It should be a bolt-action of fair weight and should be equipped with a telescope sight. The barrel should not be shorter than 22 inches nor longer than 26. With scope, the rifle should weigh no less than 8 pounds, nor more than 10½; a 9-pound rifle is about right. A Model 70 Winchester is a suitable caliber and equipped with a good scope is excellent. The Remington Model 725 is a light neat rifle. Remodeled Springfield and Enfield rifles scope-equipped and with sporting stocks are entirely satisfactory, and so are custom-built rifles on Mauser actions.

In heavy woods speed of fire is a valuable quality, but in the more open country the game is usually in sight long enough so that the slower bolt-action is fast enough. In the all-around rifle, cartridge performance is all-important, and actually a man with a single-shot rifle for an excellent high-velocity cartridge would not be greatly handicapped.

A scope-sighted Model 99 Savage in .300 Savage or .308 caliber is not a bad bet at all, particularly for the man who has never got used to the bolt action, but the .308 W.C.F. cartridge, for all its virtues, is not a .30/06 or .270. The Model 88 Winchester will do as an all-around rifle in .308 caliber, but as a rule bolt-actions are more accurate than levers.

The fairly heavy bolt-action rifle is not ideal for deer hunting in brush or woods, but it will do far better at that chore than the typical woods rifle will do in plains and mountain hunting. I use bolt-action, scope-sighted rifles almost entirely and with them I have shot many a buck in brush and woods. One good thing about the cartridges of the all-around class is that when you hit a deer with them, he stays hit!

The 7-mm. Mauser. About the lightest cartridge that I would classify as being perfectly satisfactory for all-around use is the one known in Europe as the 7 x 57, and in this country as the 7-mm. Mauser or the 7-mm. Spanish Mauser.

It is a very old cartridge—one of the first rimless, high-power smokeless-powder cartridges designed for the Mauser action. It came out in 1893, I believe, and was designed for the Spanish government to use in the 1893 Mauser rifles made for Spain by the firm of Ludwig Lowe of Berlin. As originally loaded, the 7-mm. used a 175-grain bullet at a velocity of around 2,200 foot-seconds. The Spanish used it against us in the Spanish-American War of 1898. Our military men decided it was a better battle cartridge than our .30/40 Krag cartridge, and the Mauser, with its faster clip-loading, was a better battle rifle. The lessons we learned from the 7-mm. were responsible for our designing the Model 1903 Springfield, which is simply a Mauser modified by Krag ideas, and also our .30/06 cartridge, which is simply an oversize 7-mm.

Other governments, including those of Mexico and Serbia, adopted the 7-mm., and the cartridge became very popular for big-game hunting. British custom makers turned out rifles for it on Mauser actions, and Waffenfabrik Mauser in Germany made thousands of sporting rifles in that caliber and sold them all over the world. Because they were cheap, they were used by settlers in Africa. With full metal-cased bullets these hardy Boer and British hunters made killing brain shots on elephants, buffaloes, rhinos, and other of the large African game.

After the first World War the Steyer works in Austria brought out Mannlicher-Schoenauer rifles in 7 x 57, and a great many custom rifles in that caliber were turned out by Griffin & Howe, Neidner, Hoffman, and other custom makers. The first caliber Bill Sukalle, the barrelmaker, ever tooled up for was the 7-mm.

The 7-mm. is a fine little cartridge. It will do just about anything a .30/06 will do and the recoil is much less. The late Captain Paul Curtis and Colonel Townsend Whelen both praised the caliber in their writings and were responsible largely for the run of popularity it had.

The velocity of the 175-grain loading was stepped up with new powders to 2,460 foot-seconds—but in a 29-in. barrel, which would mean that the velocity would be about 2,335 in a 24-inch barrel. This is a miniature edition of the 220-grain load in the .30/06. A further factor in popularizing the 7-mm. was the introduction by the Western Cartridge Company of the 139-grain load at 2,900 in a 29-inch barrel, which would mean something short of 2,800 in a 24-inch barrel. This load was a vicious killer—and I don't mean maybe—a one-shot killer on mule deer, sheep, and antelope. Just before World War II broke out, Winchester introduced a 150-grain load with a velocity of about 2,650 in a 24-inch barrel. I never used it on anything, but it should have been excellent.

I got a fine custom-made lightweight 7-mm. with a Sukalle barrel and a beautiful stock by Adolph Minar in 1934. I used it to shoot ten head of big game, and the experience left me with a lot of respect for the 7-mm. with that 139-grain Western Cartridge Company load. Let's look at the record:

1 mule deer, shot in chest. Dead in tracks. 1 shot.
1 mule deer, hit in rump running away in brush. 2 shots. 1 to finish.
1 javelina, hit in chest. 1 shot.
1 javelina, hit in chest. 1 shot.
1 javelina, hit in chest. 1 shot.
1 antelope, hit in chest. 1 shot.
1 antelope, hit through shoulders. 1 shot.
1 Kaibab mule deer, hit in chest. 1 shot.
1 whitetail deer, hit in guts; ran 100 yards. 1 shot to finish.
1 bighorn ram, hit in rump at about 60 yards running; went over ridge, was dead when I got to it.

All of these shots were not farther than 200 yards, and most of them were under. They show that the 7-mm. kills well.

In the past twenty years the popularity of the 7-mm. has been dropping off. The reason for this is that there isn't anything that the 7-mm. will do that the .270 will not do better. As ammunition sales slowed, the fine 139-grain load was discontinued by Western—and that brought down the popularity of the cartridge further. As this is written, the only commercial load for the 7-mm. is the old 175-grain.

I finally sold my 7-mm. rifle and got rid of my loading dies and components, not because I did not have a lot of respect for the cartridge but because 7-mm. rifles have a long throat owing to the original long loading of the 175-grain bullet. When shorter, spitzer bullets like the 139-grain are used, throat erosion is bad and accuracy life is short, because there is bad gas cutting in the leade from gas that gets by the bullet while it is jumping that throat. When the second barrel on my rifle was going bad, I got rid of it and bought another caliber instead.

However, the 7-mm. is a good choice still, particularly in the Model 70 Winchester with its tough and erosion-resistant chrome-molly barrel, for the man who wants a rifle for all North American big game but who is rather sensitive to recoil. Anyone who wants a very light but accurate and powerful custom-made rifle can get a 7-mm. built up on a Mauser or Springfield action to weigh with scope no more than 7½ to 7¾ pounds.

For long-range shooting, the 175-grain load leaves a good deal to be desired, but 7-mm. bullets in other weights are available from Fred N. Barnes, of Durango, Colorado, and from Vernon Speer, of Lewiston, Idaho. Here are some hand loads for the 7-mm.:

100-grain bullet, 50 grs. No. 4064—velocity 3,300 ft. sec.
120-grain bullet, 48 grs. No. 4064—velocity 3,100 ft. sec.
140-grain bullet, 45 grs. No. 4064—velocity 2,815 ft. sec.
160-grain bullet, 50 grs. No. 4350—velocity 2,825 ft. sec.
175-grain bullet, 46.5 grs. No. 4350—velocity 2,650 ft. sec.

As can be seen, these are a good deal better than factory loads. Pressures run right up around 52,000 pounds per square inch, and they are to be used only in good strong actions like the Model 70, the 98 Mauser, and the nickel-steel Springfield. Factory loads have to be held down because of the old Spanish and Mexican Mausers they may be shot in, and they run only around 45,000 pounds per square inch.

The .270 Winchester. Back in the late summer or early fall of 1925 I saw an advertisement for a new bolt-action Winchester rifle that was chambered for a brand-new cartridge known as the .270 W.C.F. The ballistics of this cartridge interested me because I have always been a believer in as high a velocity as possible combined with good bullet weight. According to advertisements, this new cartridge gave a 130-grain bullet a velocity of 3,160 foot-seconds. It sounded like quite a cartridge—

the best thing out until that time. Before that I had had a good deal of experience with the .250/3000 Savage, the .30/06, and also the .256 Newton, as well as with the .30/30 and .30/40. I ordered one of those new Model 54 rifles with a Lyman 48 receiver sight and chambered for the new cartridge.

I believe I killed the first deer shot in the Southwest with a .270. That first year the rifle went to the Kaibab Forest in northern Arizona, where deer were then astonishingly plentiful, and in various hands the rifle killed six deer. Every one of them was a one-shot kill. I had the rifle sighted in to hit the point of aim at 250 yards, and it didn't seem to make much difference how far away anything was. I could hold right on and squeeze off, and the bullet seemed to get there the instant the rifle recoiled.

I have been using .270 rifles off and on ever since then, and I have probably had about as much experience with the .270 as anyone. Besides that Model 54 Winchester I have owned Model 70's and three other rifles in the .270-caliber built on Mauser actions. I have hunted with the .270 from the deserts of Sonora to the mountains on the Alaskan border, and I have shot all kinds of game with the .270 from thirty-pound coyotes and javelinas to twelve-hundred-pound Alaskan moose.

When the .270 first came out, it did not catch on quickly. Outside of a few rifle nuts who were conscious of the advantage of a sharp-pointed 130-grain bullet at the then astonishing velocity of 3,160 foot-seconds, few people bought it. For a long time I didn't see an owner of another .270, in spite of the fact that I spent most of my time in the West, where the .270 was an ideal rifle.

In the first years of its experience the .270 ran into tough competition. All the gun editors of that day were singing the praises of the .30/06. Some of them went so far as to say that the .270 was less accurate than the .30/06, and there was nothing it could do that the .30/06 could not do better. Furthermore the government was selling ammunition for as little as one cent a shot for 1918 wartime ammunition in .30/06 to about three cents a shot for the late M-1 ammunition. The availability of this cheap ammunition was tough competition to buck. Furthermore, some writers claimed that the velocity figures for the .270 were inflated and that the .270 did not actually produce velocities anywhere near so high as claimed. The National Rifle Association secured five .270 Winchester rifles out of stock and had them chronographed with standard Winchester ammunition loaded with the regular 130-grain bullet. The average instrumental velocities for ten-shot strings taken at 150 feet came out as follows: 3,126, 3,125, 3,115, 3,038, 3,028, 3,109, 3,029, 3,038, 3,017, 3,034. The average for these one hundred shots checked by several different chronographs and fired from seven different rifles came out as 3,075 instrumental—that is the actual velocity over the given range. Add the arbitrary figure of 70 feet to it and you get a muzzle velocity of 3,145 foot-seconds.

A good .270 is a very accurate rifle. It has been my experience that the average factory-produced .270 will outshoot the average factory-produced .30/06 with standard factory ammunition. As a matter of fact, outside of the .220 Swift, the most accurate factory rifles that I have ever seen have been the .270's. I would say offhand that the man who wants a super-accurate big-game rifle would have a better chance of getting one in the .270 than in any other caliber. I have seen many Model 70 and Model 54 Winchesters that when fitted with a good scope would group around one minute of angle. The best .30/06 rifles are just as accurate, but I believe that for the past good many years the .270 ammunition has probably been held to closer tolerances than .30/06 ammunition. I have shot many groups of .270's running from 1 ¾ to 2 ¼ inches at 200 yards in the .270, and I have no difficulty at all in shooting 3-inch groups at 200 yards with good ammunition in any of the .270 rifles I have.

Many different factors, however, enter into accuracy. The .270 is now an exceedingly popular caliber, and thousands of .270's have been made up on Springfield and Mauser actions by all kinds and conditions of gunsmiths. In a case like this, of course, the fact that a rifle is chambered for the .270 cartridge doesn't necessarily mean that it is accurate. The best of those custom-built rifles will give beautiful accuracy; the worst, very poor.

One good thing about a good .270 is that, for whatever reason, it handles various bullet weights to approximately the same point of impact up to 200 yards. The .30/06 won't do that, nor will the .257 or the 7-mm; but with a good .270 it doesn't seem to make too much difference what sort of full-power load you put into it. The .30/06 is very sensitive to changes in amount and kind of powder and in bullet weights. As a usual thing the 150-grain bullet in the .30/06 will group a great deal higher than the 180-grain or 220-grain bullets—so much so that one would miss game at 200 yards with the 150-grain bullet if the rifle were sighted in for the 180-grain. The .270, on the other hand, will put the 100-, 130-, and 150-grain factory loads into a six-inch circle at 200 yards. It will also group the long 160-grain Barnes bullet into the same circle, and any full-power load, no matter what the bullet weight. Two other cartridges that have the same characteristic are the .250/3000 and the .22/250. I have my theories as to why this is, but I do not know for certain.

The .270's reputation was made, however, not on the target range but out in the hunting fields, particularly in the West and in Canada and Alaska, where ranges are long. Hunters using the .270 discovered that with it they could hit game at longer ranges than with anything else, and that when they hit they got a higher percentage of one-shot kills.

The explanation is that the trajectory of the .270 with the 130-grain bullet at a muzzle velocity of 3,140 foot-seconds, or the 100-grain bullet at 3,540, is very flat; for all practical purposes it corresponds to that of the Swift over 300 yards, and is flatter beyond. Consequently the hunter is less likely to under-shoot at long range. Sighted to hit the point of aim at 200 yards with a scope sight, the 130-grain bullet drops only 5 inches at 300 yards, not enough to miss even a small deer with a hold in the center of the chest.

If the hunter wants to turn his scope-sighted .270 into a real long-range rifle, let him sight in for 300 yards. In that case the bullet rises 1½ inches at 50 yards; 3 inches at 100; 4 inches at 150; 4 inches at 200; 3 inches at 250; at point of aim at 300; 4 inches low at 350; 10 inches low at 400; and 18 inches low at 500. All of which means that, so sighted, a .270 has a point-blank range of over 350 yards on even a small deer, a bighorn, or an antelope, and that by holding high on the backbone the hunter would not have to bother his pretty head unduly about trajectory even at 500 yards, which under most conditions is too far to shoot. With a higher-mounted scope, the trajectory is apparently even flatter, and under most conditions of plains and mountain hunting the rifleman needs only to put the top of the post or the intersection of the cross-hairs on what he wants to hit.

For coyotes, however, this trajectory has a bit too much rise; so for use on the little prairie wolves, the .270 would be sighted in for 250 yards. The bullet will then rise 3 inches above the line of aim at 150 and fall only 3 inches at 300.

The other part of the ease of hitting with the .270 lies in the fact that the bullet gets there fast and cuts down on necessary lead. The 130-grain Peters and Winchester sharp-pointed bullets arrive at 300 yards still zipping along at 2,440 foot-seconds, and the 100-grain gets there with a retained velocity of 2,600, or *faster than the fastest factory load for the .220 Swift*. The Swift gets the 46-grain open-point bullet to 300 yards with a velocity of 2,130, and it gets the 48-grain soft-point spitzer there with 2,570.

For the sake of comparison, the 150-grain Western open-point .30/06 bullet, which leaves the muzzle at 2,980, gets to 300 yards with a retained velocity of 2,070 and the best-shaped 150-grain bronze-point retains 2,260. For the sake of another comparison, the 180-grain Western open-point bullet for the .300 H. & H. Magnum is traveling at only 2,080 at the 300-yard mark, or only 50 foot-seconds faster than the 180-grain Remington bronze-point .30/06 bullet with its initial velocity much lower than that of the Magnum. All these little figures preach a couple of powerful lessons—that for long ranges bullet shape and sectional density are very important, and that the hunter ought to keep his eye glued to velocity figures out where the game is and *not* at the muzzle.

This high retained velocity also explains the spectacular killing power that everyone who has used the .270 has noticed at from 250 to 400 yards. Long ago I made up my mind that in order to be reasonably happy I had to live where I could do a lot of hunting. I have used four .270 rifles since 1925. In that period I have also done some hunting with three .30/06 rifles, a 7-mm., a .348, a .257, a .30/30, a .35 Remington, and a .30/40. The only cartridge with as good a record as the .270 is the 7-mm., but it happened that the longest shot I ever made with it was 200 yards.

I have shot over 100 head of big game with .270 rifles, and I have hunted with .270's all the way from Mexico to Africa. Through some strange prank of fate I have only encountered one grizzly when I had a .270 in my hands, but I have shot all other North American big game with the .270 except big bear.

The longest shot I ever made with the .270 was a big bull elk at 600 yards in Wyoming. The shortest was a whitetail buck at about 50 feet. The average shot was not far from 300 yards. I have lost only one game animal hit anywhere with a .270, and that was a whitetail buck which, as far as I could tell, was only scratched with a very slight muscle wound. With that exception, almost everything I have hit with the .270 has been a one-shot kill, including not far from one hundred coyotes. Of the two elk I have shot with the .270, one was killed in its tracks, the other took two shots—one in the jaw as it lay facing me at 600 yards, the other through the lungs. One moose took two shots, one three, and one four. One caribou took three shots through the lungs, one took two, but five were killed with one shot each —two of them at over 400 yards. Of seven black bear, six were one-shot kills; one took two shots. With only two exceptions all the deer I hit were one-shot kills, and usually they were dead so quick that they bounced. Although I have shot only one grizzly with the .270, this one was rolled with the first lung shot. One I saw killed with it was stone-dead with two quick shots through the lungs, and the grizzly is a pretty tough customer. Hosea Sarber, Alaska game warden, has killed brown bear with the .270 and finds it does very well when bullets hold together, but Sarber is a really marvelous shot, cool and deadly, and famed throughout Alaska for his shooting.

For some years the only bullet loaded for the .270 was the 130-grain. Now all concerns load a 150-grain bullet stepped up to 2,880 in 1960. Many different varieties of bullets are made by the loading companies and the bullet-makers in weights of 100, 120, 130, 150, 160, 170, and 180 grains. In Canada, a 160-grain bullet is loaded to about 2,800 by Dominion. Ammunition in .270 is loaded in Sweden and England, and the cartridge is popular in many foreign countries.

The 100-grain bullet loaded to about 3,550 by the factories is excellent for varmints if the rifleman does not mind the recoil. In Africa, handloaded ammunition with the 150-grain Nosler bullet at 2,900–2,950 has been used on antelope and leopards. For heavier game, the 170- and 180-grain bullets might be used.

Of all the bullets made for the .270, the best all-around game bullet has always seemed to me to be the old but now obsolete 130-grain pointed expanding bullet designed for the cartridge and made by Winchester. Along with the 180-grain Remington bronze-point .30/06 bullet, it is almost a perfect ballistic job, combining a sharp, wind-bucking point with good sectional density. The base is very thick and heavy; the jacket becomes slightly thinner toward the point (which in reality is a sharp soft point of lead covered with a thin jacket of copper to keep it from battering in the magazine).

I have never seen one of those bullets fail to expand well, even at long range, and I have never seen one that failed to penetrate deeply. I have found it practically perfect for medium-size big game, weighing from 100 to 350 pounds on the hoof; and hunters who have used it in Alaska and Canada agree that its penetration is adequate for moose and grizzlies. I shot my first moose with one, likewise my first caribou.

The Winchester-Western Silvertip gives a bit too much penetration and not quite rapid enough expansion for light game. It is reliable, but it will not produce as high a percentage of quick kills as the earlier bullet. For me, however, the Silvertip worked excellently on the one antelope, the few deer, and the rams I have shot with it. For moose and caribou it has proved excellent. Most deer and antelope hunters, however, have wanted less penetration, faster expansion. In wooded country where shots have to be taken through brush, I'd prefer either to the old pointed expanding. A correspondent in Michigan made extensive tests, shooting the Remington Core-Lokt through all sorts of cover, and wrote that because of the round nose and thick jacket it drives on through twigs and even small limbs with a minimum of deflection. The Silvertip, the Core-Lokt, and the Western boattail all retain less velocity than the original pointed expanding bullet does, for they get to 300 yards with a retained velocity of 2,260, as against the pointed expanding's 2,440.

I used to feel there wasn't much excuse for the original round-nosed 150-grain .270 bullet at 2,770, but since the velocity has been stepped up and Winchester has brought out a fairly sharp bullet, the trajectory is flatter. Many .270 owners do all their shooting with 150-grain bullets handloaded to 2,925–2,950 f.p.s.

For the handloader who likes to experiment and who is never satisfied with things as they are, the custom-made bullets offer definite possibilities. The original 120-grain Barnes spitzer bullet was lightly constructed and, when driven at about 3,200, the most deadly small deer, coyote, and antelope bullet I have ever seen, because of the rapid rate of disintegration. Whitetail deer, hit solidly anywhere in the body cavity with that bullet, are almost always stone-dead before they topple over. I have seen about fifteen deer and antelope killed with that bullet, and I have never seen one move three feet after being hit. On large mule deer, however, it would go to pieces too quickly to be absolutely dead sure at all angles.

A surplus military powder known as 4831, which was originally designed for 20-mm. aircraft shells, has proved to be about the best available powder for the .270. A similar powder called No. 7828 is used in the .264 and 7-mm. Magnums. I have used it almost exclusively for handloading the .270 since about 1950. With the 130-grain bullet, 62 grains gives 3,160 in a 22-inch barrel, generally over 3,200 in a 24-inch barrel. Pressure, with the Silver Tip bullet, is well under 50,000 pounds per square inch anyway. With the various 150-grain bullets, charges of from 58 to 60 grains of the powder are used, with velocities of from 2,850 to 3,000 feet per second, depending on the barrel length and also on the particular rifle. These loads are for Winchester–Western cases. Remington cases are thicker and run up pressure. I have used the 150-grain Nosler bullet with 58 grains of No. 4831 in Africa on white oryx and addax and have found its killing power excellent. A 160-grain bullet can be given 2,850 with normal pressure, and the 170-grain Speer can be loaded to 2,800.

It was the 100-grain bullets, with their very flat trajectory, their astounding accuracy, their freedom from ricochet, and their ability to buck wind, that made the varmint and coyote hunters sit up and get interested. As we have seen, these bullets retain more velocity at 300 yards than any factory load for the .220 Swift. Because of the smaller time lag, they are much less wind-senstive than the standard hot-shot .22 bullets, and they can be depended on to make longer sure hits on chucks, crows, hawks, and what not.

Many a varmint shot who has spent time and energy playing with the super .22's has discovered that the little old .270, which has been sitting in the corner all the time masquerading as a big-game rifle and nothing else, has exactly what he has been looking for. If he can manage it, he gets a ten-pound .270 with a medium-heavy barrel with a 12- or 13-inch twist, slaps an 8- or 10-X scope on it, uses those 100-grain bullets at 3,540 foot-seconds—and discovers he has the doggonedest long-range varmint rifle in the country.

Originally a good many big-game hunters were inclined to dismiss the .270 as a good sheep, antelope, and deer rifle because of the light bullets used. How a 130-grain bullet could kill game larger than deer they could not see. Now, however, long experience on the part of many hunters has proved that the .270 is not only a good cartridge for medium-size game but a highly effective cartridge on any game. Because of the flat trajectory, relatively light recoil, and good accuracy it is easy to plant shots with the .270. A shot, of course, in the chest area with a .270 will kill the largest game much more neatly than will a poorly placed shot even with a .375.

I have shot about 12 elk with the .270. Not one moved more than twenty yards after he was hit, but in all cases the shot was in the lung area. Almost all of the mountain caribou I have shot have been one-shot kills—and a mountain caribou is about as large as an elk. The overwhelming majority of sheep, caribou, antelope, and deer that I have shot with the .270 have been killed with one shot in their tracks; the small deer have been killed so quickly that they seemed to be stone-dead in mid-air, and I have had the confusing experience of having the deer disappear in low brush while he was out of sight because the rifle recoiled upward. I remember once in Sonora when I was shooting at a buck in a bunch of seven. They were all running through brush, and I was not aware that I had killed the deer that I shot at until I went down to look for blood and found him lying there. He slipped into brush and another buck came out. I was not aware that I was dealing with two bucks until I reached there. I have never used a cartridge that gave me so high a percentage of one-shot kills as the .270. It just seems to work out that way.

In the fall of 1946 my two boys and I were hunting in Sonora. I was using a .30/06 with a 180-grain bullet. My younger boy was using a .257 with a 100-grain bullet, and my older boy a .270 with the 130-grain bullet. The buck hit with the .30/06 in the chest ran about 80 yards before he fell. The buck hit with the .257 ran about 125 yards. The buck hit with the .270 turned a somersault in the air and hit like a bag of potatoes.

I do not consider the .270 an ideal moose rifle, in spite of the fact that I have killed four moose with the .270 and have never lost one. Particularly for woods hunting I should like to have a heavier bullet of larger diameter so that a good blood trail would be left at the point of entrance. When a man catches a bull moose up above timber line, where he can kill him in sight, the .270 is perfectly adequate, but in the woods it might be a different story. The first bull moose I shot with the .270 was in thick timber along the bank of Copton Creek in Alberta. I don't believe the bull was over forty yards off when he got out of his bed. He darted away from me and I drove a bullet into his abdomen and up into one lobe of the lung. The bull ran not more than fifty yards and went down. The timber was so thick that I did not see him. I tracked him up a way, and when he got up I plunged a shot right behind the shoulder into the lungs. He ran about a hundred yards this time and was dead when I got to him. Possibly the .375 Magnum would have put that bull down in his tracks with the first shot. I do not know. The same thing applies to grizzlies. I do not think that either the .270 or the .30/06 is an ideal grizzly rifle for use in the timber, just as neither is an ideal moose rifle. The time might come when a man would want to stop a grizzly quicker than he could do it with either a .270 or a .30/06. The same thing could also be true of elk under certain conditions.

For all game in open country and semi-open country the .270 is a fine and satisfactory caliber. Even for deer in timber the .270 is also satisfactory for the man who likes a bolt-action. As a matter of fact, the .270 is a good cartridge to use under those conditions because a solid hit practically anywhere means that somebody has himself a deer. On the other hand, there is no reason why the man going to hunt Alaskan brown bear should take a .270 if he has a rifle of heavier caliber—nor is there any reason why the man on the spring grizzly hunt should take one.

In a mixed fall hunt in the Rockies, however, when a man going out for sheep is likely to jump a grizzly, he shouldn't worry with the .270 in his hands. If he does his part, the .270 will not let him down.

The .30/06. The .30/06 cartridge has been kicking around a long time now—ever since 1906. It is still the most popular big-game cartridge in the United States. Its only rivals are the .270 and the .30/30. It is still one of the top choices for a cartridge to be used on all North American game.

The .30/06 originated as a revision of the original cartridge for the 1903 Springfield service rifle. The original .30/03 used a 220-grain bullet with a velocity of 2,200 foot-seconds, but in 1905 the Army Ordnance Department found that the Germans had changed their military cartridge for the Model 98 Mauser military rifle from a 236-grain round-nosed bullet to a sharp-pointed or "spitzer" bullet weighing 154 grains with an increase in velocity to around 2,800 f.p.s. and an enormous gain in flatness of trajectory and effective range. The Americans decided to apply the same set of goat lands to the .30/03, so they shortened the neck of the case one tenth of an inch and substituted a sharp-pointed 150-grain bullet at a velocity of 2,700 foot-seconds. All 1903 rifles were called back to the armory. One thread was cut off the barrel, a new thread added, and the rifles were rechambered. This accounts for the fact that ever since that time 1903 Springfields have had barrels slightly less than twenty-four inches long. Cartridges cannot be used in a .30/06, on account of the longer neck. This is nothing to brood about, however, as no .30/03 ammunition has been made for a good many years, since about the time of World War I. A few old Model 95 Winchester lever-action rifles chambered for the .30/03 are still in existence, but anyone can use .30/06 ammunition in them, if, indeed, he wants to use any at all in that superannuated musket.

It didn't take the more enthusiastic gun nuts long to find out that the new .30/06 cartridge had a good deal on the ball in the way of sporting possibilities. Theodore Roosevelt took one to Africa with him on his famous safari and used the full metal-cased 150-grain military stuff for all sorts of hunting. Very often those light fast bullets would keyhole when they struck flesh and inflict a terrible wound, but also, sadly, they would sometimes go straight through and let the animal get away.

Army and National Guard officers and members of the National Rifle Association could buy Springfields back in those innocent days before the first World War for about fifteen dollars, and soon they were being made up into sporters, with the army stock thrown away, the lousy army sight likewise, the barrel polished and blued, a receiver sight and a sporting front sight fitted, and eventually a custom sporting stock added. The novelist Steward Edward White and the gun writer Captain E. C. Crossman were among the very first to possess those sporting Springfields. Not many were made prior to World War I, however, and the only sporting .30/06 rifle made in quantity before 1914 was the Model 95 Winchester lever-action. Since then, however, thousands of Springfields have been remodeled into sporters by all kinds and conditions of gunsmiths from old Uncle George at the Fixit Shop to such artists as Bob Owen, Alvin Linden, and Griffin & Howe. In addition many other thousands of 1917 Enfields for the .30/06 have been turned into sporters, and thousands of Mauser actions have been rebarreled to that caliber. In England custom rifle-makers built .30/06 sporters and so did German custom makers. Back in the 1920's the firm of Sempert and Kreighoff of Suhl used to send some especially fine ones in. Here is a list of rifles made in regular factory production for the .30/06, more or less in the order of chronology:

The Model 95 Winchester lever action. (Discontinued in .30/06 about 1925.)

The Newton (made by the Newton Arms Co. of Buffalo and its various reorganizations in .30/06 as well as the Newton calibers. The last "Newton" concern was the Meeker Arms Co.).

The Model 54 Winchester (1925–36).

The Model 30 Remington Express. (A sporting version of the 1917 Enfield made in various models from 1925 to about 1940.)

The Model 40 and Model 45 Savage. (They came out about 1932 and in 1948 they are not being made. They are the same except for sights and checking.)

The Model 720 Remington. (Simply a final revision of the Model 30. It came out in 1941 and only a few thousand were made.)

The Model 70 Winchester (1936 to date). (Slight changes in receiver and a different safety in 1948.)

Mauser. (Various models of the .30/06 rifle were turned out for the American and African trade by the great Mauser Werke at Oberndorf am Nekar, Germany. Those I have seen are marked ".30 U.S." on the receiver ring and "7.62 x 63" on the bottom of the barrel under the fore end. Most are made on a fine, strong action with a hinged floor plate, release button in trigger guard, and a square bridge. A good one is a very fine rifle.)

Mannlicher-Schoenauer. (Many rifles in this caliber were made at the Steyer Werke near Vienna and sold in this country. Evidently a good many were also sold in Europe, and the .30/06 cartridge was regularly produced by the big German concerns like D.W.M. and R.W.S. I have had letters from a good many G.I.'s who have turned up with Mannlicher-Schoenauers marked "7.62 x 63" *and nothing else.*)

Remington 721. (This was brought out in 1948 and is Remington's bid for the bolt-action big-game rifle market.)

Remington Models 721, 725, 700 (bolt-action) and Models 740 and 742 semiautomatics and Model 760 pump.

The Savage Model 110 bolt-action in right- and left-hand models.

The Swedish Husquvarna.

The Finnish Sako.

The Belgian F. N. Mauser.

The Browning made in Belgium for Browning by F. N.

The M-1 Garand and the Johnson semiautomatic military rifles.

It wasn't too long before the .30/06 became one of the standard big-game cartridges the world over. Ammunition for it can be bought wherever men go out and shoot at animals, from Yukon and Alaskan trading posts to Mexico City, to India, to Africa. It has been used on everything from whitetails to elephants, and for the most part it has done a pretty good job.

At various times an astonishing number of bullet weights have been loaded for the .30/06: 110, 145, 150, 160, 172, 180, 190, 200, 220, and 225.

The 110-grain bullet was intended for varmint use, but it was never very successful. It had a round nose and poor sectional density and it shed its muzzle velocity of 3,350 very rapidly. Since it was greatly overstabilized in a 1–10 twist, it was never very accurate.

The best all-around bullet for the .30/06 is the 180-grain. The velocity of 2,700 foot-seconds is high enough to give a reasonably flat trajectory, and the bullet is heavy enough to penetrate well. Particularly in the bullets of heavy construction like the Silvertip and the Core-Lokt it has all the penetration I want for any American big game. I remember shooting a grizzly on a sandbar in the Yukon with the 180-grain Core-Lokt. Every bullet went clear through broadside and kicked up sand on the far side of the bear. With the same bullet I broke both shoulders of another grizzly and the bullets went clear through.

Actually, almost all the 180-grain .30/06 bullets give too much penetration and not enough expansion for the lighter game like small whitetail deer and antelope. The various 150-grain bullets at their higher velocity will give more violent action and result in quicker kills. Because of the higher velocity, the .30/06 with the 150-grain bullet at 2,960 has a flatter trajectory, and for open-country shooting a scope-sighted .30/06 can be sighted in to hit the point of aim at 250 yards. This will put the bullet 3 inches high at 100 yards, 4 inches high at 200, at point of aim at 250, and 5 inches low at 300—a trajectory not quite so flat as that of the .270 with the 130-grain bullet, but plenty flat enough for long cross-canyon shooting.

Most of the heavier bullets have been made for the .30/06,

with construction too heavy for light game, and poor expansion on animals like deer and antelope has been the result. Almost any of the 150-grain bullets are good and speedy killers on animals the size of sheep and mule deer, giving a much higher proportion of one-shot kills on animals of this class than the 180-grain bullets. Of all of them, the bullet that in my experience has given the most violent expansion is the Western open-point. But none of the 150-grain bullets with their high velocity and relatively sharp points are the things to use in brush hunting, as they will be badly deflected when they strike small limbs and twigs. The round-nosed 180-grain bullets like the Remington Core-Lokt are more reliable.

The 220-grain bullets are for the heaviest game, such as moose, Alaskan brown bear, and possibly elk in heavy timber. The controlled expanding bullets like the 220-grain Silvertip and Core-Lokt are probably best for medium-sized and dangerous African and Asiatic game like lions and tigers. With those bullets the .30/06 seems to be an entirely adequate lion rifle. From my own fairly limited experience, I am doubtful if the 220-grain bullet is needed for grizzly and I am also doubtful if it is any more effective on moose. With the full metal-cased 220-grain bullets many an elephant, rhino, and buffalo has been killed; but the boys who have hunted those monsters usually agree that no .30-caliber rifle should be used on them—that the thing is the big double-barrel rifle for ultra-powerful cartridges with very heavy bullets.

The very best .30/06 rifles with the most carefully assembled hand loads will shoot right along with almost anything, but the average factory .30/06 with over-the-counter ammunition will not shoot quite so accurately as good factory .270, .257, and .220 Swift rifles. The .30/06 of ordinary sporting weight also has the fault of shooting various loads with various powder charges and bullet weights to quite different points of impact. A .270 will usually group almost any full-power load to approximately the same point of impact to 200 yards, but a .30/06 simply will not. I have seen .30/06 rifles that would put the 150-and the 220-grain bullets 24 inches apart at 200 yards.

The .22 Hornet, the .220 Swift, and most of the wildcat .22's are far more satisfactory varmint rifles than the .30/06. For the man who wants to combine varmint and deer hunting, either the .257 or the .250/3000 is superior. For a long-range big-game cartridge for mountain and canyon shooting at sheep, mule deer and goats, the .270 has the edge. For the very largest game, the .375 Magnum is far superior.

But the .30/06 has a wider range of usefulness than any other American cartridge. Although not ideal, it can be used on jack-rabbits and woodchucks with factory 150-grain ammunition or with hand loads with bullets weighing from 110 to 150 grains. It is unnecessarily powerful for hunting whitetail deer in heavy woods, but smacks them down and keeps them down with the proper bullets. It isn't quite so good for the plains and mountains as the .270, but with the 150-grain bullet at 2,960 it isn't so far behind, and for the very heaviest game in thick cover its big 220-grain bullet beats anything the .270 can offer.

Government ammunition in .30/06 is plentiful and inexpensive, and suitable bullets, primers, and .30/06 cases are available to members of the National Rifle Association at much below ordinary rates. Worlds of loading and ballistic data are also available.

The .30/06, then, is a fine all-around cartridge for the one-rifle man who wants to hunt everything—one of the world's most useful and versatile cartridges.

Post-War All-Around Cartridges. Since the last war several new cartridges in the all-around class have been introduced. The earliest was the .308 Winchester, which in its military form is called the 7.62 mm. NATO. It is used by all the NATO countries in various types of machine guns and semiautomatic rifles. The first sporting rifle made for it was the Winchester Model 70 Featherweight, but since then Winchester has brought out the Model 88 lever-action and the Model 100 semiautomatic, Remington the Models 740 and 742 semiautomatics, the Model 760 pump, and the Model 725 and Model 700 bolt-actions. Savage has adapted the ancient but still excellent Model 99 lever-action to the cartridge.

Ballistically the .308 approximates but does not equal the .30/06, as it gives the bullets of various weights about 100 f.p.s. velocity less than the .30/06 produces. With the 110-grain bullet the .308 has a velocity of 3,340, with the 150-grain 2,860, with the 180-grain 2,610, and with the 200-grain 2,450. Because it is shorter and because it was especially designed for use in automatic weapons, the .308 is superior to the .30/06 for use in weapons of that type. It is also adapted to rifles with short actions like the Model 88 and 99. Any difference in killing power between the .308 and the .30/06 would be pretty academic. However, anyone purchsing a bolt-action rifle would be wise to select the .30/06, for it is, because of the larger case, a more powerful cartridge. It is adapted to heavier bullets, and it is more widely distributed throughout the world.

The .308 has begotten a new family of cartridges on the same case—the .243 Winchester, the .358, and with the case a bit changed a hot 7 mm., the .284 Winchester, which appeared on the market in 1963.

The other family of new Winchester cartridges is that based on the short, belted Magnum case. So far there are three—the .264 Winchester Magnum, the .338, and the .458 (which are discussed in the chapter on cartridges for heavy game). In addition, a .30 caliber Magnum on the short case, a cartridge just about identical to the wildcat .30/.338, is in the works, according to the grapevine.

The .264 is loaded with a 100-grain bullet at 3,700 f.p.s. in a 26-inch barrel and a 140-grain bullet at 3,200 in a barrel of the same length. It is a sexy-looking cartridge and has had considerable success. However, it is greatly over-bore capacity with anything except the very slowest of slow-burning powders. Even No. 4350, the slowest burning du Pont powder available in canister lots, is too quick-burning for it. It has been loaded at the Winchester factory with a slow-burning Western ball powder, but at the present time it is being loaded with a new du Pont powder called No. 7828. It is not yet available to the handloader.

Sadly enough, a 26-inch barrel is a miserable thing to lug around in the hills or to carry in a saddle scabbard, so Winchester added the .264 to the line of featherweight Model 70 rifles with 22-inch barrels. Depending on the rifle, velocity delivered with the 140-grain bullet in these short barrels drops off from 100 to 175 f.p.s. After chronographing one of these muskets, I decided that I was not about to discard my matched pair of .270 Model 70 rifles with 22-inch barrels, as they gave with my pet load 3,170 with the 130-grain bullet!

To my way of thinking, the .338 with the 200-grain bullet at 3,000, the .270-grain bullet at 2,700, and the 300-grain bullet at 2,450 is a more successful and better balanced cartridge than the .264. The other member of the family, the .458, is one of the world's best cartridges for heavy game.

Remington's two post-war all-around cartridges are the .280 Remington and the 7-mm. Remington Magnum. The .280 is a 7 mm. (.284 inch) on a modified .30/06 case. The 7-mm. Remington Magnum is a 7 mm. on the .264–.338 Winchester case. It actually belongs to the Winchester family of cartridges.

The .280 is made slightly longer from head to shoulder than the .30/06 and .270 cases, so it is impossible to fire a .280 in a .270 chamber. Ballistically, the .280 is very similar to the .270. The published velocities are as follows: 125-grain bullet, 3,140; 150-grain bullet, 2,810; and 165-grain bullet, 2,770. I found the velocity of the 125-grain on the button, but the other figures pretty optimistic. One writer said that the .280 delivered .270 ballistics with 10,000 pounds less pressure. If this were so, it would be a major ballistic miracle. Actually, the .280 seems to be loaded not only to less pressure but for less velocity with bullets of equivalent sectional density. It has been no raging success because it is so much like the .270.

The 7-mm. Remington Magnum is quite something else. When I chronographed a factory Model 700 rifle, I found the velocity to be just about what the factory claimed: the 150-grain bullet at 3,260 at the muzzle, the 175-grain at 3,020. In the Model 700 sample rifle the accuracy was very fine and at 100 yards the 150- and 175-grain bullets had the same point of impact. The recoil, though greater than that of the .30/06, was still not bad, and with the 150-grain bullet the trajectory is a little flatter than that of the fine .270. The 7-mm. Magnum should be a very effective and successful cartridge for any North American big game. By the time this book is in print, the Savage Model 110 rifle, both in right- and left-handed models, will be chambered for the .264, the .338, and the 7-mm. Remington Magnum.

The Big .300's. One of the most interesting of the post-war cartridges is the .300 Weatherby Magnum. It was designed by Roy Weatherby of Southgate, California. Its grandfather is the British .300 H. & H. Magnum and its father a wildcat known as the .300 PMVF for reasons too complicated and obscure to go into in this limited space. The .300 W. was originally "blown out" by firing a .300 H. & H. cartridge in an enlarged Weatherby chamber. Then the larger case was loaded with more powder for higher velocity and presumably greater killing power. Weatherby advertised his .300 as giving 3,400, then 3,300 f.p.s. The last Weatherby-loaded .300 ammunition I chronographed came out with the 180-grain about 3,140—still a vast improvement over the 2,920 of the standard .300 H. & H.

Weatherby is a promotional genius. He got a great deal of publicity for his rifles and cartridges, built very fancy sporting rifles with distinctive stocks, many inlaid with woods of various colors and with gold-plated metal parts. He also brought out a line of cartridges on belted cases. Calibers range from .25 to .45 He has rifles made up in Germany and his rifles and ammunition are widely distributed from Oshkosh to Nairobi. A surprising number of well-heeled Americans shoot lions, tigers, elephants, and polar bears with Weatherby rifles.

ALL-AROUND RIFLE BALLISTICS

Cartridge	Wt. Grs.	Velocity—Ft. per Sec.				Energy—Ft. Lbs.				Mid-Range Trajectory		
		Muzzle	100 Yds.	200 Yds.	300 Yds.	Muzzle	100 Yds.	200 Yds.	300 Yds.	100 Yds.	200 Yds.	300 Yds.
264 Winchester Magnum*	100	3700	3260	2880	2550	3040	2360	1840	1440	0.4	1.6	4.2
264 Winchester Magnum*	140	3200	2940	2700	2480	3180	2690	2270	1910	0.5	2.1	4.9
270 Winchester	100	3580	3160	2770	2400	2840	2210	1700	1280	0.4	1.7	4.5
270 Winchester	130	3140	2850	2580	2320	2840	2340	1920	1550	0.5	2.1	5.3
270 Winchester	150	2800	2400	2040	1750	2610	1920	1380	1020	0.7	3.0	7.8
280 Remington	125	3140	2840	2550	2280	2740	2240	1800	1440	0.5	2.2	5.5
280 Remington	150	2810	2580	2360	2130	2630	2220	1850	1510	0.6	2.6	6.5
280 Remington	165	2770	2460	2180	1930	2810	2220	1740	1360	0.7	2.9	7.4
7 mm. Mauser (7 x 57)†	140	2900	2630	2370	2190	2600	2130	1730	1480		2.5	6.0
7 mm. Mauser (7 x 57)	175	2490	2170	1900	1680	2410	1830	1400	1100	0.8	3.7	9.5
.284 Winchester	125	3200	2880	2590	2310	2840	2300	1860	1480	0.5	2.1	5.3
.284 Winchester	150	2900	2630	2380	2160	2800	2300	1890	1550	0.6	2.5	6.3
7 m. Remington Magnum	150	3260	3070	2880	2690	3540	3140	2760	2410	0.5	1.8	4.7
7 mm. Remington Magnum	175	3020	2660	2340	2050	3540	2750	2130	1630	0.7	2.5	6.2
7 mm. Weatherby Magnum	154	3260	3035	2820	2605	3621	3160	2720	2330	—	—	—
7 mm. Weatherby Magnum	175	3067	2790	2500	2270	3662	3024	2429	2002	—	—	—
.300 Weatherby Magnum	180	3350	3115	2895	2685	4477	3882	3361	2892	—	—	—
.300 Weatherby Magnum	180	3158	2935	2719	2510	3987	3440	2955	2520	—	—	—
300 H. & H. Magnum*	150	3190	2870	2580	2300	3390	2740	2220	1760	0.5	2.1	5.2
300 H. & H. Magnum*	180	2920	2670	2440	2220	3400	2850	2380	1970	0.6	2.4	5.8
300 H. & H. Magnum*	220	2620	2370	2150	1940	3350	2740	2260	1840	0.7	3.1	7.7
.300 Winchester Magnum	150	3400	3050	2730	2430	3850	3100	2480	1970	0.4	1.9	4.8
.300 Winchester Magnum	180	3070	2850	2640	2440	3770	3250	2790	2380	0.5	2.1	5.3
30-06 Springfield	110	3420	2880	2400	1970	2850	2020	1410	945	0.4	2.1	5.6
30-06 Springfield	150	2970	2670	2400	2130	2930	2370	1920	1510	0.6	2.4	6.1
30-06 Springfield	180	2700	2470	2250	2040	2910	2440	2020	1660	0.7	2.9	7.0
30-06 Springfield Match Type F.M.C.B.T.	180	2700	2520	2350	2190	2910	2540	2200	1900	0.6	2.8	6.7
30-06 Springfield	220	2410	2180	1980	1790	2830	2320	1910	1560	0.8	3.7	9.2

* Velocity taken in 24-inch barrel.

The success of the Weatherby line has led to the development of similar cartridges. The .264 Winchester is not unlike the .257 Weatherby, which is a hot .25 caliber on a short-belted Magnum case. The .338 shows the Weatherby inspiration, and the new 7-mm. Remington Magnum is quite similar, ballistically, to the 7-mm. Weatherby.

Other custom gunsmiths made reamers to enlarge .300 Magnum chambers so the .300 H. & H. case could be blown out, and still other gunsmiths tried shortening and blowing out the same case. Ballistically, all are similar to the .300 Weatherby. The Swedish ammunition firm of Norma has brought out a short .300 Magnum called the .308 Norma. The .300 Winchester Magnum which was brought out in 1963 with a 150-grain bullet at 3400 and a 180-grain bullet at 3070 should be tough competition for the other big .30 calibers.

CHAPTER XVIII

Cartridges for Heavy Game and for Foreign Hunting

THE average American has little need of a rifle more powerful than one of the .270–.30/06 class unless he plans to hunt foreign game. If he wants a more potent rifle for kicks, I am all for him, as the idea of hunting and shooting is fun and games anyway.

Writers (even gun and shooting writers) have to eat and gunsmiths have to sell rifles, so if a writer can make an honest dollar by knocking out a tale the thesis of which is that .30/06 or .270 bullets bounce off of elk and moose like baseballs off the roof of a stadium, I view his performance with a tolerant eye. I likewise view without alarm the statements that all African antelope are so marvelously endowed with life that they sneer at anything less powerful than a .375. The only time I get irritated is when someone expects me to believe these tales.

I have in my day hunted from Mexico to Alaska and from Idaho to Tanganyika, Iran, and India, and I am convinced that the placement of the bullet is by far the most important factor in killing power, and that at least ninety per cent of the world's big game can be killed very neatly with such a cartridge as the mild 7 x 57 Mauser if the proper bullets are put in the right place.

Nevertheless, the medium- and big-bore rifles have their place. Let's take a look at their advantages. With similar bullet construction, the heavy bullet will penetrate deeper than a lighter one. The heavy bullet of strong construction driven at a moderate velocity (2,200–2,600 foot-seconds) will smash heavy bones, whereas a lighter bullet might not. The impact of these heavy bullets on bone will knock a big and dangerous animal down, whereas a lighter bullet might not. The larger bullets leave a larger entrance hole and give a better blood trail. Another very real advantage (and I'd say one of the principal advantages) is that the nervous hunter confronting a potentially dangerous animal derives great comfort from the big hole in the end of this barrel and from the sight of a big, formidable-looking cartridge.

Because of the psychological angle, I heartily approve of the use of such cartridges as the .375 and the .338 on Alaska brown bear, lions, tigers, and such like. If the hunter believes he has Old Death and Destruction in his hands he'll be less nervous and he'll shoot better.

The Medium Bores

Because so little North American game is very big or very dangerous, there has until recently not been very much of a market in this country for what the British call "medium bores," rifles of .33 to .40 caliber. Until the .375 made its appearance in the Model 70 Winchester in 1936, the only cartridges for heavy game manufactured in this country were the .35 and .405 for the Winchester lever-action Model 95 rifle. The .35 W.C.F. drove a 250-grain bullet at 2,160 and gave 2,590 foot-pounds of muzzle energy. It was used to some extent by elk and moose hunters and some swore by it for Alaska brown bear. Its big brother, the .405 W.C.F., gave a 300-grain bullet a velocity of 2,220 with 3,285 foot-pounds of energy. The Model 95 in .405 was the favorite lion medicine of Theodore Roosevelt when he made his famous safari in Kenya about 1909, and is the funny-looking lever-action rifle one sees pictured in old books about African safaris written by Americans before about 1930. The Model 95 rifle has not been made since about 1936, and the .35 and .405 Winchester cartridges are no longer loaded.

THE .375 MAGNUM

One of the world's most widely used and useful cartridges is the .375 Holland & Holland Magnum. For years it has been the most useful choice for anyone who wants to add to his battery a rifle more powerful than the .30/06 but less powerful than the big "elephant" cartridges.

It is the world's most versatile cartridge—one that shoots flat enough to be used on mountain sheep and ibex, on plains game from the American pronghorn antelope to the giant eland of Tchad and the Sudan. It is one of the world's best cartridges for soft-skinned dangerous game, and yet it has enough power so that with full metal-jacketed bullets (solids) it is relatively safe to use on rhino, elephant, and Cape buffalo. Furthermore, it is a world cartridge. Ammunition for the .375 can be purchased wherever big game is shot—in Anchorage and in Delhi, in Nairobi and in Ft.-Lamy, in Cody, Wyoming, and in Capetown.

François Edmond-Blanc of Paris, one of the world's most reowned and experienced big-game hunters, a chap who not only has made a score of safaris in various parts of Africa but also has hunted in North America, India, and the Middle East, usually goes on safari with only two rifles, a pair of .375's.

The useful .375 is just about a necessity for the African battery, and it would be possible, as the experience of M. Edmond-Blanc shows, to shoot throughout Africa with but the one rifle.

The cartridge was introduced by the London gunmaking firm of Holland & Holland about 1912. It immediately became popular over the world and displaced as the best all-around cartridge the widely-used .450/.400. In the 1920's, the American custom rifle-making firms of Griffin & Howe of New York, Hoffman Arms Company of Cleveland, Ohio, and later of Ardmore, Oklahoma, and Neidner Arms Corporation of Dowagiac, Michigan, made for well-to-do clients a good many .375's on Magnum Mauser actions imported from Germany. Stoegers of New York imported some rifles in that caliber made by the Mauser Werke of Germany and by Webley & Scott of Birmingham. However, a .375 cost real money in those days—right around 300 uninflated dollars.

Winchester was aware of considerable interest in the .375, and when the Model 70 replaced the Model 54 Winchester about 1936, the .375 was one of the cartridges for which it was chambered. In those days a Model 70 in any caliber retailed for about $65. Since then the .375 has been a reasonably popular cartridge in this country. It is the favorite caliber for brown-bear guides who have to protect their clients from wounded and vindictive bears in the Alaskan bush.

In England the .375 was and still is loaded with three bullet weights—235, 270, and 300. In this country all three weights originally came out, but now only the 270-grain bullet at a velocity of 2,740 and a 300-grain bullet at 2,550 are in production. The 235-grain bullet can be pushed along at 2,850 or thereabouts and bullets in that weight are available from bullet-makers. However, there is little use for the 235-grain since the 270-grain bullet shoots flat enough for just about any hunting. Its trajectory is identical to that of the 180-grain bullet in the .30/06.

The .375 is a real powerhouse, turning up more energy than some cartridges considered adequate for elephant. Muzzle energy for the 270-grain bullet is 4,500 foot-pounds and for the 300-grain 4,330 foot-pounds. Most of the big British Nitro Express double rifles turn up only about 5,000 foot-pounds of energy.

Besides the Winchester Model 70 for the .375, Remington chambers the Model 700 for the cartridge. Many custom .375's are turned out in this country on Brevex Magnum Mauser, Winchester Model 70, and Model 1917 Enfield actions. Almost any British gunmaker will build a .375. Holland & Holland, Purdey, and perhaps other British rifle-makers will turn out doubles regulated for the American-loaded rimless belted ammunition as well as for the British flanged (rimmed) version of the cartridge.

I have two .375 rifles and have had a fair amount of experience with the cartridge. The only North American game I have ever shot with the cartridge were a couple of Alaskan brown bears, but I have used it on non-dangerous game in Africa and have shot four lions, a very large tiger, and one leopard with it. One of my .375's is a Model 70 restocked, tuned up, and remodeled by Al Biesen. The other, also by Biesen, is on a Magnum Mauser action. Both have Weaver K-3 scopes on the Griffin & Howe side mount.

Unlike some cartridges, the .375 is loaded, in the United States anyway, to full published velocities. For, whatever the reason, it is, like the .270, one of the cartridges that will generally put all bullet weights to the same point of impact to about 150 yards. In addition, a tuned-up .375 usually delivers very fine accuracy. Recoil is a bit severe but anyone who does considerable rifle-shooting can stand it. Kick is about like that of an 8-pound 12-gauge shotgun with the 2¾-inch Magnum loads with 1½ ounces of shot.

THE .338 WINCHESTER

Another very fine medium-bore is the relatively new .338 Winchester, a .33 caliber on a short-belted Magnum case. The Model 70 Winchester rifle is chambered for it and so is the Browning bolt-action and other European-made rifles imported into the United States.

The .338 is loaded with three bullet weights—a 200-grain bullet at 3,000 foot-seconds, a 250-grain at 2,700, and a 300-grain at

2,450. Energy with these various bullets is 4,000 foot-pounds or a bit above—somewhat less than the energy of the .375.

In reality the .338 and the .375 are so much alike that the hunter could use them alternately for a lifetime and never be able to tell the difference. The .338 has a bit less recoil and with the 200-grain bullet has a flatter trajectory than any bullet available for the .375. The 250-grain bullet of the .338 should do about anything the 270-grain bullet would do in the .375 and the trajectories of the two bullets are almost identical. Theoretically, the 300-grain bullet of the .338 should give a little deeper penetration than the bullet of the same weight in .375 caliber. I'd just as soon use one cartridge as the other, but the .375 has the advantage of wider distribution. The .338 should do nicely on Alaskan brown bear, on tiger, and as the medium-bore in an African battery. Like the .375, it is loaded to advertised velocity.

THE .358 NORMA MAGNUM

Another medium-bore which will about duplicate the performance of the .375 Magnum is a new Swedish cartridge called the .358 Norma. Like the .338 it has a short-belted Magnum case with a sharp shoulder. The over-all length of the .358 is less than that of the .375—about that of the .338 and the .30/06. It uses a 250-grain bullet at a velocity of 2,790 and with 4,322 foot-pounds of energy at the muzzle. Husquvarna and, I believe, the Danish Schultz and Larsen rifles are made for it. Cases and loaded ammunition are imported into this country, and some custom rifles are being made in that caliber.

There is nothing much against owning a .358—and nothing much in favor of it. It will not do anything the .338 or the .375 will not do and ammunition is not so widely distributed.

MEDIUM-BORE WILDCATS

Dozens of medium-bore wildcats have been introduced in the United States but most of them have not been popular. P. O.

Ackley, the Salt Lake City rifle-maker, says that the .358 Norma is identical to his short Magnum .35 caliber wildcat, which he designed and introduced a decade or more ago. The .333 O.K.H., designed by Charles O'Neil, Elmer Keith, and Don Hopkins, is the .30/06 case necked up to take .333 bullets used by the .333 Jeffery rifle, and the .333 Belted is a short Magnum case for the same cartridge. The .35 Whelen is the .30/06 necked up to .35. It has enjoyed some popularity, but there is little excuse for it now. At one time it was widely used because rifles for it could be built on standard-length Mauser-type actions. Now such actions can be used for the better (and factory-produced) .338 Winchester cartridge.

FOREIGN CARTRIDGES

Just as a few American cartridges are used and loaded all over the world, so are a few foreign big-game cartridges loaded in this country. Our .30/06 is popular wherever big game is shot, and the .270 is also widely used. The .30/30 has been fairly popular in Europe for 3-barrel guns (drillings) and is of course widely used in Latin America.

The only German cartridges now regularly loaded in the United States are the 7 x 57 and 8 x 57. The 7 mm. became popular because thousands of Spanish Mausers in that caliber were captured in 1898 and the 8 mm. owes its acceptance to the fact that tens of thousands of Model 98 Mausers in that caliber were brought back by servicemen from two world wars. At one time the 6.5 and 8 mm. Mannlicher-Schoenauer cartridges were loaded here but they have been discontinued.

The .303 British cartridge sells well in the United States today because many thousands of obsolete British short Lee-Enfield rifles have been sold here for a few dollars.

The British and the Germans both load excellent cartridges, but very few of them offer much advantage over American cartridges. The 7 x 64 Brenneke is a sort of German .270 Winchester or .280 Remington. The 6.5 x 88 is on the order of the .257 Weatherby and the 8 x 68 is much like a .300 Weatherby.

A widely used German medium-bore is the old 9.3 x 63 Mauser, which is about the same as the American wildcat .35 Whelen, and the German 8 x 60 is much like the .30/06. The .404 Jeffery, with its 400-grain bullet at 2,125, is a good enough cartridge but inferior to the American .458 Winchester Magnum. All European cartridges are loaded with Berdan primers with twin flash holes. They cannot be decapped with American loading tools and, in general, owning a rifle for a cartridge not made in the United States is a pain in the neck.

THE BIG BORES

The well-to-do British were the big-game hunters of the world in the days before two world wars squandered the accumulated treasure of Britain and dissolved the British Empire. As a consequence, most of the cartridges suitable for the heaviest game such as rhino, buffalo, and elephant are of British origin. Double-barrel rifles to shoot British Nitro Express cartridges are a British specialty. Beautiful doubles by such firms as Jeffery, Rigby, Holland & Holland, Purdey, and Westley Richards are cherished by gun lovers all over the world.

Such a rifle is expensive. The cost of a British double in London runs from about $750 to as high as $3,500. They are made in ejector and non-ejector types, engraved and plain, and in calibers from the obsolete .22 Savage High Power to .600 Nitro Express.

The American is primarily interested in such rifles for heavy, dangerous game. For this type of hunting the double has its advantages. For one thing, it is very fast in the brush because the low line of sight enables the man behind it to point it by roughly aligning the muzzles as he would a shotgun. It is the fastest powerful rifle in the world for the vital second shot at a charging animal. In effect, it is two rifles with two barrels and two sets of locks.

Many of the fine old British rifle-making firms have folded up. Jeffery, for example, is a recent casualty. Others, like Rigby, no longer make double rifles. Some of the cartridges have become obsolete. The .476, the .450 No. 2, and the .475 No. 2, for example, are no longer being loaded in England.

Smallest of the Nitro Express cartridges considered adequate for elephant and rhino are the .450/.400–3¼ and the .450.400–3 inch or .400 Jeffery Nitro Express. Ammunition for both is still loaded in Britain and both use 400-grain bullets at 2,125 foot-seconds and deliver about 4,000 foot-pounds of muzzle energy. The cartridges are not interchangeable. With solid bullets these two .40 calibers are adequate for heavy, dangerous game, and with soft-points they are favorites for both lion and leopard. They have probably killed more Indian tigers than any other cartridges. The famous Jim Corbett, who wrote *Maneaters of India*, used a .450/.400 double. India is full of old single-shot and double rifles in the two .450/.400 calibers.

An American buying a double rifle to take on an African safari today, however, would be wise to select either a .470 Nitro Express or a .465 Nitro Express (also called the .500/.465). These are the two most popular cartridges of the thick-skinned, dangerous-game class, and ammunition is available not only in London but all over Africa. The .470 uses a 500-grain bullet at 2,150 and turns up 5,140 foot-pounds of energy. The .465 Nitro Express (another cartridge designed by Holland & Holland) drives a 480-grain bullet at 2,150 and gives 4,930 foot-pounds of energy. Killing power of the two cartridges should be just about identical.

The cartridge that set the style for the British "elephant" cartridges was the .450 Nitro Express, which came out in the 1890's. It used a 480-grain bullet at 2,150 and gave slightly less than 5,000 foot-pounds of energy. Hunters of elephant, rhino, and buffalo found that it killed just as well as the ponderous and brutal 8- and 10-bore black-powder *rifles* they had been using, that it shot flatter, kicked less.

Then the importing of any .45 caliber rifle was prohibited in India and the Sudan, as there were great caches of old .45 caliber ammunition that could be used in them hidden away. The London gunsmithing firms all raced to bring out cartridges which would be legal but which would give about the same ballistics. Ammunition for the .450 Nitro is still manufactured, and many second-hand doubles in that caliber can be picked up in London and Nairobi.

Anyone thinking of buying a second-hand double should first find out if ammunition is still made for it. Many of the old Nitro cartridges have been discontinued, and of course most of the old black-powder express cartridges are no longer in the land of the living. The fearful 600 Nitro Express with its 900-grain bullet and 7,600 foot-pounds of energy is obsolete and I doubt if the .577 will last long.

A double rifle costs important money, and consequently many Britishers have always preferred the cheaper large-bore bolt-action rifles. An outstanding cartridge for these big rifles is the .416 Rigby. This is a big rimless cartridge with a sharp shoulder. It drives a 410-grain bullet, according to claims, at a velocity of 2,371 and turns up 5,100 foot-pounds of energy. Be that as it may, British ammunition shows only about 2,300 foot-seconds on the chronograph in my own .416. Pre-war Rigby .416 rifles were all built on genuine Magnum Mauser actions, but for a time after the last war, Rigby could not obtain them and made many rifles on Belgian FN actions opened up. These were too weak and chopped up for the big cartridge and were not satisfactory. Rigby is now using the excellent Brevex Magnum Mauser action made in France.

The .416 is what is known as a "proprietary" cartridge. This is a quaint British custom by which Kynoch makes all the ammunition but sells it only to the gunmaker. The gunmaker tacks a fancy profit on it and resells it. The last .416 ammunition I bought in New York cost me 85 cents for each cartridge.

However, there is an easy way out for the American who is also a handloader. Cases for the .378 and .460 Weatherby are exactly the same as those for the .416 except that they are belted. For my own .416 I get these Weatherby cases, turn the belts off on a lathe. Then I run them through a full-length R.C.B.S. .416 die, prime them with one of the hotter varieties of American large-rifle primers, load them with 400-grain bullets of correct diameter made by Fred Barnes of Durango, Colorado. I am then in business. My powder charge is 105 grains of No. 4831. Velocity is 2,450, pressure is a bit under 45,000 pounds per square inch, and energy well over 5,000 foot-pounds. This way I do not have to monkey with the miserable Berdan primers in the British cases. For the record, 110 grains of No. 4831 gives the 400-grain bullet 2,600 at moderate pressure, but recoil is still pretty grim.

It is no trick at all to get an American-made .416. Rifles in the caliber have been built by Al Biesen and Tom Burgess, both of Spokane, Washington, by Griffin & Howe of New York, and by Apex Rifle Company of Sun Valley, California. Bolt-action and double-barrel rifles for the .416 are also made in both Belgium and Austria.

The .404 Nitro Express is another popular "elephant" cartridge loaded in Britain. It uses a 400-grain bullet at 2,125 and turns up 4,020 foot-pounds of energy. I'd much prefer the .416. The .425 Westley Richards duplicates the ballistics of the .416, but is seldom seen nowadays in Africa. Again I'd prefer the .416.

The American entry in the elephant-cartridge field and probably the best bet for an American is the Winchester .458 Magnum. It uses a short, straight belted case that headspaces on the belt. Ballistics duplicate those of the famous .470 Nitro Express —a 500-grain bullet at 2,125 with 5,010 foot-pounds of energy. The solids for the cartridge have very thick steel jackets and have won an excellent reputation in Africa. Since a Model 70 rifle in .458 can be purchased for a bit over $300, the .458 is a good buy for the American going to Africa. Many have been purchased by residents of Kenya, Tanganyika, and other African countries.

THE AFRICAN BATTERY

For my first African safari I took enough rifles and ammunition to start a small war, and my white hunter still regards the episode with horror. On my next two safaris I saw the light and took only two rifles and a shotgun.

For a general hunt in the great game fields of Kenya, Tanganyika, or Portuguese East Africa, three types of rifles are necessary—a light, a medium, and a heavy. The light rifle will be used on the smaller antelope and will be used more than any other in the battery—for meat, for lion and leopard bait, and for trophies. It will be used on everything from Tomson gazelle, which are about the size of coyotes, to such animals as zebra, which weigh around 600, and kongoni and topi, which weigh around 300.

The medium rifle will be used on lion, eland, perhaps on kudu and sable, possible on leopard (although the light rifle will do as well). In a pinch the medium will take anything from gazelle to rhino or elephant. However, it is illegal to use anything less than a .375 caliber on dangerous game in Tanganyika and anything less than a .40 caliber in Kenya.

The heavy rifle will be used on rhino, elephant, Cape buffalo, and can be used with soft-point bullets on lion.

Here is a list of satisfactory calibers in the three categories:

Light. .270, .280, 7 x 57, .308, .30/06, 8 x 57, .318 (a British cartridge on the order of the .30/06), 7-mm. Remington Magnum, or .300 Weatherby.

Medium. .375, .338, 9.3 x 74-R (a German cartridge on the order of the .375 Flanged), .378 Weatherby.

Heavy. .458 Winchester Magnum, .465 or .470 Nitro Express, .425 Westley Richards, .416 Rigby, .460 Weatherby.

To be perfectly safe, the American on his first African safari who wants a collection of most game should take about 200 rounds of ammunition for his light rifle, about 60 for his medium, and about 40 for his heavy, equally divided between soft-points and solids.

Rifles of all kinds can be rented, but such rifles usually have open iron sights, 9-pound trigger pulls, and look as if they had been stepped on by twenty-one horses. Most ammunition can be purchased in Nairobi in British or American make.

Some of the finest wing shooting in the world is available in Africa—guinea fowl, francolin, sand grouse. In East Africa all shotguns that hold more than two cartridges are illegal. A good double shotgun is a useful addition to the battery, not only for birds but with buckshot for wounded leopard.

On my second African safari I hunted in the Tchad Republic, for the rare desert game (white oryx, addax, dama and dorcas gazelle, desert cheetah, and Barbary sheep) in the southern Sahara, and for lion, giant eland, various antelope in the brush country north of Ft. Archambault. My battery consisted of two restocked and remodeled Model 70 Winchesters, one a .270 with a 4-power telescope sight and the other a .375 with a 2¾-power scope. I used the .270 on the open desert and the .375 in the brush. For a shotgun I rented a French 16-gauge double.

On my third safari I went to Tanganyika and took my wife along. It was to be a specialized hunt for plains game, eland, leopard, lion, kudu, and sable. Our combined battery consisted of a 7 x 57 which my wife used, a .30/06 custom-made by Al Biesen with a Lyman 48 receiver sight, and a Lyman 2½-power Alaskan scope on Griffin & Howe mount, my old Model 70 .375 restocked by Griffin & Howe and fitted with a Lyman 48 and Bear Cub 2¾-X scope on Griffin & Howe side mount. In addition I took a Winchester Model 21 double-barrel shotgun in 12 gauge bored modified and improved modified.

BALLISTICS OF THE MEDIUM-BORES

Caliber	Bullet Weight	Muzzle Velocity	Muzzle Energy
.338 Winchester	200	3,000	4,000
.338 Winchester	250	2,700	4,050
.338 Winchester	300	2,450	
9.3 × 62	232	2,630	3,535
9.3 × 74-R	286	2,360	3,530
.35 Whelen	250	2,450	
.358 Norma	250	2,790	4,322
.375 Magnum	270	2,740	4,500
.375 Magnum	300	2,550	4,330
.378 Weatherby	270	2,940	5,181
	300	2,800	5,223

BALLISTICS OF THE BIG-BORES

Caliber	Bullet Weight	Muzzle Velocity	Muzzle Energy
.450/.400—3-inch (.400 Jeffery Nitro Express)	400	2,100	3,920
.450/.400—3¼	400	2,150	4,110
.404 Jeffery	400	2,125	4,020
.416 Rigby	410	2,371	5,100
.425 Westley Richards	410	2,350	5,010
.450 Nitro Express	480	2,150	4,930
.458 Winchester	500	2,150	5,140
.465 Nitro Express	480	2,150	4,930
.470 Nitro Express	500	2,150	5,140
.577 Nitro Express	750	2,050	7,010
.460 Weatherby	500	2,725	8,245
.600 Nitro Express	900	1,950	7,600

THE BATTERY FOR ASIA

As is the case with Africa, the most useful single cartridge for India is the .375 Magnum. With the 270- or 300-grain expanding bullets it is the medicine for tigers, and with 300-grain solids it does very well for bison and guar, both large members of the wild cattle family. As a second rifle anything of the 7 mm.—

.30/06—.270 class does nicely. When I was shooting tiger in India in 1955, my battery consisted of a .270 and a .375. With the .270 I shot chital (spotted axis deer), wild boar, hog deer, and black buck. I used the .375 only on tiger.

For the exceedingly interesting mountain game of Asia, I cannot imagine a better rifle than a good .270 with the 130-grain bullet and sighted to hit the point of aim at 275 yards with a 4-power scope. I have used a .270 on Persian red sheep, urial, ibex, and wild boar on two hunts in Iran, in 1955 and 1959.

Some of the rarest and most interesting game in the world is found in the mountains of Asia, but most of it is not very large or very tough. Some of it has to be taken at rather long range, but it isn't hard to kill. Game includes the little red sheep of Iran, Turkey, and Iraq; various species of ibex from Arabia to India; wild boar almost everywhere; the great Ovis poli, an enormous wild sheep, in Hunza, Afghanistan, China, and Asiatic Russia; the various related sheep of the argali family; the handsome urial, a medium-size wild sheep found in India, Pakistan, and Iran; markor, a wild goat; various large deer related to our elk; and, among the big cats, the leopard and tiger.

On a remarkable expedition to Hunza in 1959, my two friends Herb Klein and Elgin Gates took .300 Weatherby rifles. They were the first Americans to shoot Ovis poli in over thirty years. Prince Abdorreza Pahlavi, brother of the Shah of Iran and one of the world's most experienced big-game hunters, does most of his shooting with a 7 x 57 Mauser. Many Iranian sportsmen use the .270, a cartridge which is also used by the King of Afghanistan.

Wildcat Cartridges

THE term "wildcat cartridge" has a rather sinister sound, as if there was something downright dangerous about such cartridges. Actually the term means nothing more or less than a cartridge that is not in regular production by one of the big loading companies.

A wildcat originates in a real or fancied need for a cartridge somewhat different from any factory-produced cartridge. Sometimes the wildcat is so successful, so fills an existing need, arouses so much enthusiasm among riflemen, that a factory begins to make rifles for it and furnishes ammunition. Then it is no longer a wildcat. In the majority of instances, however, the new wildcat comes along, has its little blaze of glory, and is forgotten because it performs its job no better than an existing factory cartridge, or not as well.

Wildcat can be produced in one of several ways. Perhaps the most simple is to neck down an existing cartridge case to smaller caliber, keeping the same slope of shoulder. This is the way the famous .270 Winchester cartridge was developed—not as a wildcat, but by the Winchester factory. The .30/06 case was simply necked down to .270. Another method is to neck down and shorten a case. The .250/3000 Savage is the .30/06 necked down to .25 and shortened. The .257 is the 7-mm. Mauser case necked down to .25. The .22 Savage Hi Power and the .219 Zipper are based on the old .25/35 case.

Another method is to neck *up* or expand a case to a larger caliber. The .35 Whelen is a .30/06 case with the neck expanded to .35, and the .400 Whelen was the same case expanded to .40.

If the experimenter wants to he can simply blow out or fireform a case to give larger powder capacity, less body taper, and a sharper shoulder by firing a factory case in a rechambered rifle. Brass is pliable and under pressure it will expand to fit the chamber—even one considerably larger than the one for which it was designed. Probably the first gunsmith and experimenter to do this was Lysle D. Kilbourn, of upper New York State, who rechambered Hornet rifles to give a sharper shoulder, less body taper, and more powder capacity. Then a regular Hornet cartridge was fired in the chamber and emerged as a K-Hornet, which would hold more powder and give more velocity. The same thing has been done with a good many rimmed cases, because the head space is controlled by the rim. Fire-formed wildcats are the Improved Zipper, the Mashburn Bee, and even "Improved Krags."

Roy Weatherby's big .300 Weatherby Magnum is simply the regular .300 H. & H. Magnum case given more powder capacity and less body taper by firing it in a specially chambered rifle. In these instances regular factory ammunition can be used in the so-called improved chambers, *but* the fire-formed or blown-out cases cannot be used in an unaltered chamber. The Mashburn Long .300 Magnum is another blown-out .300 wildcat based on the H. & H. case. Blowing out permits putting more powder behind the bullet and consequently more velocity. The Holland & Holland series of cases (.300 and .375) are belted, with the belt just forward of the extraction groove, taking care of the head spacing, and this practice, within reasonable limits, is safe.

In recent years rimless cartridges have also been blown out. In this case the head space is presumably taken care of by the cartridge stopping its entry into the chamber at the junction of the neck with the shoulder. Just how safe this is I wouldn't say, but people seem to get away with it. This is the method used in producing the "improved" .257's, .270's, and .30/06's. I do not recommend it. Not much powder capacity is added, and to obtain real improvement pressures have to be run up beyond the safety point. An "improved" .270, the history of which I followed, shot its barrel out in about three hundred rounds. Among my correspondents have been a good many men who have submitted their pet .270's and .257's to this rechambering job and who have then been bitterly sorry.

Still more complicated is the wildcat case based on a factory case that has been shortened, necked down, and then fire-formed. The Ackley series of wildcats designed by P. O. Ackley, the Trinidad, Colorado, gunsmith, are made by shortening, necking down, and *then* fire-forming Holland & Holland Magnum cases. So are the .257 and .270 Weatherby Magnum cartridges. In either instance the making of cases is a slow and painful procedure of running cases through two or three dies, trimming, and fire-forming.

For the confirmed rifle crank of an experimental turn of mind who is mechanical by nature and who enjoys the details of his loading bench, the ownership of a wildcat is no hardship. For the busy man who is not a rifle crank and who does not do his own reloading, the ownership of such a rifle is a pain in the neck. If he wants to dispose of his rifle, he will do so only with difficulty because it is not standard. Of all the wildcats, the easiest to own is the type that uses factory ammunition, fire-forming it by shooting it in the new chamber. In a pinch then over-the-counter ammunition can be used.

The wildcatters have had a good deal of influence on cartridge design, and in the past they have given rifle nuts something to think about and gun editors something to write about. Many cartridges now in regular factory production have been developed from wildcat prototypes.

In a previous chapter I mentioned that the inspiration for the .244 Remington was the .243 Rockchucker wildcat cooked up by Fred Huntington, the loading tool and die maker of Oroville, California. The .280 Remington is simply the 7 mm./06 wildcat made a bit longer from head to shoulder so it will not chamber in a .270. Loads for the wildcat 7 mm./06 and the .280 are identical.

Winchester's highly successful elephant cartridge, the .458 Magnum, was by no means the first .45 caliber elephant cartridge with a straight case which headspaced on the belt. Its ancestor was a now forgotten wildcat, the .450 Watts. It was brought out about 1950 by Harvey Anderson, a Yakima, Washington, gunsmith. I used a .450 Watts loaded with British Kynoch bullets for the .450 No. 2 in Africa in 1953 and shot buffalo and rhino with it.

Anyone who has seen a case for one of the Ackley short Magnums and who has then seen a Winchester .264 or .338 will note that like the Ackley wildcats the Winchester cases have short, straight bodies and sharp shoulders—both features which Ackley said promoted greater efficiency twenty-five years ago. In most ways the Winchester .338 is very similar to the .333 O.K.H. belted, a wildcat which Don Hopkins used extensively in Africa.

Roy Weatherby's line of cartridges has greatly influenced cartridge design. Weatherby has sold a lot of rifles, and his cartridges have acted as a thorn in the pants of the big loading companies. The Weatherby cartridges will be discussed later in this chapter.

Many wildcatters are sensible people with considerable mechanical and technical knowledge, and their experiments have been of great value. Others are plain nuts. Many of the claims made by the nuttier of the wildcatters have been enough to make anyone with any knowledge of ballistics come down with an attack of night sweats.

Over the years I have learned to take the statements of most aficiondos of the wildcat cartridge with large portions of salt. Just before the war broke out, many pages in various magazines were devoted to a mysterious wildcat 7 mm. on the .30/06 case. Those who developed it described the velocity as "crazy." They guessed something like 3,300 foot-seconds with a 180-grain bullet. Trajectory was so flat, they said, that one could sight in at 300 yards and hit an apple anywhere up to 400. Animals struck with this magic bullet didn't move out of their tracks. Instead they lay as rigid as an equestrian statue of General Grant. Smoke with a slightly sulphurous odor drifted slowly out of the wound.

All this struck me as pretty phony. In my dull peasant way I could not figure out how it was possible to get enough powder in a .30/06 case to give that velocity with acceptable pressures. I reasoned that the velocity could not be over 2,800 foot-seconds and was probably less. Then I got a report from a chap with a chronograph. Velocity was indeed about 2,750. Trajectory was like that of any other bullet of the same ballistic coefficient at the same velocity. All the virtues of this now-forgotten wildcat were simply in the minds of those who had developed it.

I have long since learned to be very skeptical of testimonial evidence. Once a chap who had developed a .30 caliber wildcat on a blown-out .300 H. & H. case brought me a sample cartridge.

"What velocity are you getting with the 180-grain bullet?" I asked innocently.

"I don't know," he said, "but when I sight in to put the bullet one inch high at 100 yards it is only one inch low at 400. What do you think I am getting?"

"About 10,000 feet per second," I told him.

In the old days most wildcatters did everything with the seats of their pants. They had no chronographs, no pressure equipment. They tried guessing their velocities from bullet drop and estimated the pressure from the appearance of the primer and the looks of the case. Nowadays, there are many electronic chronographs scattered over the country and velocity dope is not difficult to come by. Pressure equipment, however, is concentrated in the hands of the arsenals and the loading companies.

Pressures of many wildcat cartridges run very high. Some experimenters conclude that if their rifles don't blow up with a blinding flash they have nothing to worry about. Others think a primer leak is nothing serious and if they drop their loads down a couple of grains after they get leaking primers they are all right.

Some years ago I asked one of the big loading companies to load some cartridges up in good brass until they began getting primer leaks and then run pressure tests. A leaking primer generally shows that pressures are up to about 70,000 pounds per square inch or more. A blown primer shows pressures in the neighborhood of at least 80,000 p.s.i.

There is a lot of leeway built into a modern bolt-action rifle and into a modern brass cartridge case. This leeway is necessary for the protection of the shooter. Let us suppose that a factory cartridge is loaded to a mean pressure of about 53,000 p.s.i., which is about as high as factory cartridges go. Let us say it gives a 150-grain bullet a velocity at the muzzle of about 3,000 foot-seconds. Our wildcatter comes along, changes the shape of the case a bit, rams more powder into it, and gets a velocity of 3,250. His rifle does not blow up. He can extract the cases. He lays his increased velocity onto a more "efficient" case. Actually he is getting more velocity because he is working with higher pressure—at least 10,000 p.s.i. more than the factory load. Use that much pressure in the factory case and the velocity would be the same.

A pal of mine stoutly maintained that the 7 x 57 case was more "efficient" than the larger .270 case. To prove it, he showed almost as much velocity with a 130-grain bullet in the 7 mm. case with 50 grains of No. 4320 (a medium-slow burning powder) as I was getting with a bullet of the same weight in front of 62 grains of very slow burning No. 4831. I sent the two loads off for pressure testing. The 7 mm. got its velocity with about 53,500 p.s.i. pressure, the .270 with about 44,000 p.s.i.

Something the wildcatters forget is that to a great extent velocity and pressure go hand in hand. On a dozen occasions or more I have found, when pressure data is available, that when a small case delivers as much velocity as a large case it does so with substantially more pressure. One gunsmith has a line of cartridges based on the .30/06 case. He gets velocities that would do credit to the much larger .375 Magnum case necked down. But his pressures must run around 70,000 p.s.i., and every now and then one of his customers discovers that his rifle has come apart in his hands.

Some of the claims made by the wildcatters really give me pause. An example: The .257 Roberts case is simply the 7 x 57 case necked down to .25 caliber. One wildcatter necked the .257 case up to .270. His bullet then measured .277 instead of the original .284 bullet of the 7 mm. This magic 7/1000-inch difference in bullets for some reason, he testified, made his .270 wildcat flatter shooting, more deadly, more efficient!

SOME GOOD WILDCATS

In preparing this new edition of *The Rifle Book*, one of the most melancholy tasks I have faced has been the revision of this chapter on wildcats. The manuscript of the first edition was completed in 1948, and I am revising the book in the summer of 1961. When I wrote the original chapter I included some dope on what, back in 1948, were the most useful and widely used wildcats. Where are most of them now? Gone with the wind!

I haven't heard anything about the .218 Mashburn Bee for years. It was the .218 Winchester Bee blown out for a straight body and a sharp shoulder by firing in an enlarged chamber. The blown-out K-Hornet is equally dead and Roy Weatherby's blown-out .220 Swift called the .220 Rocket has been dropped. When I wrote the original version of this chapter, many rifles on single-shot actions were being made for the .219 Improved Zipper cartridge. This little number is likewise dead, and the single-shot fad has played itself out. I haven't heard of the .285 O.K.H. (just about identical to the .280 Remington) in years, and most of the .25 caliber wildcats are as dead as Jonah.

When this book was first written, there were some large holes in the factory cartridge lists, but most of these have now been filled. At one time there was a big gap in the .22 varmint cartridges between the .218 Bee and the .22 Hornet and the Swift. It was partially filled by the .219 Zipper, but no good rifle was available for it. Now the .222 Remington and the .222 Remington Magnum have filled the gap.

The .300 H. & H. Magnum was not a very efficiently designed case for American powders, and the woods were swarming with blown-out .300 caliber wildcats. Now the .300 Winchester cartridge is widely distributed in factory loads and anyone getting a big .30 other than the Winchester is making it hard on himself.

Americans started swarming to Africa after the last war, but there was no American-made cartridge of the elephant class. There was some reason for the .375 case necked out to .45 and called the .450 Watts. Now that the .458 Winchester is in factory production, the Watts is exceedingly dead. Some chaps started playing with various cartridges necked up or down to 6 mm. right after the war. Now that the .243 Winchester and the .244 Remington are in regular factory production there is not much need for them.

There are still some wildcats that fill holes in the factory list. One is the .22/250, or .22 "Varminter," as it is sometimes called. In some ways it has advantages over the Swift, and the handloader who wants a hot .22 would not be too unwise to consider it.

The .25/06 (the .30/06 case necked to .25 with the same shoulder slope retained) has the edge on any other varmint cartridge on a windy day, as good velocity can be given bullets of excellent ballistic coefficient.

For years there was room for a long-range 7 mm. on a Magnum case. Remington has filled it with the 7 mm. Remington Magnum.

For the most part the wildcat cartridges are no better than similar factory-loaded cartridges. Owning a wildcat rifle is a headache. Ammunition has to be handloaded and cannot be obtained in sporting-goods stores. Often the cases must be fire-formed with trouble, expense, and barrel wear. Sometimes the case must be cut off, necked down (or up), and then fire-formed. May the saints preserve me from such an ordeal!

One enthusiastic wildcatter shipped a whole battery of wildcat rifles to Africa. His ammunition went along in a separate box. When he arrived his rifles were there but his ammunition was lost. He made his safari with *rented* rifles.

If the owner of a wildcat rifle wants to sell it he gets less money for it. All in all, a person should do a bit of thinking before he invests in a wildcat or believes the pitches put out by wildcat-cartridge designers.

Some Semi-Wildcats

One of the most indefatigable cartridge designers of this generation is Roy Weatherby of Southgate, California. Weatherby dashes off a cartridge design with the same speed and aplomb that the late Edgar Guest used in knocking out a poem. Since he went into business right after the last war, he has designed the .220 Rocket, the .257, .270, 7 mm., .300, .375, .378, and .460 Weatherby Magnums. His firm also designed a new and very strong action of the Mauser type which incorporates features of the Arisaka, the Remington Model 721, and the old Newton. He imports telescope sights made to his design in Germany. His cartridges used to be plain and unadulterated wildcats. His .220 Rocket was a blown-out .220 Swift. His .300 was a blown-out .300 H. & H. case, and his .375 a blown-out .375 H. & H.

At first his short Magnums were made by first trimming the .300 H. & H. cases to length, then running them through the proper die to neck them down and put a shoulder on them, and then blowing them out by loading them and firing them with powder and bullet in a Weatherby chamber.

His .378 and his .460 (in reality a .45) were developed on the British .416 Rigby case. Weatherby is a great believer in horsepower and the .416 case was the biggest he could find.

Now, however, the Weatherby cartridges are out of the wildcat class. Weatherby's cases are made for him in Sweden. In this country he primes them and loads them with American bullets and American powder on automatic machines in his Southgate, California, plant. His cartridges are not loaded by Remington or by Western, but they are widely distributed over the United States and Canada and anyone who owns a Weatherby and doesn't care to reload has no trouble obtaining ammunition. The cartridges are even obtainable in Nairobi.

Weatherby is a promotional genius, and his rifles and cartridges have gained wide acceptance. I would make a guess that about fifty per cent of those who hunt in East Africa take with them at least one rifle in a Weatherby caliber. His stock design seems a bit bizarre to the conservative, but his rifles have a lot of dash and glitter. Many are gold-plated, elaborately engraved, and the stocks are inlaid with contrasting wood, ivory, mother-of-pearl, and whatnot. They are favorites with Hollywood movie stars, Texas oil millionaires, Far Eastern potentates, and other well-heeled characters.

Most famous and popular of the line is the .300 Weatherby, which began life simply as the .300 H & H. case blown out. At one time Weatherby claimed a velocity of 3,400 foot-seconds with the 180-grain bullet and probably got it, but his latest catalog claims 3,300. His figures are for 26-inch barrels, but his standard rifles now have 24-inch barrels. Not long before I wrote this I purchased some Weatherby factory ammunition for the .300 at a local sporting-goods store and chronographed it. Instrumental velocity in a 24-inch barrel was about 3,120 and muzzle velocity would be about 3,170. This is not as high as is claimed, but when you consider that the standard .300 H & H. factory loads produce only about 2,825 muzzle velocity in a 24-inch barrel, the Weatherby is a great improvement.

I have had a fair amount of experience with the .300 Weatherby in North America and in Africa. It is a flat-shooting and deadly cartridge on any soft-skinned game. In North America I have shot with it only grizzly bear, a couple of antelope, a Rocky Mountain white goat, and a few mule deer. However, when I was in Africa in 1953 I used my .300 W. more than any other rifle and shot everything with it from Tomson gazelle to sable and greater kudu.

The load I have used more than any other for years in the .300 Weatherby is 78 grains of No. 4350 with the 180-grain bullet. Velocity about 3,160, or about that of the .270 with the 130-grain bullet. Since the .300 W. case is over-bore capacity, the best powder is No. 4831, and 83 grains of this will give 3,230 with what seems to be perfectly usable pressure.

The .300 can be used as a medium-bore for the larger soft-skinned game when loaded with the 200-grain bullet with 80 grains of No. 4831 to give a flat 3,000 or with 73 grains of No. 4350 to give the 220-grain bullet 2,990.

About the only thing that can be said against the .300 is that the recoil is a bit severe and that barrel life is not too long. Recoil is about like that of the .338 Winchester, and 1,000 rounds, in my experience, will show considerable erosion at the throat.

To my way of thinking, the best of the Weatherby short Magnums is the 7 mm. Recoil is much less than that of the .300, and it is just as effective as the larger cartridge on anything up to elk and caribou in size.

Recently chronographed factory 7 mm. Weatherby Magnum loads gave me 3,200 with the 140-grain bullet in a 24-inch barrel. The Speer Handloader's Manual lists 3,347 with the 145-grain Speer .284 bullet in front of 73 grains of No. 4831 and 3,198 with 72 grains of the same powder with the 160-grain bullet. I have played with a good many wildcat 7 mm. Magnums, with the British .275 H. & H. Magnum, and this is the best of the lot.

The .270 Weatherby Magnum is more popular than the 7 mm. Magnum, but probably a bit less efficient, as the hole in the barrel is a bit small for the powder capacity. However, it is an excellent long-range cartridge. Most widely used load is 65 grains of No. 4350 with the 130-grain bullet for 3,300.

The .257 Weatherby Magnum has been surprisingly popular, and spectular long-range kills have been made with it. With top loads the 100-grain bullet can be driven about 3,600 (70 grains of No. 4831) or 66 grains of No. 4350, and the 120-grain bullet about 3,325. Barrel life is somewhat short, but this is a high-performing outfit for the plains or mountains.

The .375 Weatherby is the .375 Magnum blown out to handle a bit more powder, but improving the .375 Magnum is to my way of thinking a bit like improving the looks of Elizabeth Taylor. The .378 Weatherby is something else again—the .375 Magnum bullets pushed at higher velocity out of the big belted case based on that of the .375 Rigby. Velocity with the 270-grain bullet, according to Weatherby figures, is 3,200 f.p.s. and with the 300-grain bullet 3,000.

The .460 Weatherby produces more foot-pounds of energy than any other cartridge being made today. It is the .378 Weatherby case necked up to .45 caliber to take the same bullets as the Winchester .458. In it the 500-grain bullet has a muzzle velocity of 2,725 foot-seconds and a muzzle energy of 8,245 foot-pounds! This exceeds the energy delivered by the .600 Nitro Express!

Other Semi-Wildcats

Back in the early 1950's a good deal of publicity was given a cartridge known as the 7 x 61 Sharpe and Hart. It is a short-belted Magnum taking 7 mm. bullets and was designed by the late Phil Sharpe and a gunsmith named Hart. Rifles were made in that caliber in Denmark by Schultz & Larsen and imported into this country and sold by Sharpe and Hart. Ammunition was likewise imported as made by Norma of Sweden.

Sharpe wrote that developing the cartridge had cost $10,000 or $25,000 or something. What for, I cannot say. Reloading dope sheets were sold for $5. One factory load was furnished—a 160-grain bullet at a claimed velocity of 3,100. A Schultz and Larsen rifle with a 26-inch barrel produced slightly over 2,900 on the Speer electronic chronograph for me, about the velocity one can get with the .280 Remington. However, 67 grains of No. 4831 will produce about 3,100 with a 160-grain bullet, but at what pressure no one knows. Loading data furnished by Sharpe was pretty optimistic and didn't check out on the chronograph.

Few wildcats or semi-wildcats come up to claims, and I for one am pretty dubious about most of the wildcat tribe.

Reloading

Reloading the better known and more widely used wildcat cartridges does not offer much of a problem, as information is quite generally available. Loads for some of the older cartridges can be found in the Phil Sharpe's *Complete Guide to Handloading* and loads for the more widely used wildcats are found in the *Speer Manual for Handloading Ammunition*, which is published by Speer Products, of Lewiston, Idaho. It is available from the publisher or from most dealers in handloading supplies.

Such wildcat cartridges as the K-Hornet, the .22/.250, the .25/06, and the .35 Whelen have been around for a long, long time and good loads for them are more or less standard. Numerous charge tables and velocity data for them are available, but of course no pressure dope.

An enthusiast who is keeping up one of the wilder wildcats will find that his best source of information is, probably, the gunsmith who dreamed it up. However, a word of warning. Designers of wildcat cartridges tend to be an optimistic lot. They make their creations to look good and some of their loads are pretty hot. It is wise to start about 10 per cent below most recommendations.

The chap who has fallen heir to some esoteric creation that goes under some fanciful name such as the .221 Timiskenko Tornado—all he can do is to interpolate. He must compare the capacity of the case and the weight and bearing surface of the bullet with those of a similar cartridge for which loading data is available. Then, staying on the conservative side, he can make an educated guess. I have worked up loads for some odd ones by this means, and with safety. Among them are the British .275 Magnum and the .416 Rigby.

CHAPTER XX

Trajectory and Sighting In

ONCE upon a time a cynical gunsmith who in his lifetime had worked on thousands of rifles and had talked to hundreds of hunters wrote me that he did not believe that one deer hunter in ten went out into the woods in the fall to shoot his buck with a rifle sighted in well enough to knock over a standing buck at two hundred yards, even with a perfect hold. I am inclined to believe him correct. Not a day passes but what I receive letters from men who apparently haven't the faintest notion how to sight in a rifle. I have known men to embark on long and expensive hunting trips with rifles they have never fired, content in the notion that the rifle has been correctly sighted in at the factory.

Let's find out some truth as a basis for this chapter:

(1) Some but not all rifles are sighted in at the factory, and the sights are adjusted usually to hit the point of aim, in the big-game rifle at one hundred yards.

(2) However, no one can sight in a rifle for another and be sure that it is on the nose, particularly with open sights. Ways of holding a rifle differ and ways of seeing sights differ. With open iron sights two equally good shots may put their groups a foot apart or more at two hundred yards *with the same rifle.*

(3) Very few rifles put bullets of different weights into the same point of impact, and if bullets are changed the rifle is usually shooting off. Even with the same bullets a different powder

with different burning characteristics will usually cause a change of point of impact, though the bullets may be loaded to the same velocity and pressure. Rifles should be sighted in to hit the point of aim with the same ammunition that is to be used on the hunt.

(4) Rifles change point of impact from month to month, from year to year. Sometimes this is because of loosening of the guard or tang screws. Sometimes it is because of warpage of the wood in the stock. *It is never safe to assume that because a rifle was sighted in last year, it is still sighted in this year.*

Now let us assume that the reader of this book doesn't know too much about rifles and wants to sight in. Perhaps he has a new and unfired rifle from a factory or from a custom gunmaker. Perhaps he has had a scope or receiver sights installed. At any rate, let us assume that our reader does not know where his rifle is shooting.

Many people have the notion that if the sights can be lined up by bore-sighting (aligning the sights by training them on an object seen through the bore of the rifle), all their troubles will be over. As a matter of fact, bore-sighting is only a rough and ready method of seeing that the bullet will land *somewhere* on the target. The reason for this is that barrels vibrate when a bullet passes through them and no two barrels vibrate exactly alike. Many people also have the notion that if they could clamp a rifle in a vise and thus eliminate all human error, sighting would be simple. Actually the point of impact of a rifle sighted in even with a machine rest is usually different from what it is when shot from the shoulder.

To bore-sight a rifle, cut two V's in a wooden box, so that the rifle can rest in line without being held. Then remove the bolt so you can look right down the bore. Train the rifle on a dark brick in a wall, on the white globe of a street light—anything, just so you can see it right in the middle of the bore. Then adjust the sights so that they also rest on the same object. Sights and bore are now lined up, *but the rifle is not sighted in.*

Sometimes, with a very stiff, uniform, and well-bedded barrel, you can point the bore a little higher than the sight to take care of the bullet drop and find you are pretty well on. *But only sometimes!* Usually bore-sighting will only put the bullet somewhere on the target. In installing scopes and receiver sights good gunsmiths always bore-sight, so usually the shooter does not have to bother.

Since the reader wants to get his rifle to shooting where it looks, he should put up a good, clear target at twenty-five yards and then get himself some sort of rest. A regular bench rest is excellent, and many large target ranges have them. If one is not available the shooter can do well by shooting prone from a padded box, or even by shooting out of the back seat of a car with the rifle rested on a bedroll, a pillow, or anything comparatively soft so that the bullet will not fly high.

Do the first shooting at twenty-five yards, and the bullet will be somewhere on the target. If the shooting is done at two hundred or even at one hundred yards, the bullet will often miss the target entirely—and then the shooter knows no more than he did before.

We are all set. We have our target up and our rest. We also have a supply of the proper ammunition. Now shoot a group of three shots. Take the center of the group as the point of average impact. Then measure the distance between the point of impact and the point of aim, or where the sights rested. Make the adjustment.

Let's get specific. We are sighting in a .30/06 rifle, let us say, with the 180-grain factory hunting load at a velocity of 2,700 f.p.s., and our rifle is equipped with a Lyman Alaskan 2½-X scope with clicking minute-of-angle adjustments.

The distance between the center of impact of the three-shot group we fired to the center of the bull's-eye, where the crosshairs of the scope rested is 3 inches low and 1½ inches right. Now, our scope (and also most receiver sights) is marked or graduated in minutes of angle, which is equal to one inch at 100 yards. At 25 yards, therefore, the minute of angle is one fourth of that, or ¼ inch, just as the minute of angle is equal to two inches at 200 yards, three inches at 300 yards, four inches at 400 yards—or ½ inch at fifty yards.

We remove the caps that guard the adjustment dials of the scope. We see that the elevation dial on top has an arrow pointing to the word "UP." This means that turning the dial in that direction raises the point of impact. Therefore let us turn the dial in the "UP" direction twelve clicks, because at 25 yards the minute of angle has the value of ¼ inch. We count the clicks as we turn and stop at twelve.

We now remove the cap from the windage dial on the right side of the scope and discover an arrow pointing to the letter *R*, which stands for "right." We want to move our point of impact to the left, so we turn the dial in the direction opposite to the way the arrow points and count off six clicks.

Now we shoot another group of three shots and, much to our gratification, we find it right in the middle of the bull.

"But," you say, "who wants to sight in for twenty-five yards?"

You have forgotten the fact that the bullet starts below the line of sight, rises until it crosses the line, rises farther to the top of the curve of trajectory, then falls until it crosses the sight line again. It is at this distance that the rifle is said to be sighted in for—this second place where the bullet crosses the sight line.

In the case of our .30/06 with the 180-grain bullet at 2,700 f.p.s. and a telescope sight 1½ inches above the line of bore, let us see what has happened.

The bullet has crossed the line of aim at 25 yards. It continues to rise. At 50 yards it will strike 1 inch high, at 100 yards 2½ inches high. At 150 yards it is down to 2 inches above the line of sight again, and at 200 yards it again crosses the line of aim. The rifle can be said to be sighted in for 200 yards.

Remembering this fact, that the bullet crosses the line of aim *twice* and that a rifle sighted in for 200 yards, in the case of the .30/06, is also sighted in for 25 yards, has got me many a mess of grouse and rabbits when I had nothing but a big-game rifle along. Once up in northern British Columbia I had been hunting caribou on top of a mountain and had killed a fine big bull at about 200 yards. As we neared camp a whole covey of fat blue grouse flew up in a tree and perched. I took the heads off of six out of seven with the .30/06 by holding right where the head and neck join.

Let us also see what this 25-yard preliminary sighting does in the other calibers:

A .270 with a scope sight mounted 1½ inches above the line of bore and hitting the point of aim at 25 yards with the 130-grain bullet at a velocity of 3,120 will return the bullet to the point of aim again at 250 yards with a maximum trajectory height at 150 yards of 3 inches.

A .30/06 using the 150-grain bullet at 2,960 and so sighted with scope will return the bullet to the line of aim at 225 yards with a maximum rise at 150 yards of 3 inches.

A .30/30 with the 170-grain bullet and with iron sights will return the bullet to point of aim at 100 yards.

We have our .30/06 hitting on the nose at 25 yards, but we must not assume that it is absolutely perfect at 200 as yet. Let's check it. We put up a target at 200, fire a group, then either look it over through a useful spotting scope or, if we don't have one, go down and check. Usually the group will be right on. Sometimes ways of seeing the sights at different ranges differ a bit and slight changes in sight adjustment will have to be made to bring the group right in at 200 yards. One should remember, too, that any error at 25 yards will be *eight* times as great and hence eight times as apparent at 200.

Now, for further check, let us shoot at 200 yards from the hunting sitting position. We may find that the rifle that was so prettily sighted in from the bench rest or from prone with a padded rest is a bit off from the hunting position. This is often so, and no rifle will hit exactly in the same spot from different positions. That is something the hunter ought to know. In my case a rifle sighted to hit the point of aim from a bench rest at 200 yards will usually shoot a bit high (about 3 or 4 inches) from my particular brand of sitting position. But that is something I know. Now we have our rifle sighted in. We must continue to practice, however, and also to check the sights from time to time.

Until now we have taken the arbitrary distance of 200 yards for sighting in. That is a pretty good compromise with a rifle of a muzzle velocity of at least 2,500 f.p.s. For special cases, however, other distances can be selected. With a rifle of a velocity of around 2,000 f.p.s. and to be used mostly at short ranges in the woods, the thing to do is to sight in so that the bullet will not rise more than 2 inches above the point of aim at the highest point in the trajectory. On the other hand, with a rifle to be used at long and uncertain ranges in the mountains, where 300-yard shots are much more common than 100-yard shots, I like to sight in so that the maximum trajectory height is 4 inches. Holding one third of the way up an animal's body, this high a trajectory is *not* going to cause any mid-range misses, and shots up to considerable range can be taken with no allowance for bullet drop. I have done most of my mountain hunting with .270 rifles sighted to hit 4 inches high at 150 yards. The bullet is right at point of aim at 275 yards and only two inches low at 300. At 350 the bullet falls only 7½ inches, which means that a .270 so sighted has a point-blank range of about 350 yards.

For the same sort of hunting with the .30/06 and the 180-grain bullet with scope sight, one can sight in to put the bullet 4 inches high at 150 yards and the bullet will strike the point of aim at 240 yards. At 300 yards the bullet will strike only 7 inches low and a hit with a center hold is possible.

But if the same rifle were sighted in to hit the point of aim at 100 yards, the 18 inches low and a dead-on hold would result in a miss. *For mountain use the rifle should always be sighted in for the longest possible range that will not give mid-range misses.*

[274]

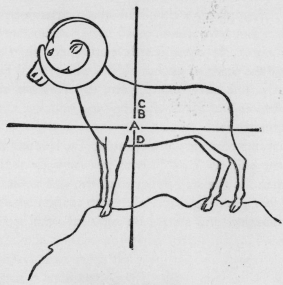

With this hold and a .270 sighted to hit the point of aim at 250 yards the bullet will strike at A at that distance, at B at 100 yards, C at 200, and D at 300.

Even with the deer rifle to be used in country where the average shot is 100 yards or less, I think it the best idea to sight in for 150 yards. In the case of the rifle of the .30/30 class with a velocity of a bit over 2,000 f.p.s. The bullet will strike only 2 inches high at 100 yards and fall only 5 inches at 200 yards, as against a fall of 9 inches at 200 if the rifle is sighted in with iron sights to hit the point of aim at 100.

So far I have spoken of bringing the bullets to point of aim only with a scope clicking in minutes of angle. The majority of scopes are marked in minutes or fractions of a minute. The Weaver K series with screw adjustments (K-S) are graduated in two minutes of angle. The Weaver K scopes with the click adjustments (K-C) are graduated in ¼ minutes. Depending on the individual model, receiver sights are graduated in clicks with the value all the way from ¼ minute to 1 full minute. Manufacturers' sight catalogues give the dope.

With the open sight, which is really now obsolete, *exact* adjustment is often pretty tough. The crude steps one commonly sees for elevation have a minute-of-angle value running all the way from 4 to 8. In other words, putting the sight up a step may change the point of impact all the way from 4 to 8 inches at 100 yards. The only way anyone can find the value is to shoot a group at 100 yards, then put the sight up a notch and shoot another group.

If the first step puts the point of impact too low and the second too high, the only thing to do is to put the sight in the second step and then file the step down until the rifle shoots where it looks. But let me repeat, open sights with crude step adjustments are really obsolete and should be replaced with scopes or receiver sights.

TRAJECTORY

It is difficult to discuss the correct sighting in of a rifle without some reference to trajectory, as the trajectory of any cartridge must necessarily govern the distance for which the rifle is sighted.

The principles of trajectory are really simple.

All bullets begin immediately to fall to the earth from the line of bore the instant they leave the muzzle because they are acted on by gravity exactly like any other free-falling body. If the barrel is pointed exactly level with the earth, the bullet's course is a gradual downward curve that never reaches the line of bore but is always below it. For this reason rifles are so sighted that the bore points slightly upward, and we have seen how the bullet climbs to the line of sight, crosses it usually at about 25 yards, and continues above until it reaches the height of the trajectory curve.

It is paradoxical, but even though the bullet is rising, *it is falling constantly below the line of bore.* All bullets fall at the same rate of speed because they are acted upon by the same force, gravity. If a .22 bullet at 1,100 f.p.s. and a .220 Swift bullet at 4,140 were fired at the same instant from rifles parallel to the ground, they would both strike the earth at the same instant—and so would a bullet dropped from the hand. The Swift bullet, however, would fly farther because it is flying faster.

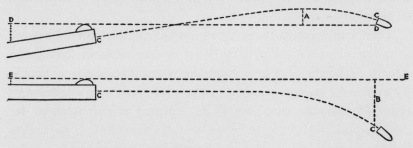

Because the rear sight is higher than the front sight when a rifle is sighted to hit the point of aim at any distance, the bullet rises as in the top picture until it crosses the line of aim (D-D) near the muzzle. It is, however, always dropping below line of bore. It continues above line of aim until it reaches the top of the trajectory curve. Then it falls until it crosses the line of aim the second time. In the second picture the line of aim (E-E) is parallel to the bore and the trajectory curve of the bullet never rises to cross it.
The total fall (B) of the bullet is roughly four times that of the height of trajectory over a given range (A).

The most important factor in trajectory is velocity—not merely muzzle velocity, but *average* velocity over a given range. The greater the speed at which a bullet travels, then, the greater the distance it will cover when fired at a certain angle of elevation before gravity pulls it back to earth.

To retain this *average* velocity the bullet should be relatively long and with a sharp point. Such a bullet will shoot much "flatter" than a short, blunt bullet at the same velocity. Often people are fooled by the high muzzle velocity of some such load as the 110-grain .30/06 bullet at the muzzle velocity of 3,350, whereas actually that bullet has a greater drop over 300 yards than the 150-grain .30-caliber spitzer bullet at 2,960.

Because the pull of gravity remains constant whereas velocity falls off rapidly, the trajectory is not a segment of a circle but an irregular curve known as a parabola. The farther the bullet travels, the greater its downward motion as compared to its forward motion. The more efficient the bullet is in retaining its initial velocity, the flatter the other end of the trajectory curve. The poorer the bullet, the more pronounced the far end of the curve.

The loading companies in their catalogues publish trajectory data for various cartridges, usually in the form of mid-range trajectory height over certain ranges, usually 100, 200, and 300 yards. These figures are from line of bore, *not* from line of sight. The actual rise of the bullet above the line of sight depends, obviously, on how high the line of sight is. The higher the line of sight, the flatter, apparently, the trajectory.

The *total fall* of a bullet over a given range is figured as the drop below the line of bore. This amounts roughly to four times the height of the mid-range trajectory. Taking the 180-grain .30/06 bullet at 2,700 f.p.s., for example, the mid-range trajectory (from line of bore) over 200 yards is three inches. *The total fall is 12 inches!*

Often people ask: how far will a bullet shoot flat? The answer is *no distance at all.* Let me repeat that any bullet begins to fall the instant it leaves the muzzle. Even the .220 Swift bullet at the tremendous muzzle velocity of 4,140 has a total fall over 200 yards of about 5 inches. It is for this reason that it is important that the rifle be sighted in for the longest possible range that will not cause mid-range misses, and it is for this reason that it is the height of foolishness to sight in such a rifle as the .30/06 for 100 yards. An iron-sighted .30/06 with the 180-grain bullet sighted for 100 yards puts the bullet 6 inches low at 200 yards and 12 inches low at 250, whereas the same rifle sighted for 200 puts the bullet about 2¾ inches high at 100, on the nose at 200, and only 5 inches low at 250. Since a bullet rise of 2¾ inches is not enough to cause a mid-range miss, sighting in for 200 yards instead of 100 has increased the range a full sixty yards.

With a heavy rifle to be used in stopping dangerous game at the very closest range and placing bullets precisely in small areas as in the case of brain shots on elephants, it is probably wise to sight in to hit the point of aim at 75 or even at 50 yards, but otherwise such sighting is foolish because few men can shoot well enough offhand to place a bullet in a six-inch circle at that distance anyway.

RECOMMENDED RANGES FOR SIGHTING-IN RIFLES

Caliber	Distance at which Bullet First Crosses Sight Line	Recommended Range	Bullet Fall at Longer Ranges		
.22 LR high-speed	20 yards	75 yards	100 3 in.		125 yds. 7 in.
Rifles of .30/30 class with velocity of around 2,200 f.p.s. iron sights	10 yards	150 yards	175 2 in.	200 5 in.	250 14 in.
Rifles with 2,500–2,600 f.p.s., 8-mm. Mauser, .22 Hornet, 180-gr. .30/40, .348 200-gr., .300 Savage 180-gr. iron sights	15 yards	175 yards		3 ins.	9 in.
Rifles with around 2,700 f.p.s. velocity .30/06, 180-gr. .300 Savage, 150-gr. iron sights	20 yards	200 yards	250 4 in.	300 10 in.	400 35 in.
Rifles with 3,000–3,150 f.p.s. .30/06 150-gr., .270 130-gr., etc.	25 yards	250 yards		4 in.	18 in.

NOTE: These figures are *relatively* accurate, but they are intended only to give the rifleman a notion of bullet fall and of what distance he should sight in. Bullet drop will vary over the longer ranges according to the shape of the bullet, and every rifleman should check his own rifle.

CHAPTER XXI

The Elements of Rifle Shooting

T HE average man who has learned to shoot a rifle has almost always begun his practice in exactly the wrong way. He has started off without any supervision whatsoever, and as a usual thing he has acquired bad habits. He has done his first shooting from the offhand position, the most difficult of all positions from which to shoot a rifle. He has never learned to call his shots. He jerks the trigger and flinches.

The United States is not exactly full of good rifleshots, and the average man who hunts deer once a year and who occasionally shoots at a tin can is really a pretty poor shot. I once helped three deer hunters who had just purchased new Model 94 Winchester rifles in .32 Special to sight their rifles in. From a sitting position two of these hunters could just about keep their shots in a 2½-foot circle at 100 yards. That is pretty poor shooting, but even shooting as bad as that will get deer. The third hunter could not even begin to keep his shots in a 10-foot circle at 100 yards. He must have been closing his eyes and jerking the trigger. I have seen hunters miss standing deer at 50 and 100 yards, and once I saw five hunters fire twenty-five shots at a running buck that got up within 10 yards of the closest hunter and ran 150 yards up an open hillside and over a crest. One would think that the law of averages would get that buck, but he got over the ridge and out of sight without even having a hair ruffled.

Learning to shoot a rifle is not difficult. I believe that learning to shoot a rifle well enough to kill deer consistently is really exceedingly easy if one goes about it right. Shooting a rifle at a stationary mark is actually one of the easiest of all sports. It is far easier to learn, for example, than good shotgun handling.

All that is necessary to hit a mark with a rifle (assuming that the rifle is correctly sighted in) is to get the sights lined up on the mark and then to let the trigger off without disturbing the aim. This, in theory at least, is utterly simple. If a rifle could be held absolutely steady and the trigger squeezed off each shot, the bullets would land in a very small group on the mark.

All good rifle shooting is based on the rifleman's assuming as steady a position as is possible under the circumstances and then letting off the trigger at exactly the right time. One soon finds out, however, that except from a bench rest it is impossible to hold a rifle even approximately steady, and even with most bench rests a rifle cannot be held *absolutely* steady. When using iron sights from a bench rest it is possible for a man to believe that he is holding steady, but let us put an eight-power scope, say, on the rifle, and we discover that even when we are sitting at a bench rest with the rifle resting across a sandbag, there still is wobble and tremor to the piece. Whatever the position, then, we learn that we have to complete the trigger squeeze at exactly the right time, when the sights are properly aligned.

Most men begin shooting from the offhand position. The rifle wobbles, and in an attempt to get the shot off when the sights are aligned, the beginner yanks the trigger. He does not learn to call his shots or to have a mental picture in his mind of exactly how the sights looked when he felt the recoil. The yank he gives the trigger throws the rifle off. Anticipation of the recoil and muzzle blast makes him flinch and it adds this flinch to the jerk of the trigger. Many people will fool around with offhand shooting for years and get no better.

If it were possible, it would be best to begin every shooter from the prone position with a sandbag rest, or from a bench rest. Then the problem of keeping the rifle steady does not amount to much. The shooter can concentrate on squeezing the trigger and learn to let off his shot without disturbing the aim. He will gain confidence in his rifle and in himself. He will learn that when the sights are correctly aligned, the bullet strikes within the bull's-eye as he has intended. After a week of rest shooting and concentration on squeezing the trigger and avoiding the flinch, the beginner should be able to shoot a relatively small group at 100 or 200 yards.

The next step should be shooting from the prone position, which is the steadiest of all positions. When the prone position is assumed, the shooter lies with his legs outspread and his body at about a forty-five degree angle to the left of the line toward the target. The left elbow should be directly under the rifle, and the rifle itself should rest on the heel of the palm. In that position there is much less tendency for the rifle to shake and wobble because it is supported by the bones of the forearm, acting as a pillar in direct contact between the rifle and the ground. In this position the rifle is relatively but not absolutely steady even with the help of a sling.

The ability to squeeze the trigger and to call the shot will increase in usefulness here. For many years the army has taught that the rifleman should not know when his rifle is going to go off. The theory is that when the rifleman gets his sights lined up approximately he should take up the preliminary pull of the double military pull. Then when his sights are on the bull correctly, he should increase the squeeze by a few ounces. When the sights wobble off he should stop. As the rifle comes back again on the target, he should increase the pull once more. Finally, theoretically at least, the rifle will go off unexpectedly, and because he is not expecting the recoil, he will not flinch. Since he has increased the pressure on the trigger only when the sights are correctly aligned, every shot should land within the bull's-eye. For whatever reason, this theory never worked with me. I have always known when the gun was going off. As soon as I learn the trigger pull I press the trigger until all except the last two or three ounces of pull are taken up. Then when my sights swing onto the target in correct alignment, I squeeze the shot off.

Our beginning rifleman, then, should practice from no other position but prone for some time. He should keep shooting until the majority of his shots land within the bull. Not until this essential prone position has been mastered should he move on to a more difficult one.

Under most hunting conditions the prone position has little value. In other words, there is practically no chance that a man can shoot at a whitetail deer or any other forest animal from a prone position. In the Southwest with its rocks and cactus the position can seldom be assumed and it cannot be used in canyon country because to lie down the rifleman needs relatively level ground. For plains shooting at antelope the prone position is very handy. It can also be widely used above timber line in the Rocky Mountains, where a typical shot will be from a smooth, round ridge down into a basin below. The most useful of all hunting positions under any other conditions except the jump shooting of forest game is the standard sitting position, which is almost as steady as prone. The sitting position puts the rifle much higher than the prone position and it can be used in fairly tall grass or small bushes. It can be assumed on a hillside. For my part, I have probably killed seventy-five per cent of the game I have shot from the sitting position. In the canyon country of the West, even when a buck jumps up and goes off at a hard run, I drop to the sitting position and I have trained myself to get the sights on almost the instant I touch the ground.

To assume the sitting position, the hunter should face away from the target at an angle of about forty-five degrees. Then he should lean over so that the flat part of his upper arm above the elbow comes in contact with the inside of the knees. As in the prone position, the left elbow should be as nearly under the rifle as possible so that the bone of the forearm acts as a pillar to support it. In the standard sitting position the heels are hard against the ground, and if the shooter has the time he should make little holes in the soil so that his heels will not slip. A good variation of the sitting position is the same as the one just described except that the shooter sits cross-legged. Many prefer this cross-legged position on level ground; of course, it cannot be used from a steep hillside. From a good steady position it is not too difficult for a good shot who can squeeze them off and call them to stay in a ten-inch circle at three hundred yards and to drive the bullets well within the lung area of an animal the size of a mule deer or sheep at the same distance. At four hundred yards, however, the prone position should be used whenever possible; usually an animal that far away is not greatly frightened and the rifleman will have a chance to assume the steadier position.

In the sitting position the most fatal mistake that can be made is to put the elbows on top of the knees. When this happens the loose cartilage of the elbows and the kneecaps causes the rifle to wobble. It is actually no better than shooting offhand—if, indeed, it is as good.

The sitting position is made much steadier by the proper use of a good tight sling. If a hunter has time to get his left arm through the loop of the sling and tighten up all along the line, he can do the best work from the sitting position. One of the smallest groups I ever shot from the sitting position under any circumstances was at a big mountain sheep. He was on a hillside about two hundred yards away. I had been watching him with glasses to decide whether I wanted his big head or not. When I decided I did, I laid my binoculars down, slipped my arm through the loop, drew the keepers up tight, and then put the cross-hairs right behind a foreleg. That rifle seemed as steady as from a bench rest. Because that ram was on a steep slope, his off side was higher than the near side. The bullets I was using did not open up much. The shots went through the body and almost tore the left leg off where it joined the body on the off side. I believe a silver dollar would have covered my three shots.

The kneeling position is much less steady than sitting. In fact, it is not greatly superior in that respect to shooting offhand. There are times, however, when it is useful. It can be assumed slightly quicker than a sitting position and it holds a rifle a little higher. Where there are tall grass and small bushes it is often impossible to sit and yet one can kneel and get the rifle over the obstructions. As I write this, the last deer I shot was from the kneeling position. I was down in the Mexican state of Sonora. I could see two deer across a wide arroyo. They were partially concealed by brush and I was standing in high grass and bushes. I watched those deer for a moment; then I could see that one of them was a big buck. I dropped to a kneeling position and as the rifle steadied I squeezed off the shot with the crosshairs resting right on the chest of the big buck as he faced me. I heard the bullet plop into him and saw him go off on a mad dash. I crossed the arroyo, picked up his track, and found him dead about seventy-five yards from where he had been hit. The bullet hole was almost exactly in the spot for which I had aimed.

To assume the kneeling position, one should face away from the target at an angle of about 45 degrees, squat firmly on the right heel, and hook the left arm well over the left knee. The tension of the back muscles causes the upper arm to pull against the knee and establish a relatively steady state of equilibrium. Above all, the shooter should avoid having his elbow right on top of the wobbly kneecap.

The offhand position is the most widely used, one of the most useful, and also the least steady of all positions. It is a position that must be learned, however, and no one who cannot shoot well from it can be called a good all-around shot. Almost all game in wooded areas is killed from the offhand position.

A good shot from the sitting position at 200 yards can keep most of his shots in the 8-inch bull, but the good offhand shot is one who can keep *all* his shots in the 30-inch 4-ring, picking up an occasional bull as he goes along. If he can average a score of 43 out of 50 he is a good offhand shot. If he can place *half* his shots in the bull with the rest in the 4-ring he is very good indeed. It is seldom, however, that a skillful shot will take a pop at a big-game animal offhand at 200 yards. If the game is that far away, he'll usually have time to sit or kneel.

For cool, deliberate offhand shooting, the right elbow should be held horizontal, almost exactly level with the shoulder, and the butt should rest on the big pad of muscles thus formed at the conjunction of the shoulder and the upper arm. The work of holding the butt firm against the shoulder should be done with the last four fingers of the right hand and with the thumb *around* the small of the stock. The left hand should be rather far back, just about on the floor plate of the rifle, and the weight of the rifle should rest on the heel of the palm. The elbow should be directly below the rifle itself, as if it is to the side it causes sway and trembling. The shooter should stand so that a line drawn between his toes points almost directly at the target. In other words, he should stand so that if he is shooting east he is just about facing south.

This is the offhand target position and one which will occasionally be used for a fairly long shot on game if the cover is such that one cannot kneel or sit. The last moose I shot was from the offhand position. I was standing in arctic willows almost waist-high and the bull was about two hundred yards away. My three shots could have just about been covered by a twenty-four-inch circle, which isn't too good, yet not too bad either.

The best offhand shot I ever made—one of those a man will always remember—was down in Sonora many years ago. I was standing on a point in waist-high chaparral when I saw a big buck standing under a tree about three hundred yards away across the canyon on the next point. It seemed as if it took me a couple of minutes to get the shot off, but when I did the buck fell on his nose. In that case my single shot for record was a pin-wheel "5."

For woods shooting at running game, the left hand is much

farther forward to control the swing of the rifle and the shooter does not face away from the target so much. In woods hunting the accent is on speed, rather than accuracy, since the target is large, usually not far away, and very often moving.

TRIGGER CONTROL

When good positions are learned and become natural, the next step is to control the trigger and call the shot. No man ever learns to become a good rifleshot unless he develops his co-ordination to the point where he can let his shot off at the exact instant he wishes. This is as true of shooting running game as it is on the target range. The best trigger is one with a light, crisp pull. It can be a double-stage military pull or a single-stage sporting pull, *but it must be crisp*. If the last stage is draggy, rough, and creepy, no one can use it. A heavy crisp pull is far superior to a light creepy pull.

When a good shot learns his pull, he takes up by his sensitive sense of touch all but a couple of ounces of the pull; then when his sights are correctly aligned, he squeezes off those last few ounces. The final stage of the pull should always be thought of as the most gentle of squeezes, even though the squeeze is a rapid one at a charging grizzly. If the motion that lets the trigger off is anything but a gentle squeeze, it will disturb the aim and the shot will not go where it is supposed to.

The difference between the good shot and the fair shot is that the good shot gets his bullet on the way when he wants it to go, and the fair shot gets his off *about* when he wants it. This getting the shot off at the precise instant takes a lot of practice and the good shot who isn't shooting up to par has let his co-ordination fall down. This is why offhand shooting is such fine practice. You either have to control that trigger—or else!

No one can ever be a good shot unless he can *call his shot*. He should be able to say where his sights are aligned when the rifle

[287]

goes off. Particularly in the offhand position it is impossible to get the shots off exactly at the right instant every time. In the interval between the time the brain says to let off and when the laggard muscles actually do so, the rifle has moved a bit, from a pinwheel "5" to a "4" at two o'clock let us say. But the shooter should know it. If he calls a "5" and gets the "4" he is getting nowhere.

Shots on game should be called just as carefully. The first moose I ever shot was in very heavy timber along the bank of a little creek up in the Alberta Rockies. I was still hunting and was within thirty-five yards of the moose when it got up. It ran quartering away, and when the rifle went off, the cross-hairs in the scope were against the curve of the abdomen, so that the bullet should have driven up into the lungs.

But away went the moose, giving absolutely no sign of being hit. I thought it over. I just couldn't see how I could have missed the bull. I took up his track. He had gone down in a patch of willow not more than fifty yards from where he had been struck by the bullet. My shot was right where I had called it—which wasn't much of a feat at that, since a moose is a very large target. Many times the fact that I always call shots has paid off in big-game hunting.

Always know how the sights are aligned when the rifle goes off, and you are on your way to becoming a good shot!

Getting enough practice with the rifle isn't easy for the average city dweller. If possible he should belong to a rifle club so he can have range facilities at his disposal and be able to shoot for a half-day every week or two. If he cannot get anything better, an indoor range for three-positional .22 shooting helps enormously. He should not confine himself to the prone position alone, as so many small-bore enthusiasts do, but should shoot offhand and sitting as much as possible.

Handgun shooting is beautifully adapted to training for rifle shooting as the very smoothest trigger pull is even more vital with the handgun than with the rifle. To some extent training acquired at skeet and trap shooting is also transferable. Those games teach one to swing and to shoot fast, both skills applicable to running game.

If nothing better is available, "dry shooting" at miniature targets or silhouettes of game in one's own living-room is helpful and far better than nothing. The man who religiously squeezes off and calls ten shots a day with an empty rifle is going to be surprisingly good if he can also have a little practice with live ammunition between times.

From the patio of my home I can see a chimney with a dark brick. Every day I take a rifle out and get off ten dry shots from the sitting position at this brick and as many offhand. The neighbors think I'm slightly nuts, but it keeps the trigger finger limbered up!

CHAPTER XXII

The Rifle on Game

LIKE anything else, shooting big game well is easy if a man is good at it—difficult if he is not. Actually, however, it is usually easier to become a passable big-game shot than it is to become a passable shotgun shot. The difficult shot at big game is the exception. Most shots are relatively easy if the excitement, glamour, buck fever, and so forth are stripped from them. Big game offers a relatively large mark. Although the whitetail deer is a small animal as big game goes, it really is pretty large when compared with a prairie dog or even a woodchuck. It is incredible that every year thousands of hunters miss standing shots at whitetail deer within one hundred yards. Even the running shots that are so often obtained at whitetail deer are not very difficult if the hunter keeps his head and reacts quickly and coolly. A moose at close range in the timber, even though he is trotting and partly obscured by brush, is almost as difficult to miss as the side of a house if a man keeps cool. The moose will measure around three feet from the top of his shoulder to the bottom of his brisket. That is quite a target to shoot at from a few yards! An elk in the timber offers a mark that, although not so large, is comparable.

For the most part, the shooting in the Rocky Mountain region is not very difficult. Of the game that I have killed in the Rockies the great majority have come through easy shots. The animals have been standing or moving slowly at no great distance.

In plains shooting at antelope it is often necessary to take long shots at from 250 to 400 yards. These are not too easy, but they are not too difficult either, for a man who has had plenty of practice and who knows his rifle. Even the long cross-canyon shots in the West at mule deer, whitetail deer, and sheep can be mastered.

What causes so much game to be missed is primarily buck fever. Most men will deny that they ever have it. They think it is something discreditable. As a matter of fact, I think almost all hunters suffer from it to some extent. Buck fever is simply another word for excitement, and the man who gets no excitement out of big-game hunting really does not care much about it. At its mildest, a bit of buck fever only adds spice to the hunt. At its worst, it makes the hunter a slavering idiot who couldn't hit the side of a house at thirty yards. Men have often at the sight of fine bucks been unable to pull the triggers of their rifles. They have shaken so violently that they could not keep their shots in a ten-foot circle at fifty yards. Some have pumped every cartridge, unfired, from their weapons and then have wondered why the deer didn't drop. Basically buck fever is caused by a combination of overeagerness and lack of self-confidence. The only thing that will cure overeagerness and reduce it simply to *eagerness* is a lot of experience. The man who has never killed a fine buck would almost give his right leg to get one. When the opportunity offers itself, particularly if it is unexpected, this tyro is apt to lose control of himself. This is particularly so if he hasn't much confidence in himself as a shot. He is in a frame of mind to get an uncontrollable attack of buck fever.

I have had buck fever many times myself. Years ago I used to have it badly. Now I have it only slightly. Sometimes I do not have it at all. Sad to say, on the occasions when I do not have just a little bit of buck fever I do not have much fun.

The best way for the hunter to go about curing or reducing it to reasonable limits is to gain the utmost confidence in his capabilities as a competent rifleshot. He can do that in only one way—by practice. He can know absolutely that his rifle is sighted in correctly. He can also know that when he places the front sight or the reticule of the scope against an animal, that means curtains for the animal. Practice enables him to become a good shot and also make his movements automatic so that even when he is excited he is still a good shot—a good shot because his muscles and his subconscious mind are trained. Training and practice are the only things that make a good shot. Some people who are superlatively gifted in eyesight and muscular co-ordination can become good shots with less practice and less experience, but no one can become a good shot without practice.

In times of strong excitement, training and habit take over without the conscious mind having much to do with it. I use both bolt-action and lever-action rifles. I use several different kinds of safeties. In an emergency, however, my subconscious mind practically always takes over and I never have to think what sort of an action or safety I am using. Practice, then, is the whole key of success in successful big-game hunting.

As I have said, the typical shot at a whitetail deer, although it may seem exceedingly difficult to the beginner, is really not too tough. The whitetail is usually shot at short range. Sometimes the hunter is on a stand. He is motionless and the buck does not see him. Probably the hunter hears a noise or catches a movement and the buck walks out at seventy-five yards or less and stops. Such a buck is really a sitting duck in spite of the fact that thousands of such shots are missed every year. There is nothing for the hunter to do except to line the sights up on the chest area and squeeze the trigger. Such easy shots are missed because the hunter gets the shakes; he flounces around in trying to get into action, makes a lot of noise, and frightens the deer. Hunters also miss those shots because, even though they are not conscious of it, they will give a big quick flinch, jerk the trigger, and throw the bullet over the buck's back. Under such circumstances the cure is to pause an instant to be sure the sights are dead on, then squeeze the trigger. Let us say, however, that in your particular case we are still hunting hunting. We steal quietly along through the woods, endeavoring to rustle no leaves, to break no twigs. We are hunting upwind, straining our eyes to catch glimpses of the gray body of a buck before the buck sees us. Suddenly just on the other side of a windfall there is a terrific clatter as a buck that has been bedded there leaps to his feet and starts quartering away at a dead run, his big white flag up and his antlers looking as though you could hang the family wash on them.

Under such circumstances the beginning hunter jumps about a foot; his heart contracts for an instant, then pounds madly. His breath catches in his throat. It seems to him that that buck is moving with incredible speed, that he cannot possibly raise the rifle to his shoulder and get off a shot before the buck disappears in the timber. Wildly he throws his rifle to his shoulder. He does not see the sights. He can see nothing but the buck. With his rifle only pointed in the general direction, he yanks the trigger and the bellow of a rifle disturbs the quiet of the woods. The buck vanishes. The woods are silent. The hunter stands, with his heart racing and his mouth open, half wondering if this has all been an illusion. That night the hunter goes back to camp.

"Did you see anything?" his companions ask.

"Yes, I saw a buck with a head like a rocking-chair. I bet he didn't go up thirty yards away, but all I got was a snap shot at him and I missed. I looked all over after he ran off to see if I could find hair or blood, but I never touched him."

Snap Shooting

One of the first things the woods hunter must get out of his head is that there is a mysterious thing called "snap shooting"— some magic by which the hunter "instinctively" points his rifle in the general direction of the game, touches her off, and gets the bacon. Every year thousands of bucks live another season and grow another set of antlers because excited hunters point their weapons at them, shoot, and miss.

The beginning woods hunter feels terribly pressed for time. The big buck that is really moving at a rate of fifteen miles an hour or so seems to be going like lightning. The hunter is afraid he will disappear before he can get him. He points his rifle with a wild lunge, yanks the trigger, and that's that. A deer may be a large animal, but the atmosphere surrounding it is even larger!

No weapon can be shot accurately unless the sights are correctly aligned and the shot is called.

Now let us take a good whitetail shot. He has been slipping quietly along upwind in good bedding country and he is convinced he is going to get a shot. He is carrying his rifle as a quail hunter carries a shotgun at ready. Then suddenly, off thirty-five yards or so to his left, he hears a crash, whirls, and sees a big buck with a shining brown crown of antlers going out of there, head back, white tail up. His rifle comes up smoothly. His cheek is at the comb and his eye is on the sights. The swinging front sight follows along the buck's gray body for an instant, and as the hunter squeezes the trigger, he notes that the gold bead is bright and sharp against the bounding buck's shoulder. As the rifle recoils, he sees the buck turn a somersault. The bullet has struck a few inches back of the shoulder in the lungs and the buck never knew what hit him.

Our hunter has shot rapidly but smoothly. He has taken his time because in actuality he has had plenty of time. The interval of time was not much, but it was plenty and the old and skillful hunter has known that.

The good game shot takes his time, but he has taught himself that he must shoot the exact instant his sights are first aligned correctly. The target shot who has never gone in for rapid fire can dawdle, check, and recheck; but the man who shoots running game has to learn to shoot right but *fast*. Press that trigger the instant those sights are on! *But know they are on.*

[294]

Shoot fast and *call the shot*. The whitetail hunter should never just shoot at the whole deer, but at some particular part. Have the bead or scope reticule right on the point of the shoulder, just behind the shoulder, on the neck, but *somewhere*. For whatever reason, shooting at the whole deer is something like shooting at a flock of ducks. Shoot at a particular duck in a flock and you'll usually get the duck and maybe another or two. Shoot at the flock and you'll hit nothing. So it is with deer shooting.

For training for fast, relatively accurate brush shooting I have a stunt that may be worth imitating. On the range at the local rifle club are a series of boulders about a foot in diameter at 150, 100, 75, 50, and 25 yards. I get fast offhand practice by shooting at the farthest stone and working up to the nearest or starting at the nearest and working back to the farthest, keeping the butt at the shoulder and firing every shot the instant the sights are on. The man who goes through that routine once a week is not going to be a bad game shot when the deer season rolls around.

Most brush and forest shooting requires quickness, coolness, and only fair accuracy. The man who can keep all his shots in a one-foot circle at fifty yards but who can shoot quickly is going to be a deadly whitetail hunter under most conditions, and also a deadly hunter of any game that is jumped and shot in the woods under those conditions—elk, moose, bear, or even woodland caribou.

Most running deer in the woods are missed by overshooting. The first reason for this phenomenon is that most hunters cling to the obsolete open sight. Many use the Rocky Mountain buckhorn with its narrow *V* and its big ears. The light at the bottom of the *V* is dim, and under the stress of excitement the hunter does not draw his front bead down fine. He shoots and the bullet flies high. In poor light this is almost impossible to avoid with a sight having a deep cut for a *U* or *V* notch. The best open sight for deer hunting is the very shallow *U* or *V* as seen on the British double rifles.

With a peep sight with a large aperture it is much easier to avoid overshooting, but with any sight it is to be guarded against because the deer is seen most plainly at the top of his bound, and that is when the temptation is to shoot. Under those circumstances one should hold a bit low because one is aiming at a falling deer.

Another factor, particularly on going-away shots, is that the white tail is so conspicuous. The hunter shoots at the tail, believe it or not, and misses. I have done it myself. I remember taking a shot at a big whitetail buck that jumped about forty yards away. Off he went, leaving only a half-dozen white hairs floating in the breeze. I had unconsciously shot at his tail. I had hit it, but a lot of good it did me!

Shooting running game in more open country and at longer ranges requires another sort of skill—to me, anyway, a skill that is the very apex of marksmanship. Now and then the hunter of Eastern whitetail will get a running shot across a field at from 100 to 300 yards, but such shots are the exception. In the open country in the West, country where the long shot at moving game across canyons is the rule rather than the exception, these running shots are very common. They are seen at their most difficult, possibly, when antelope hunting in the plains of Wyoming, New Mexico, and other states that hunt that fleet plains-dwelling animal. In the high Canadian Rockies, where most hunting is above timber line, the hunter must occasionally make a long running shot at all animals—caribou, sheep, and even moose and grizzly.

The best practice for such shooting is hunting jackrabbits and coyotes. In the woods, where ranges are short, not much lead is necessary, but the hunter of plains and mountain game soon learns that if he is going to hunt running game he must lead—even with the highest-velocity rifle. Take a shot at a scared jackrabbit running broadside even with a .220 Swift, hold right on, and you'll miss every time. Running game must be laid with a swinging rifle.

For running shooting at the longer ranges a good scope has it all over any iron sight ever invented, because with one the hunter can see so much better and estimate his lead more exactly. The two best reticules I have ever found for this sort of work are the medium cross-hair and the Lee dot subtending (covering) 4 inches at 100 yards in the 2½-power scope or 2½ inches in the 4-power scope. With these one gets a good unobstructed view above, below, and on all sides of the target, and with them it is easy to maintain a constant elevation. For this work I do not like the post reticule and have a tendency to overshoot with it.

Let us suppose that the game is running broadside. I like to start behind the game, swing the horizontal cross-hair evenly along the animal, then touch off the shot when the vertical hair is the correct distance ahead. The faster the rifle is swung, the less the lead necessary. This is true with rifle shooting just as it is with shotgun shooting. As in shooting at woods game, this type of "fast swing" demands that the hunter be *fast*, that he touch off his shot the instant the vertical hair or wire is the correct distance ahead.

As in any kind of sport, practice makes perfect. No one can

Two methods of shooting running game, as illustrated by an antelope running broadside at about 150 yards. The first method (A) is the fast swing. The sights are started behind, then swung ahead for the proper lead. The shot is taken with the rifle still moving.

The second method (B) is the sustained lead. The sights are held the proper distance ahead and kept there, the sights moving apparently as fast as the antelope.

[297]

learn this type of shooting on big game alone. A running deer target at the range is better than nothing, but the best target of all is the running jackrabbit. Some years ago, when jacks were plentiful on the arid ranges around my Arizona home, I shot once a week for about two years straight, killing from five to thirty jacks a day with everything from a .22 Varminter to a .30/06. I missed a lot of jacks, but I also killed plenty, many of them at ranges that were astonishing. One day when I was as hot as a pistol I killed three running jacks at about 150 yards with three shots. I'd hate to have to do it again before witnesses, but I did it that day—and with a witness on hand.

The whole thing is to swing the rifle fast but precisely, keep the horizontal hair on the jack, and then, when the vertical hair is the correct distance ahead, touch her off smoothly. As a man practices, his co-ordination speeds up so that he finds himself with plenty of time—so much that even the most difficult shots appear easy. A good shot should not miss a running jack more than a foot up to three hundred yards, and what such a man can do on running deer is really something.

Practice and luck go a long way. Once for four straight years, hunting on a little ranch belonging to friends and on the Mexican border, I shot four bucks all running and all at between two hundred and three hundred yards away. I killed one with my first shot, three with my second. Usually a puff of dust will enable the hunter to correct his lead, and the second shot should do the trick. I have also missed plenty of running bucks, incidentally, but that was when I was in form from jackrabbit shooting.

Another style of running-game shooting, and the one that probably should be adopted by the man with slower reactions, is the sustained lead. In this case the hunter gets the reticule of his scope or the front sight the proper distance ahead of the game, swings along with it, and then pulls the trigger. This type of shooting requires more lead than the fast swing, but it is easier to learn because it gives the man behind the rifle more time. I once knew an old rancher who was adept at it. He would ride along with a running buck until anyone with him wanted to scream, but when he finally shot, it was curtains.

Much running shooting, even in open country, requires little lead. Let us suppose you shoot at a buck climbing out of a canyon. Then it is only necessary to hold high with a stationary rifle and he is your meat, since he will move into the shot. The same is true of a buck climbing out at a slight angle. Hold high and a bit to the side.

LONG-RANGE SHOOTING

About the first thing to be said on the long-range shooting of big game is that much that is written about it and most that passes by word of mouth is unreliable. From long experience I have found that most hunters say that when they have killed a deer at 50 yards they have killed it at 100 yards. When it is shot at 100, they stretch it to 200, and when they actually do kill a deer at 200 yards, the distance grows to anywhere from 300 to 400 yards. The deer shot at an actual 300 yards becomes one of those famous quarter-of-a-mile kills.

I am not belittling long-range shooting, but I am going on record as saying that most game, even in the West, is killed at 200 yards or under. A lot of long-range shooting is wind, of course; but there is also a lot of wind from the boys who insist that the real he-hunter always sneaks up and shoots his game in the eye. Much of this comes from men who couldn't stalk a hungry horse at a hayrick.

For the sake of something to start with, let us call any shot up to 200 yards a short-range shot, anything from 200 to 300 yards a medium-range shot, and anything over 300 yards a long-range shot. Before we go further *let me go on record again* as saying that ninety per cent of *all* big game is killed at 200 yards or under. That goes for the West as well as for the East.

One day, having nothing better to do, I sat down with a pencil and paper and tried to remember the occasion of shooting each of the fourteen mountain rams of various species I have killed. Now, mountain sheep are traditionally shot at long ranges, yet the average shot came out at only a bit over 200 yards. The last Mexican ram I shot, for example, was 35 yards away. The largest Canadian bighorn I ever shot was not 100 yards away.

On the other hand, the occasion arises now and then when the hunter has to knock over a prize trophy at long range or not shoot at all. The whole success or failure of a long and expensive trip may depend on the skill, wisdom, and preparation that go into making a long shot. Up in the Yukon in 1945 I had to take my best Dall ram at about 450 yards and I got him. It wasn't in the cards that time for me to get any closer.

Probably of all the game I have hunted the longest *average* shots I have taken have been at Arizona whitetail deer, which usually have to be shot on the far side of wide canyons—and, more often than not, when they are running. I believe my *average* shot at those little whitetails is about 300 yards. In certain areas mule deer are shot at long range more often than not, and on the open plains antelope are almost always long-range game. Even elk often have to be taken at long range, particularly when the big bulls are above timber line in the early part of the season.

Successful shooting at long range demands that the man behind the rifle learn to squeeze and hold and to assume a steady position. Nothing in the world is more futile and silly than standing on the hind legs and firing a barrage at a disappearing buck a quarter of a mile away. Long-range shooting also demands a good scope on a flat-shooting *accurate* rifle *and* ability to judge range.

In the first place, long-range shooting requires a rifle of high velocity and flat trajectory. I wouldn't take anything less effective than the .30/06 with the 180-grain bullet at 2,700 feet per second. The .300 Magnum with the 180-grain bullet at 2,930 is also good. I have done most of my own long-range shooting with the .270 Winchester with the 130-grain bullet at 3,120 and it has proved a deadly and effective load.

If the hunter can handle a pretty hefty recoil without flinching, one of the .30 Super Magnums—.300 Weatherby, .308 Norma, or .300 Winchester, is very potent medicine for long-range shooting. All give approximately the same trajectory over 400 yards as the .270 W.C.F. with the 130-grain bullet. Sighted in with the 180-grain bullet to strike 3 inches above the point of aim at 100 yards, they are on at somewhere between 270 and 300 yards.

However, as I grow old and cynical and a bit weary of wonders, I am inclined to be skeptical of these long-range terrors. They kick like the devil in a rifle of weight light enough to be carried around comfortably in the mountains, where long shots are the rule. Few people who own them can shoot them as accurately as they would shoot rifles of less recoil. Les Bowman, the famous guide and outfitter of Cody, Wyoming, says he sees more game missed and wounded with rifles of this class than of any other. I am inclined to believe that they belong with the medium-bores, rather than with the high-velocity long-range jobs. However, if a man can handle one (and I have seen plenty who could), they are poison.

Best scope for the long-range open-country rifle is a good 4-power, I am convinced. Nothing is gained by the higher power, for the sacrifice in field in a 6-power is a definite handicap. The 8-power is strictly for varmints. I have used the Weaver K-4 in various versions and have found it satisfactory. I have also used the 4-power Bear Cub made by Redfield, the 4-power Lyman All-American, and the 4-power Leupold Stevens. All are excellent scopes.

For this work I prefer them mounted on a good, solid top mount. Of these my particular pet is the Tilden. It is made of strong steel, and it is the one top mount I have never had any trouble with.

It is best to sight in a long-range rifle for the longest possible range that will not cause mid-range misses. I sight in a .270 with the 130-grain Winchester Silvertip bullet to hit the point of aim at 275 yards. That means that the bullets strike 4 inches high at 150 and 200 yards, 2 inches low at 350, and 8 inches low at 400. With the better shaped but now obsolete Winchester pointed expanding bullet and a special hand load I used to sight in for 300 on the nose. A .270 sighted in as I have described gives a point-blank range with scope of close to 350 yards, and on a deer-sized animal a hold on the backbone will strike in the chest cavity up to 400 yards in a large mule deer, a goat, or a sheep, and even farther in a moose, caribou, or elk.

With the .30/06 and the 180-grain bullet I sight in to hit the point of aim at 225 yards. The bullets strike 3½ inches high at 125 yards, 2 inches low at 250, and about 8 inches low at 300. A backbone hold is good up to about 350 with a large deer.

With the .300 Weatherby Magnum I sight in to hit at the point of aim at 300 with the 180-grain bullet at 3,300 f.p.s. The bullet hits 4 inches high at 200 yards, 8 inches low at 400, and apparently only about 24 inches low at 500. It works out so that at 500 I try to hold enough above the backbone of an animal so that I can see a white line between the bottom of the horizontal cross-hair and the top of the animal's back. A .300 Weatherby is the easiest rifle to hit with at long range I have ever seen and it has enough soup for grizzly or moose 'way out there. For the average man, however, I think the .270 is still the best long-range rifle because of its great accuracy, relatively light recoil, flat trajectory, and high velocity, and the easy availability of factory ammunition.

For most shooting at long range—which means to 350 yards or so—a man with the .270 can forget trajectory, simply hold dead on and hit. The same is true of the .300 Weatherby Magnum. The rifles of the .30/06 or 7-mm. class require sharper figuring. For almost all the Western deer hunting I have done I have simply held dead on with a .270 if the animal was standing or have concentrated on how far I was going to have to lead if the animal was on the move.

Nevertheless, some dope on the judgment of range should be in order. One of the first things to learn to do is to mark the distance off between the gun and the animal by comparing it with known distances. A buck appears to be about four 100-yard units away. Learn what 100 yards looks like. Practice guessing ranges to various objects and then pacing the distance off as a check.

Another helpful device is the range-finding reticule. The Lee dot in a 2½-X scope should subtend 4 inches per 100 yards of range. Knowing this, the hunter can compare the size of the dot with the size of the animal from back to brisket and arrive at an approximation. If it checks pretty well against the estimate arrived at from units of 100 yards, it cannot be too far wrong.

The W. R. Weaver Company, of El Paso, Texas, is furnishing a range-finding reticule with their better scopes now. There are two cross-hairs—the upper of medium width, the lower fine. They are separated by a space that covers 6 minutes of angle.

When the hunter has a good notion as to the depth of an animal's body and can compare it with the reticule, he has a pretty fair notion of the range. Here are some approximate figures, back to brisket:

Small whitetail deer	14–15 inches
Medium-size deer	17–18 inches
Large mule deer, sheep	20–22 inches
Goat	22–24 inches
Elk, caribou	24–26 inches
Moose	30–36 inches

Now let's see how this works. When I was hunting for antelope between Lander and Rawlins in Wyoming in 1944, my guide and I spotted a bunch that included several bucks the instant we poked our heads over a little rise. The guide said the herd was 500 yards away. I did not think so, and I found that I could see hair both above and below the 4-minute Lee dot I was using in the 2½-power scope on my .270. Assuming that the antelope measured 15 or 16 inches from back to brisket, that meant that, instead of being 500 yards away, the antelope was probably about 300 yards away, because at that distance the dot would cover about 12 inches. I held dead on and killed the antelope.

The Lee dot here covers 4 in. per 100 yards of range and shows the antelope to be around 350 yards away.

Once when I was hunting elk in Wyoming, the finest bull I had seen in a ten-day hunt was in an open basin a long way off. There was no cover and I decided it would be better to take a long shot at a standing elk than attempt to get a bit closer and risk a running shot.

First I tried to divide the distance off in units of 100 yards. The elk appeared to be about 600 yards away. Then I put the 4-minute dot against him and found that it just about exactly covered him from the top of the shoulder to the bottom of the brisket. That too checked out as around 600 yards. At that distance the bullet would drop about four feet, since the rifle was sighted to hit the point of aim at 300 yards with the 130-grain bullet, the bullet to strike at 300 yards where the middle of the dot rested.

I found two boulders, one that would do for a seat, and the other for a rest. I sat down on the lower boulder, put my down jacket on the larger boulder, and rested my rifle on it. This made an improvised bench rest, which gave me a very steady hold.

Then I held the width of the dot over the bull's back, deciding that if I had guessed right the bullet would strike within the chest cavity. The bull was lying down when I shot. He lurched to his feet and stood there. As I fired my second shot, the guide, who had been watching with glasses, saw dust fly right behind the bull's shoulder. A moment later he fell over on his side. Both shots had been hits.

The man who shoots at long range should not scorn a rest. Using a coat, a jacket, even a hat, to keep the shot from flying high, he can take a rest on a log, a stone—anything. Hunting antelope and shooting at long range in Wyoming, I have put a down jacket over scrubby sagebrush, and the result is a fine, steady rest.

If something of the sort is not available, one should shoot prone with a sling if the terrain permits it. Sitting is not bad for the long shot, and I have made most of my own shots at from 200 to 300 yards sitting.

No one should take a long shot if he has a good chance to get closer, however, and no one should take a long shot unless he is using a powerful rifle *that he has learned to shoot!*

CHAPTER XXIII

Killing Power and the Placement
of Shots

IN ALL the lore of the rifle no single subject is more calculated to start an argument than killing power. Practically everyone who has ever shot so much as one deer has decided opinions on the subject and will defend them almost with his life. One man, let us say, swears that he can kill a grizzly with one shot at 800 yards with a .30/30, and the next declares that a .30/30 cannot be counted on to knock over a whitetail deer in its tracks with a neck shot at fifty feet. One hunter of experience will swear by lightweight high-speed bullets, the next by heavy bullets at moderate velocity. One man may kill everything on the continent with a .30/30, the next may feel that he is undergunned with a .30/06.

One thing that can be said for certain is that, in the study of the subject, individual instances do not amount to much, and no conclusion based on a few examples is worth anything. Species vary in vitality. Individual animals vary. Conditions under which the animal is shot vary. The animal may be close and receive the bullet when it is traveling at maximum velocity. It may be a long way off and be struck by a bullet that has lost most of its velocity. An organ may be full or empty when struck. The bullet may be partially opened by striking leaves or twigs. Any hunter of wide experience will see things that apparently contradict all his previous experience.

My own conclusions are based on a good deal of hunting experience from Mexico to Alaska, on a wide variety of game, ranging from little southern Arizona and Mexican javelinas weighing about thirty to forty pounds dressed to moose weighing more than a thousand. It includes herbivorous animals and predators, game shot at close range in the brush and at long range in the mountains. More important than my own experience, however, is the fact that I receive many hundreds of accounts of kills every year from all sorts of other hunters. From them I believe I can get a pretty good picture.

Animals are killed by two means. The first is by having the life processes interfered with. The second is by one of the varieties of shock. If shots are placed in vital areas like the brain, the forward portion of the spine, or the heart, large animals may be killed with small-caliber rifles. Pot-hunters often lie in wait around water holes and salt licks and kill deer at a distance of a few yards with head and spine shots with .22 rifles. If a bullet strikes the brain, or the spine forward of the shoulders, death is instantaneous, *no matter how small the bullet.* Death will also come quickly, but usually not instantaneously, from a heart shot. When the heart is injured and stops functioning, the brain begins to die from lack of oxygen and the animal perishes.

A curious thing about heart shots is that they seldom result in *instant* death. Actually, in my experience, a shot *near* the heart will kill quicker than one through the heart itself. Many times I have seen animals shot squarely through the heart make one last wild run of maybe fifty yards—or a hundred. Once I saw an antelope shot through the heart run close to a quarter of a mile. Typically, the animal shot through the heart runs wildly off, then falls kicking and dies. The heart shot is no good when the hunter wants to stop a dangerous animal quickly, but more of that later.

In Africa the resident Europeans often hunt elephants with light rifles like the .303 British and the 7-mm. Mauser, but they work in close to their game and carefully place their shots in the brain by aiming between the eye and the orifice of the ear. An elephant so shot is just as dead as if he had been hit with a bullet from a .465 or .470.

The shot through the heart, brain, or upper spine is deadly, then, with practically any sort of bullet just so it penetrates deep enough and does the damage.

Animals are also killed by surgical shock. When a high enough proportion of tissue is destroyed on an animal, it will perish no matter where the tissue is located. A jackrabbit or a woodchuck with his abdomen blown away will be instantly killed, even though this tissue is located a long way from the vital area. Often an animal the size of a deer or antelope is instantly killed with a paunch shot from a powerful high velocity rifle if enough tissue is destroyed. The messages from the damaged nerves so overload the brain that the animal dies.

The first buck I ever shot with the .270 (and surely one of the first deer ever killed in the Southwest with a rifle of that caliber) was running at about 250 yards. I didn't lead him enough and the bullet struck him in the paunch with a tremendous thump. He went down, struggled convulsively for a moment to get to his feet, then fell over dead. His stomach had exploded like a bag of water and his intestines were all messed up. But no area ordinarily thought of as vital had been hit at all. What had killed that buck was *shock*.

Shock is also probably transmitted to the brain by the blood vessels in the form of hydraulic transmitted shock, which works in exactly the same manner as the hydraulic brakes of an automobile. The sudden violent, pressure applied by the striking bullet is transmitted through the veins and arteries right to the brain. The sudden blow kills the animal. Surgical shock is in direct proportion to the amount of destroyed tissue. Hydraulic transmitted shock depends surely on the number of blood vessels involved and the violence of the transmitted pressure.

Tissue destruction and the consequent surgical shock depend on several factors: the weight of the bullet, its caliber, the velocity at which it is traveling when the animal is struck, the amount of penetration, the violence with which the bullet expands, and the character of the tissue struck. If all other factors are equal, the heavier the bullet, the more destructive it is. The greater the diameter, the more destructive the bullet; and the higher the velocity, the more the destruction. Bullets striking muscle that has little moisture will be less destructive than the same bullet striking a moisture-filled area like the paunch.

Yet let me repeat again that often one sees incidents that seem to contradict. Once in Mexico I had to take a fast shot at a big desert ram just about to disappear over a ridge and at a distance of not more than fifty yards. The 139-grain open-point 7-mm. bullet hit him in the rump and blew up so fast that I was conscious of a great red wound blooming like a flower against the ram's dun-white rump as I pressed the trigger. The ram got over the ridge, fell and rolled a couple of hundred feet, and was dead from shock when I got to him. The bullet had not penetrated more than three or four inches at the deepest.

In Alberta I stalked a Canadian bighorn to within about 75 or 100 yards. The 130-grain .270 bullet blew up in his rump, and the animal got up and ran off on three legs until a shot through the lungs stopped him. The same hit, but two different reactions.

It is absolutely necessary that the bullet get *inside* the animal, but once it is in the vital area, the more rapidly it sheds its energy, the more violently it transmits surgical and hydraulic shock. For some time I used a thin-jacketed .270 bullet made by Fred Barnes and loaded to 3,200 f.p.s. in the .270. With these loads I killed about fifteen deer and antelope and every one of the animals was dead instantly from hits anywhere in the body cavity. Those bullets went to pieces so quickly and thoroughly that I could never find more than a few bullet fragments. In no case did a single particle of the bullet come through on the far side. Once inside the animal, the bullets exploded like bombs, hurling fragments in every direction. In almost every case a hit in the lungs meant that there would be a fragment through the animal's heart.

On the other hand, the Winchester pointed expanding bullet does not open up so quickly and does not give so high a percentage of instantaneous kills. The Silvertip opens still more slowly and gives still fewer spectacular kills. The Remington Corelokt opens still more slowly and almost never kills a deer in its tracks.

The faster the bullet opens and the more violently it goes to pieces once it is inside the animal, the quicker the kill. A full metal-cased bullet that drives straight through an animal, leaving a pencil-sized hole, will not kill at all unless heart, spine, or brain is struck. *Yet that bullet will have the same velocity, the same energy, and the same weight as a corresponding expanding bullet.*

A .257 with a rapidly expanding bullet weighing 100 grains will kill a small deer or antelope in its tracks with a lung shot. One make of bullet that I used in that weight and caliber opened so slowly that I had to chase down and finish off five deer shot with it. I changed bullets, and instead of being a crippler the .257 became a deadly rifle.

No one can count on side shots exclusively, however, and the bullet should be to some extent a compromise. It should hold together well enough to break shoulders on light and medium-sized animals, get into the vitals and to reach up into them with a rear-end shot, yet at the same time expand well to deliver shock.

Killing power can be increased, then, by increasing the bullet weight, by increasing the velocity, and by perfecting the expansion of the bullet.

From my own experience on all North American big game with the exception of the Alaska brown bear, I am inclined to believe that the most important factor in killing power is velocity, just so long as the bullet is heavily constructed enough to get into the vitals. The .22 Long Rifle bullet weighs 40 grains and leaves the muzzle at 1,375 f.p.s. The muzzle energy is 168 foot-pounds. The .220 Swift bullet weighs only 48 grains, or slightly more than the .22 rim-fire bullet. The .22 Long Rifle isn't even a very good jackrabbit cartridge, while the Swift has killed elk and moose in their tracks. What makes the difference? The Swift's terrible velocity of 4,140 f.p.s.! As long as it retains that velocity it is a killer. When it falls off to .22 Long Rifle speed, it is no more deadly than the .22 rim-fire.

In my experience on soft-skinned American game, the 130-grain .270 bullet at 3,140 is a quicker killer than the 150-grain .270 bullet at 2,770; the 180-grain .30/06 bullet at 2,700 a quicker killer than the 220-grain bullet at 2,450; the 139-grain 7-mm. bullet at 2,850 better than the 175-grain bullet at 2,300. Why? *Velocity!*

There seems to be a critical velocity at which a bullet must strike before the devastating effects of shock are noted. That is apparently around 2,500 feet per second. This would mean that with the 130-grain bullet in the .270 the effect would be noted to between 250 and 300 yards depending on the shape of the bullet, with the 180-grain .30/06 bullet to within 100 to 150 yards. Adding 100 foot-seconds retained velocity out at 200 yards is enormously important.

All things being equal, the larger the animal, the harder it is to kill because the smaller the proportion of tissue a given bullet can disrupt and destroy. A deer is harder to kill than a coyote, and an elk is harder to kill than a deer. Likewise, because it is larger, a moose is harder to kill than an elk.

A black bear is, in my experience, no harder to kill than a deer of equal weight. The grizzly is harder to kill than the black because he is larger, and the brown bear, they tell me, is still harder to kill.

I have killed six moose and never one with one shot, in spite of the fact that most of the moose I have shot have been hit with the first shot right in the lung-heart area. If they had been deer or sheep they would not have moved out of their tracks. A .270 or .30/06 cannot be depended on to make one-shot kills on moose with lung shots. Possibly a .375 Magnum with the 300-grain bullet at 2,540 would do the trick—or a 180-grain .30-caliber bullet speeded up in the .300 Weatherby Magnum to 3,300 f.p.s.

When animals get so large, they simply cannot be killed by shock alone because no man alive can carry and shoot a rifle heavy enough. With his ponderous .465, .470, and even .600 double rifles the elephant hunter can only hope to slow down and maybe halt one of those big beasts with a poorly placed shot. He kills his elephants with well-placed shots in the heart, lungs, or brain. Nothing short of a 75-mm. cannon could destroy enough tissue on an elephant to kill it as a .220 Swift will kill a jackrabbit or a woodchuck with just any solid hit.

Some species of animals are are more susceptible to shock and more easily killed than others. I have found bobcats and mountain lions quite easy to kill for their size, with a bobcat hardly more difficult than a jackrabbit. On the other hand, the Rocky Mountain goat is a very difficult animal to kill, and most hunters swear the goat is harder to kill with one shot than a larger elk or moose.

An unfrightened animal is easier to kill than one that is angry and fearful. A fleeing animal that has been frightened from a superficial wound sometimes has to be shot almost to pieces before it is brought down.

No matter how powerful the cartridge is, it is essential that the shots be as well placed as possible. A deer hit through the lungs near the heart with a .25/35 will ordinarily be brought to death quicker than a deer hit in the guts or the hams with a much more powerful .30/06. A deer hit in the brain with a .22 will be a dead deer, but a deer that has its leg broken by a .375 Magnum will get away. The placement of shots is very important, but in many cases proper placement is very difficult. Hunting whitetail deer in heavy woods and forest where a high percentage of the time the deer is shot on the run makes necessary a relatively powerful rifle that will disable with any solid body hit because placement of shots is so difficult. Very often a whitetail deer is running

Vital points on deer: (A) *Heart area,* (B) *Lung area,* **(C)** *Spine,* (D) *Shoulder for crippling shot.*

away from the hunter. Only the rump and the bobbing white fan will be presented for the shot. No poorer place to hit a deer can be imagined, yet a high proportion of all whitetail deer killed are hit in the rear end and broken down. It is for that reason that people who say such a rifle as the .25/35 is entirely adequate for deer under all conditions give me a pain. The .25/35 in the hands of a calm, unhurried hunter who will place his shot carefully in the lung cavity is an entirely adequate deer rifle. The .25/35 in the hands of the ordinary hunter who is excited and overeager and who shoots the minute he sees horns, no matter how the deer is facing, is not an adequate deer rifle. Under most deer-hunting conditions a man is lucky to hit a deer hard anywhere, and far more deer are missed than are hit at all. In all brush shooting, then, shots are usually hard to place, and under modern deer-hunting conditions where the woods are full of hunters and the deer are wild, the best marksman in the world cannot be sure of placing his shots. I am not one to decry the correct placement of shots. I am simply saying that in many instances good placement is so difficult as to be impossible, and the only way a hunter can make up for his poor placement of shots is to use a rifle powerful enough to disable a deer even with shots in the rump or in the abdomen.

One thing that most big-game hunters have noticed is that if an animal is hit in a non-vital area and wounded, he is much more difficult to kill with subsequent shots. The wound makes the animal angry and frightened. His ductless glands pump adrenalin through his system. He becomes wild with fright and rage and much more difficult to kill than if he had been hit well the first shot in a vital area. Under those conditions the amount of lead an animal can carry is amazing.

Once in southern Arizona when I was hunting whitetail deer, I heard three shots from over the ridge and presently a hunter appeared and asked my wife and me to help him track a wounded buck. I found a little blood, which appeared to be from an abdominal wound. I tracked the buck and decided it was in a canyon below us. I told my wife and the hunter to get ready. Presently the buck came out running up the opposite hill slope. Before that buck went down, it had been hit twelve times with a .348 Winchester, a .30/06, and a .257. There was hardly a bit of edible meat left on it. The animal had absorbed enough lead to kill half a dozen grizzlies, yet it did not go down until a shot from my .30/06 broke its spinal column. The trouble was that most of those shots were in non-vital areas, and the first shot that had wounded it had gone through the fleshy part of the ham and into the abdominal cavity.

Assuming that one gets a broadside shot at not dangerous game, the best place to aim at is right behind the forelegs about one third of the way up from the brisket. This is where I almost always try to drive a shot. A bullet so placed has a good deal of leeway. If it flies forward it will break the shoulders. It can fly high and still rupture the lungs. Ordinarily I do not try to hit the heart, as an animal shot near the heart in the lung cavity is much more likely to be killed instantaneously than an animal shot right through the heart itself. Many times I have seen animals shot directly through the heart run off madly for from fifty to one hundred yards and then fall down dead. A shot in the heart-lung area, then, with any fairly powerful rifle will almost always result in a quick kill. The animal may run a little way if the cartridge is on the light side, but the lung cavity will fill with blood and the animal will quickly drown in its own blood. With a powerful rifle driving a high-velocity bullet the shock of the bullet striking near the heart will almost always stop it and result in instantaneous death. This heart-lung area is large and relatively easy to hit, and a shot there results in quick death.

A shot back of the diaphragm in the abdominal cavity should be avoided if it is at all possible to do so. In the first place, an animal hit there is a miserable thing to dress. The area is non-vital. Struck in the abdomen with a high-velocity bullet, animals are often killed in their tracks. Very often they will go down, but if they are not killed the shock will wear off and then, as any experienced hunter knows, a gut-shot animal can run all day to escape and die a lingering and painful death. As a matter of fact, I once saw a bighorn ram that was shot with a .300 Savage in Mexico lose almost the entire contents of the abdominal area and still run several hundred yards.

If an animal is too large and too tough to be killed quickly with a shot in the heart-lung area, the hunter should aim high on the shoulders to break the shoulders and destroy the power of locomotion. Then the animal can be finished with a second shot in the head or neck. Most experienced moose hunters try to hit the shoulders of a moose and break it down because experience has taught them that with ordinary powerful rifles a moose will almost always run off with a heart-lung shot, and then it becomes necessary to track him.

This same shoulder shot is almost a must for dangerous game.

[315]

If an animal's power of locomotion is destroyed he ceases to be dangerous. Hence old grizzly hunters try with their first shot to break a shoulder. Then when the bear leaps he will fall to the side of the broken shoulder. When a bear or a lion charges and the charge must be instantly diverted, the cool deadly shots try to break the shoulder, particularly on the downhill side.

Ordinarily I cannot agree with the feasibility of shooting at the neck of an animal. The spinal column is small and difficult to hit, and if the bullet misses, a shot in the neck is no more deadly than a shot in any other muscular area—the rump, for instance. I have seen deer run miles when shot in the neck and the vertebræ missed. I saw a caribou shot in the neck run for a considerable distance bleeding from a severed artery. It ran until so much blood was pumped from its system that it died.

For North American game I think there is but little use for a brain shot. In the first place, if a man is a trophy hunter the head and antlers would be destroyed, and even in a bear the skull is ordinarily needed in mounting. In the second place, the brain area is small, and again it is difficult to hit. If I should get in a jam at close range with a grizzly and want to stop it instantly, I would not hesitate to shoot for the brain if I thought I could hit it. Otherwise I would far rather place a shot somewhere else.

In woods hunting at running animals it is ordinarily exceedingly difficult to place shots exactly. On stalked game where the animals have not seen the hunter and are standing unfrightened, the placement of shots is ordinarily quite easy, and a really good shot should be able to drive the bullet into a vital area with little trouble even at fairly long range. Under those ideal conditions the hunter should take every care to make his first shot a deadly one. Many times I have shot from the prone position with a sling, particularly above timber line in the Rockies. On other occasions I have used a rest by padding a rock with a down jacket or even a hat so the gun would be held absolutely steady. If the animal is not broadside, then aim should be taken so the bullet will drive up into the heart-lung area. The first shot is the important one. If it goes into a vital area the animal will either be killed instantly or knocked down and disabled so that a second shot will finish it off. If the animal is only wounded and goes off frightened, it may well be lost.

The Care of the Rifle

A RIFLE that is well taken care of will give perfect satisfaction for many years. One that is poorly taken care of can be ruined in one season. Actually, taking proper care of a rifle is simplicity itself, yet many fine weapons are ruined through neglect and some are ruined through loving but ill-advised care.

Before the invention of non-corrosive priming, thousands of rifle barrels rusted out annually. Too few people knew how to care for a rifle barrel and many of those who did know would not bother. Today there is no excuse for allowing a barrel to rust out. With a few minutes' care at the end of every day that the rifle has been used, the weapon should last indefinitely.

Now let's take a look to see what should be done when a rifle has been used in the field. Probably the first thing to do is to run a clean patch through the bore. With the bolt-action rifle one should remove the bolt to give access to the bore from the breech. Then one should saturate a cut flannel patch of proper size, put it on a cleaning rod, and push it slowly through the bore. When the patch emerges from the other end, it should be thrown away, as it has carried with it dirt and grit. That cleaning will suffice if the rifle is to be used again within a few days. Most people, however, run another patch through the bore, also saturated with some good powder solvent or oil. If the rifle is to be left for a week or more, an additional patch on which is some oil of good body or some gun grease is used. Rig, a preparation for sale in most sporting-goods stores, will protect the bore for a long time. It is a light neutral grease that seals the moisture off from the steel. Another satisfactory rust-preventive is an oil called Sheath, which leaves a tough protective film over the steel and seals off the air and moisture. Where a gun may actually be stored for months or years, as in a jobber's warehouse or a government arsenal, all metal parts, including the inside of the bore, are covered with a heavy grease known as Cosmoline. Protected by this, a gun can be kept rust-free indefinitely even in sections where it is very damp.

Most new guns come from the factory filled with Cosmoline, by the way. It should be scrubbed off with a gasoline-saturated rag or brush before the gun is used.

A .22 if used with either greased or waxed bullets does not need to be cleaned at all. The non-corrosive priming leaves a harmless deposit and the grease leaves a thin protective covering over the bore. Many youngsters do their .22's more harm than good by cleaning them assiduously and trying to remove all traces of the harmless carbon compounds that come from the combustion of powder and leave a cleaning patch dark.

All modern commercial priming is now non-corrosive or non-rust-producing. On the other hand, millions of rounds of .30/06 government ammunition will be used by civilian riflemen. All government ammunition has potassium-chlorate priming. When one of these primers is fired, the potassium chlorate is changed to potassium chloride, a substance not very different from common table salt. Like ordinary table salt this attracts moisture and causes rust. In the old days the reason for the rusting out of barrels was not understood. Smokeless powder got the blame. In some calibers where the proportion of the priming mixture to the powder charge was very high, the barrels would rust out very rapidly and nothing apparently could be done about it. For years the "acid primer fouling of smokeless powder" received the blame. In the later 1920's it was discovered that the fault lay nowhere except in the priming. With non-corrosive priming, the ordinary .22, which used to be almost impossible to keep from rusting out, became almost indestructible.

There is only one thing that will dissolve salt. That is water. A thorough job of cleaning a rifle fired with corrosive priming cannot be done by any solvent that does not contain water. The best way to clean a rifle in which a corrosive primer has been fired is as follows:

Remove the bolt. Put on the stove a small pan of water with a very few soap flakes in it. Heat the water until it boils. Then put the rifle, with the muzzle down, into the water. Then take a cleaning rod with a patch of proper size on the end and pump it back and forth through the barrel. The suction of the relatively tight patch will draw the water up behind it, and the hot water will dissolve every vestige of the harmful primer salt. When the barrel is very hot, it should be removed from the water, and three or four dry patches run through it. Then the rifle can be put aside. The heat will drive all the moisture out of it. Then the barrel can be oiled or greased, depending on how long it is to be set away.

The best type of cleaning rod to use is a one-piece steel rod. Joined rods tend to jump around and endanger the delicate rifling of the bore. Brass rods pick up dust and grit, which do the same thing. Cut patches of the proper size made of Canton flannel can be purchased at any sporting-goods store. If one feels economical, one can buy a yard of the same material and cut it up into patches of the proper size as the need arises.

Lever-action rifles have to be cleaned from the muzzle. When this is done, care must be taken not to damage the delicate lands near the muzzle. Actually this is not a difficult thing to do.

When the bore of the rifle is clean, all outside metal parts should be wiped over lightly with an oily rag. In the summertime particularly, damp hands can cause rust, and a rifle should be wiped off every time it is handled. It is disheartening in the extreme to pick up a treasured weapon from the gun rack and find fingerprints rusted into the black and shiny bluing.

Most people put too much lubricating oil in a rifle action. They take an oilcan with a spout and squirt the oil indiscriminately here and there. This surplus oil often squirts back into the shooter's eye when the rifle is fired. It runs down into the action, collects, and eventually much of it gums. Lubricating oils made from petroleum products are definitely not good for wood. Rifles are often brought into gunsmith shops with the wood all soaked up and spongy from this surplus oil.

It is sufficient to put a small drop of good lubricating oil occasionally on the working parts of the mechanism. No more oil is needed. If the rifle is to be used in sub-zero weather, the action should be very carefully cleaned in gasoline to remove every vestige of oil, as ordinary oil will freeze up. The bolt of a bolt-action rifle should be taken apart and washed in gasoline. In former years, to avoid this freezing up in cold weather, rifle mechanisms were lubricated with powdered graphite. During the last war several oils came out that did not freeze up. These should be used in cold countries, but first every trace of ordinary oil should be removed.

The Care of the Gunstock

Most factory stocks are finished with lacquer or varnish. Such a finish shines nicely when the rifle is new. It is cheap and quick to apply. It is relatively waterproof. Even some custom gunsmiths use varnish finishes of one kind or another. The only thing wrong with finishes of that type is that they are not durable. The ordinary factory gun, after a few years' use, has big hunks of varnish chipped off with the bare wood showing beneath. There isn't any way to avoid this. There isn't any real way to preserve such a stock. It isn't a bad idea to go over a varnished stock with a slightly oily rag to wipe off the dirt and fingerprints, but this does the stock no real good.

Sooner or later the time will come when such a stock should

be refinished and an oil finish put on. Here's the way to go about it: First take the barrel and action out of the stock. Then obtain a commercial varnish-remover. In applying it follow directions. Most of those varnish-removers soften the varnish so that it can be scraped off with a dull-bladed knife, leaving the bare wood underneath. Sometimes two applications of the remover are necessary because streaks of varnish may be left. Then the stock should be smoothed up with fine sandpaper, great care being exercised not to harm the checkering. After the first sanding the stock should be rubbed over with a wet rag, then dried quickly over a flame such as the burner of a gas stove. This will make the "whiskers" rise—little pieces of wood that have been forced down by the sanding. Now one should go over the wood again lightly with fresh fine sandpaper. Then the wetting, drying, and "whiskering" should be repeated. One should repeat this several times until the stock is glass-smooth. One should always finish up with the *finest* sandpaper.

Now the stock is absolutely smooth. If the wood is of good grade and reasonably dense, one can simply use pure linseed oil. It is best to warm it and sop on all it will take. Then the stock should be allowed to sit in a corner for a couple of days. All the oil will be absorbed. Then another application of oil should be made. Probably not all of the second coat will be absorbed. The gun should then be wiped off with water and powdered pumice on a rag. One should scour hard to see that all of this old gummed oil is off. When this is done, one should put a few drops of linseed oil on one's palm and rub it well into the stock, polishing carefully. After ten or fifteen minutes of polishing it is wise to go over the stock with a dry rag and wipe off any surplus oil. Then the stock should be allowed to set for a week or so. This treatment should be repeated at intervals and eventually it will build up a rich glossy durable finish, the handsomest of all finishes. If, on the other hand, the wood is spongy, soft, and open-grained, the first application should be of a half-and-half mixture of spar varnish and linseed oil. It should be put on, allowed to gum, and then cut away. If the wood is exceptionally dense and fine-grained the first application of oil should be mixed half-and-half with turpentine to give deeper penetration.

In recent years it has been the fad to denounce the oil finish. Many fine stockers have used other types of finish, like the French polish. Many of these substitute finishes look well for the time being. None of them can stand the beating in the field that the oil finish can stand. With an oil-finished stock it is not difficult to go over a slightly scratched and marred stock, rub in a coat of oil, then wipe it off. The damage will disappear. With finishes of the varnished-stock type a scratch that gets in the stock is there to stay. I have an old Springfield with a fine English-walnut stock. It has had very rough usage from northern Mexico to the Alaska border. It is true that there are dents and mars in the stock and yet applications of linseed oil from time to time have kept it looking handsome even today.

Minor Adjustments

The owner of a rifle should have two or three screwdrivers to fit the various screws on his rifle. A screwdriver that does not fit the slot of the screw will mar it and detract from the appearance of the gun. If the screws are not kept turned up tight the rifle cannot be accurate. Often I have seen receiver sights on rifles that were so loose that they were almost ready to fall off. The same thing holds true with scope mounts. The loose scope mount is inaccurate and unreliable. With the bolt-action rifle the guard screws should be kept turned up tight or the rifle will change its point of impact. This is particularly important to watch on a long pack trip where the rifle may be carried on a pack horse or in the scabbard on a saddle horse for hundreds of miles.

THE TRIGGER PULL

This is not a book on gunsmithing, so I am not going into the details of trigger-pull adjustment. Nevertheless a good, clean, crisp trigger pull is one of the most important factors in accurate rifle shooting. The trigger should have no drag or creep. Probably the best type of pull for all-around use is the one-stage pull seen at its best with the fine trigger mechanism of the Model 70 Winchester. A well-adjusted double-stage military pull is also quite satisfactory, and actually an experienced rifleman has little trouble shifting from one to the other. Whatever the type of rifle, however, the pull should be clean and crisp, with the final let-go as clean and sharp as the breaking of a glass rod. It isn't wise to get a pull too light. The finest adjustment should be at between 3½ and 4½ pounds. A pull lighter than 3½ pounds is often dangerous with the bolt-action rifle. If the pull drags and the rifle goes off erratically so that the man behind it cannot control it, he can never do good shooting with it. Any competent gunsmith should be able to make a clean, crisp trigger pull. No matter how light or how heavy, a creepy pull is one of the worst things that can happen to a rifle.

Now and then a bolt-action rifle will develop a habit of letting the firing pin fall as the bolt is closed. This could be caused by a worn sear, but most often it comes from too little leeway in the inletting. The trigger is hanging up in the cut of the stock. When this happens it is not much of a trick to take the rifle out of the stock, go in with a small sharp chisel, and trim out some of the wood to free the trigger. It is surprising how often that condition exists.

Another annoying condition that develops with the bolt-action rifle is a weak, light, and creepy pull, coupled with an easy and soft lift of the bolt handle. In cases like this, the accuracy falls off and now and then one will get a pierced primer. The

[324]

trouble here is that the mainspring has lost its tension. The firing pin isn't hitting the primer hard enough. The weak mainspring has caused the trigger pull to become light and unsatisfactory.

The only remedy for this is to get a new mainspring. One of the principal reasons for this condition is that often amateur gunsmiths and even professionals who should know better cut off several coils of the mainspring. This will result in an easy bolt-handle lift, but the firing pin is weakened and, as it ages, it becomes too weak. If an easy bolt-handle lift is desired, the thing to do is to polish the cams.

Sometimes a rifle will shoot too high even with the lowest adjustment of the rear sight. With rifles made by custom makers who do not know what it is all about, this often comes through putting on too low a front sight. The remedy there is a higher front sight which in effect lowers the rear sight. In a factory rifle, however, this condition is usually brought out by the warping of the fore end too hard against the barrel. If you suspect this condition, take the barrel and action out of the stock and see if toward the fore end you do not find a place where pressure has rubbed the fore-end channel bright and dark. The thing to do then is to relieve the wood a little bit with a fine hollow chisel or a special rasp. In cases of very slight pressure, even sandpaper could be used if the job is done carefully. I have had letters from correspondents whose rifles were shooting a foot high at one hundred yards with the lowest adjustment of the rear sight, but who brought them down to where they wanted them with this relieving of the too great upward pressure of the fore end.

The ideal place for storing a gun at home is in a glass case to keep the dust away from it. The gun that is simply stood in the corner of a closet will eventually get knocked about and nicked up. In these days of small houses and apartments, however, that is about all there is to do. A word of caution must be said about storing a gun for a long period in a fleece-lined gun case. Very often the fleece will collect moisture from the air and cause rust.

That same gun case, however, is an excellent gadget in which to carry a gun in an automobile. Every man should have one if he values his gun; many a nick and scratch will be avoided.

It is not difficult, then, to keep a gun in good repair. A few minutes of care after the gun is used will keep it in good shape for years. The gun shouldn't be dropped or thrown around, not only for the sake of its appearance, but to prevent possible danger to the sights and body.

CHAPTER XXV

Slings, Scabbards, Carrying Cases

On THE target range the man who does not use his gun sling for shooting is greatly handicapped, but in the hunting field the sling is most useful for carrying the rifle. Now and then a skilled target rifleman will use a sling in steadying down for a long shot, but I doubt if one game animal in five thousand is killed with a rifle held by a sling.

I wouldn't have a rifle for hunting that would not take a sling. With one the carrying of even a fairly heavy rifle is easy, by putting the sling over the right shoulder, rifle back, butt down. If it is necessary to use both hands for climbing, the rifle can be strapped across the back with the sling across the chest.

Sporting use of the sling began with the British long before it did with the Americans. Most British double rifles are equipped with eyes through which the narrowed end of the plain leather sling can be passed. Anyone who has ever hefted one of those eleven- to fifteen-pound doubles can well understand why the sling, as an aid in carrying, met with a warm welcome. American sportsmen came late to the use of the sling because before the first World War most of our rifles were lever-actions with no provisions for sling attachment. As a matter of fact, the first Model 54 bolt-action Winchesters, which made their bow twenty years ago, and the first Model 30 Remingtons simply had eyes instead of swivels, and the slings one could buy for them were handy for carrying, but almost useless for shooting.

Nowadays good swivels, and in some cases slings, have become accepted factory equipment of many rifles. Bolt-action rifles like the Model 70 Winchester come equipped with swivels or swivel bases as a matter of course, as do the fancier lever-actions like the Winchester 64 deer rifle, the Model 71, and the Savage 99-RS. Actually it ought to be considered a crime for a factory to put out almost any standard rifle without some provision for a sling, which is handy even on a .22.

The first sling with which American sportsmen became acquainted was the government job on the 1903 Springfield. Its 1½-inch width is all right for the target range and for the carrying a heavy rifle on marches of from twenty-five to forty miles day after day. But a narrower, lighter sling is in order on the sporting rifle. There are now two kinds in regular use, both from ⅞ to 1 inch wide. One is a two-piece sling very similar in construction to the one on American military rifles. The other, the Whelen sling, consists of a single piece of leather 52 inches long, with a claw hook on one end. The strap is punched with holes into which the hook will fit. A short piece of rawhide, or a shoestring if the rawhide gets lost, is laced through these holes to hold the sling together. Two leather keepers come with slings of this type.

The two-piece sling is a bit heavier and more complicated than the one-piece, but to my way of thinking it is handier. It consists of a short tailpiece attached to the butt of the rifle, and the much longer loop portion. Each has a claw hook for adjustment, and the loop portion has two leather keepers. When the two-piece sling is adjusted correctly, it is a good idea to lace the forward portion together so it will stay put. The claw hooks have a way of working out, and the lacing will assure that the sling does not separate in an emergency.

For shooting, the loop for the upper portion of the left arm should be made by adjusting the claw hooks and lacing. This same adjustment will also be about right for carrying the rifle, with the sling over the right shoulder. Then, if the hunter wants to strap the rifle across his back so that both hands will be free, the strap can be lengthened by merely loosening the lower claw hook and putting it in another set of holes.

The rear swivel or swivel base is attached to the stock 2½ or 3 inches forward of the toe of the butt. Front swivels are located from 14 to 18½ inches ahead of the center of the trigger, depending on how they are placed on barrel or fore end. The distance on both the Linden-stocked .270 rifles in my rack is 16½ inches, and that seems to me to be about right.

The placement of this forward swivel and the way it is attached to stock or barrel are of great importance, because the more pull there is on the barrel from sling tension, the less accurately the rifle will shoot. And it makes no difference whether it is a run-of-the-mill swivel or a complicated detachable one fitting on the fancy and more fashionable swivel base.

The worst place to attach the front swivel is directly on the barrel forward of the fore end. This arrangement was very fashionable some years ago and many de-luxe sporters are still floating around with swivels so attached. Almost equally bad is the method used on many fine tailor-made sporters of having the swivel screw into a base in the rear of the fore-end tip and connected with a barrel band. Better but not perfect is Linden's method of tying the barrel to the fore end by a band about 2 inches to the rear of the front swivel. Similar is the Winchester method, used on the Model 70 sporter, of having the screw which ties barrel and fore end together about 3¼ inches behind the front swivel.

The best of all is to let the barrel alone and not tie it to the fore end at all. The fore end should be so made that full tension can be given the front swivel without materially altering the relationship of barrel and fore end. That is why I am a devout believer in full fore ends of dense strong wood so cut that the grain runs diagonal to the barrel.

It is a smart move for every hunter who uses a sling to determine the difference in point of impact at various ranges between

[329]

shots taken without a sling and shots taken with a tight sling. Many a hunter who has sighted his rifle in without a sling has wondered why he missed an easy shot when using a tight sling.

A rifle of mine, a .270 Mauser, has the front swivel 2 inches forward of the band that ties the barrel to the fore end. With a tight sling it puts the bullets 5 inches lower at 250 yards (or about 2 minutes of angle lower at any range) than without the sling. That is enough to result in a lot of misses, when the aim is taken at the heart region at a distance of 250 yards and more. If I use a tight sling with this rifle I compensate by holding on the chest cavity. I must confess, however, that I often use no sling at all, even on long shots, because the pesky little white-tail bucks I chase around on the oak-covered ridges of the Southwest and Mexico can get out of sight before you can say scat; they seldom wait for a hunter to climb into his sling and do the thing up right.

The sling is a handy piece of equipment that makes hard, close holding easier, but no one should become so dependent on it that he thinks he cannot shoot without it. I have seen riflemen accustomed to varmint shooting and target work spend precious seconds getting into a tight sling while a big buck was tearing up the opposite side of the canyon and about to disappear. That is ridiculous!

On the hunting rifle, be it for large game or for varmints, the sling should be adjusted to give a good loop for the left arm and then *left that way.* The so-called "hasty" sling adjustment isn't of much use; it affords little or no more accuracy than no sling at all. Nor does a sling, hasty or other, help from the offhand position. For a quick running shot it is an actual handicap.

For a long, deliberate shot at standing or slowly moving big game, or for almost any shot at more than 150 yards, the sling is extremely helpful in sitting or prone positions. The loop should be short enough so that, when it is put *high on the upper arm* and the keeper pulled up to hold it there, the butt bears *hard* against the right shoulder with the left hand *tight* against the forward swivel—so tight that in a long string of shots at the target range the shooter needs a heavy glove to protect the hand. So adjusted and so used, the sling holds the rifle steadily without any work by the right hand.

THE RIFLE SCABBARD

It is a sad fact that good rifle scabbards for scope-sighted rifles are almost impossible to buy over the counter in a retail store. Most of those sold are for short lever-action carbines, and those designed for scope-sighted bolt-action rifles are so short as to leave the butt of the rifle exposed to nicks and scratches and to fail to protect scope and mechanism from rain or snow.

I am giving dimensions for a good scabbard of generous size which will protect the average bolt-action, scope-sighted rifle with a 24-inch barrel:

Length: 38½ in.
Width: 6¼ in. from open end to 9¼ in.
Width: 13 in. from open end to 7½ in.
Length of straps for attaching to saddle: 42 inches.

The mouth of the scabbard should be split back for about five inches so the rifleman can reach in, grab the rifle by the grip, and yank it out. Good stiff leather should be used to hold the rifle firm and keep it from flopping around in the scabbard and wearing off the bluing.

For hunting on horseback, where game is likely to be jumped while the hunter is mounted, the rifle scabbard should be attached to the left side, pointing muzzle-down at an angle of about forty-five degrees. The scabbard should go *under* the stirrup leather and the butt should be about level with the horse's rump or a bit below. So attached, the scabbard will hold the rifle and it will not fall out, even when going up very steep hills.

The hunter can dismount (on the left side, of course) when

he sees game, grab the rifle, and pull it out. Often rifles are carried butt-forward along the horse's neck, but grabbing for a rifle by the horse's head often frightens it and the rifle so carried causes the scabbard to fill up with leaves and twigs. Rifles are also carried on the right side, butt to the rear, but that is unhandy, with no possible gain.

In the far north, where horses have a lot of Percheron blood in them and are round-backed and also where game is seldom actually hunted on horseback, the rifle just about has to be carried on the right side, butt to the front. In this position the rifle tends to equalize the pull of the hunter's getting aboard on the left side, and there is less tendency to pull the saddle over, because the weight is carried close to the cinch. This method is not necessary where real saddle horses with backs shaped for the saddle are used. It is really a method for transporting the rifle on the trail, *not* for carrying when hunting from horseback.

CARRYING CASES

For many years fleece-lined leather carrying cases have been made for rifles. They are excellent for carrying a rifle in a car to protect it from scratches. They are worthless, however, for any real transportation. Now various firms are making heavy sole-leather, full-length cases lined with fleece. These do beautifully for carrying a rifle on a plane or in the bedroom of a train —and even for packing a spare rifle on a pack horse for a long hunting trip.

Index

N.B. *For complete coverage on any article of rifle equipment it will be necessary in using this index to consult general headings such as* rifle, scope, sight, *etc.,* manufacturer's names, such as Remington, Winchester, Lyman, *and trade names, such as* Core-Lokt, Silvertip, *etc.*